FEAST OF FEAR

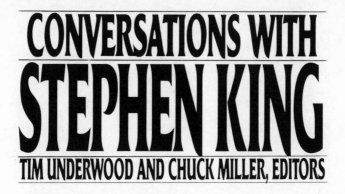

CONVERSATIONS WITH
STEPHEN KING

TIM UNDERWOOD AND CHUCK MILLER, EDITORS

FEAST
OF FEAR

Carroll & Graf Publishers, Inc.
New York

This edition published by arrangement with Underwood-Miller, Inc.

First Carroll & Graf edition 1992

Carroll & Graf Publishers, Inc.
260 Fifth Avenue
New York, NY 10001

Library of Congress Cataloging-in-Publication Data is available.
Manufactured in the United States of America

This collection was compiled by Don Herron. We also wish to thank
Stanley Wiater for his editorial assistance, and Craig Goden of Time
Tunnel books for help in tracking down several of the interviews
which appear in these pages.

ACKNOWLEDGEMENTS

Chapter One: "Genesis"

Chapter Two: "Early Years"

"Eyeglasses for the Mind" by George Christian. Published in *Houston Chronicle*, September 30, 1979. Copyright © 1979 by Houston Chronicle. All rights reserved. Reprinted by permission.

Chapter Three: "A Brand Name Is Born"

"It *Is* You, Mr. King . . . Isn't It?" by Jerry Harkavy. Published in *Portland Press Herald*, October 31, 1979. Copyright © 1979 by Guy Gannett Publishing Co. All rights reserved. Reprinted by permission.

"Stephen King: A 1981 Interview" by Bill Munster. Published in *Footsteps* Number Seven, November 1986. Copyright © 1986 by Bill Munster. All rights reserved. Reprinted by permission.

"Has Success Spoiled Stephen King? Naaah." by Pat Cadigan, Marty Ketchum and Arnie Fenner. Published in *Shayol* Volume One, Number Six, Winter 1982. Copyright © 1982 by Flight Unlimited, Inc. All rights reserved. Reprinted by permission.

"The Stephen King Interview" by David Sherman. Published in *Fangoria* Number Thirty-five, April 1984, and *Fangoria* Number Thirty-six, July 1984. Copyright © 1984 by David Sherman. All rights reserved. Reprinted by permission.

"Stephen King Talks about *Christine*" by Randy Lofficier. Published in *Twilight Zone* Volume Three, Number Six, February 1984. Copyright © 1984 by Randy Lofficier. All rights reserved. Reprinted by permission.

Chapter Four: "Going Hollywood"

"Stephen King on *Carrie, The Shining*, etc." by Peter S. Perakos. Published in *Cinefantastique* Volume One, Number Eight, Winter 1978. Copyright © 1978 by Frederick S. Clarke, Publisher. All rights reserved. Reprinted by permission.

"King of the Night" by David Chute. Published in *Take One*, January 1979. Copyright © 1979 by David Chute. All rights reserved. Reprinted by permission.

"Watching *'Salem's Lot*—with the King" by Chris Palmer. Published in *Bangor Daily News*, November 17, 1979. Copyright © 1979 by Bangor Daily News. All rights reserved. Reprinted by permission.

"Fright King's World Grips Convention-Goers" by Tom Wood. Published in *Nashville Tennessean*, May 5, 1980. Copyright © 1980 by Guy Gannett Publishing Co. All rights reserved. Reprinted by permission.

"The King of Horror Novels," by David Chute. Published in *The Boston Phoenix*, June 17, 1980. Copyright © 1980 by David Chute. All rights reserved. Reprinted by permission.

"New Adventures in the Scream Trade: A Non-Stop King Takes on TV" by Ben Herndon. Published in *Twilight Zone*, Volume Five, Number Five, December 1985. Copyright © 1985 by TZ Publications. All rights reserved. Reprinted by permission.

"Interview with Stephen King" by Paul R. Gagne. Portions published in *Famous Monsters* Number 162, April 1980, and in Number 164, June 1980; in *Cinefantastique* Volume Ten, Number Four, Spring 1981, and in Volume Fourteen, Number Two, December-January 1983–84. This version copyright © 1989 by Paul R. Gagne. All rights reserved. Reprinted by permission.

"King of the Road" by Darrell Ewing and Dennis Myers. Published in *American Film*, June 1986. Copyright © 1986 by The American Film Institute. All rights reserved. Reprinted by permission.

"Interview with Stephen King" by Jessie Horsting. Portions published in *Stephen King at the Movies* by Jessie Horsting, Starlog/Signet 1986, and in *Fangoria* Number Fifty-six, August 1986. Copyright © 1986 by Jessie Horsting. All rights reserved. Reprinted by permission.

Chapter Five: "Scream Partners"

"Stephen King and George Romero: Collaboration in Terror" by Stanley Wiater. Published in *Fangoria* Number Six, June 1980. Copyright © 1980 by Stanley Wiater. All rights reserved. Reprinted by permission.

"Interview with Stephen King" by Paul R. Gagne. Portions published in *Cinefantastique* Volume Ten, Number One, Summer 1980. This version copyright © 1989 by Paul R. Gagne. All rights reserved. Reprinted by permission.

"Interview with Stephen King" by Paul R. Gagne. Portions published in *Cinefantastique* Volume Twelve, Number Two-Three, April 1982 and Volume Thirteen, Number One, September-October 1982, and in *The Zombies That Ate Pittsburgh: The Films of George A. Romero* by Paul R. Gagne, Dodd, Mead, 1987. This version copyright © 1989 by Paul R. Gagne. All rights reserved. Reprinted by permission.

"The King/George Conversations" by Tony Crawley. Published in *Starburst* Numbers Fifty-Four and Fifty-Five, 1983. Copyright © 1983 by Marvel Comics Ltd. Book rights retained by Tony Crawley. All rights reserved. Reprinted by permission. With thanks to Frederic Albert Levy for providing a tape of the unedited interview.

"Interview with Stephen King and George Romero" by Jessie Horsting and Mike Stein. Portions published in *Fantastic Films* Number Thirty-two, February 1983. This version copyright © 1989 by Jessie Horsting and Mike Stein. All rights reserved. Reprinted by permission.

"Interview with Stephen King" by Paul R. Gagne. Previously unpublished. Copyright © 1989 by Paul R. Gagne. All rights reserved. Published by permission.

Chapter Six: "Highway to Horror"

"The Director is King" by Stephen Schaefer. Published in *Film Comment*, June 1986. Copyright © 1986 by Stephen Schaefer. All rights reserved. Reprinted by permission.

"Stephen King: The Maximum Overdrive Interview" by Stanley Wiater. Portions published in *Prevue* Number Sixty-Four, May-July 1986, and in *Valley Advocate* (Hatfield, MA), July 21, 1986. Copyright © 1986 by Stanley Wiater. All rights reserved. Reprinted by permission.

"Interview with Stephen King" by Stephen Schaefer. Portions published in *Boston Herald*, July 27, 1986, and in *Men's Guide to Fashion* (MGF) Volume Two, Number Nine, October 1986. Copyright © 1986 by Stephen Schaefer. All rights reserved. Reprinted by permission.

"Interview with Stephen King" by Robert Strauss. Portions published in *Chicago Sun-Times*, July 1986, and in *Monsterland* Number Fifteen, 1986. Copyright © 1986 by Robert Strauss. All rights reserved. Reprinted by permission.

"Interview with Stephen King" by Paul R. Gagne. Previously unpublished. Copyright 1989 © by Paul R. Gagne. All rights reserved. Published by permission.

Chapter Seven: "Personal Demons"

"Horror Writer Stephen King is Afraid There's Something Awful Under His Bed" by Michael Hanlon. Published in *Toronto Star*, October 5, 1983. Copyright © 1983 by Toronto Star Syndicate. All rights reserved. Reprinted by permission.

"The King of the Macabre at Home" by Michael J. Bandler. Published in *Parents Magazine*, January 1982. Copyright © 1982 by Michael J. Bandler. All rights reserved. Reprinted by permission.

"Steve King on Baseball" by Bob Haskell. Published in *Bangor Daily News*, October 16, 1980. Copyright © 1980 by Bangor Daily News. All rights reserved. Reprinted by permission.

Chapter Eight: "Beyond the Brand Name"

"The Book Business Interview" by Ted Koppel. Broadcast on ABC News *Nightline*, January 13, 1984. Copyright © 1984 by American Broadcasting Companies, Inc. All rights reserved. Reprinted by permission.

"Reality Too Frightening, Horror King Says" by William Robertson. Published in *Miami Herald*, March 25, 1984. Copyright © 1984 by Miami Herald. All rights reserved. Reprinted with permission of The Miami Herald.

"Cosmo Talks to: Stephen King" by T. N. Murari. Published in *Cosmopolitan*, December 1985. Copyright © 1985 by The Hearst Corporation. All rights reserved. Reprinted by permission.

"Stephen King" by Mike Farren. Published in *Interview* Volume XVI, Number Two, February 1986. Copyright © 1986 by Interview Enterprises. All rights reserved. Reprinted by permission of New York Times Syndicate.

Chapter Nine: "Recent Years"

"I Am a Hick, and This Is Where I Feel at Home" by Elaine Landa. Portions published in *Inside* Volume Seven, Number Four, April 4, 1986, the newspaper of Orono High School, Orono, Maine; Sanford Phippen, advisor. Copyright © 1986 by Inside. All rights reserved. Reprinted by permission.

"Stephen King: The Limits of Fear" by Jo Fletcher. Portions published in *Knave* Volume Nineteen, Number Five, 1987. Copyright © 1987 by Jo Fletcher. All rights reserved. Reprinted by permission.

"The West Interview: Stephen King" by D. C. Denison. Published in *West Magazine, San Jose Mercury News*, July 19, 1987. Copyright © 1987 by D. C. Denison. All rights reserved. Reprinted by permission.

"Interview with Stephen King" by Ed Gorman. Published in *Mystery Scene* Number Ten, 1987. Copyright © 1987 by Ed Gorman. All rights reserved. Reprinted by permission.

"He Has the Last Word on What's Scary" by Martin Booe. Published in *Los Angeles Herald Examiner*, January 31, 1989. Copyright © 1989 by Los Angeles Herald Examiner. All rights reserved. Reprinted by permission.

Epilogue: Has Success Spoiled Stephen King?

"Midas with the Common Touch: Why Hasn't Success Spoiled Stephen King?" by Edgar Allen Beem. Published in *Maine Times* Volume Eighteen, Number Forty, July 11, 1986. Copyright © 1986 by Maine Times. All rights reserved. Reprinted by permission.

CONTENTS

FEAST OF FEAR

CHAPTER ONE

†

GENESIS

†

With David Bright

Steve King can't make quite make up his mind whether or not he should retire. The 25-year old Hampden Academy English teacher, his wife, Tabby, and their two children will be coming into a sizable amount of money by virtue of King's authorship of *Carrie*, a novel scheduled to be published by Doubleday in January of 1974.

For King, the book marks his first hit after three strikeouts in trying to break into the novel business, and Doubleday is so excited about his book that more than six months before the presses are scheduled to roll the firm is calling the book a bestseller.

The book is about a high school girl named Carrie who lives in Chamberlain, Maine, a town built in King's mind out of experiences in his home town of Lisbon Falls and the numerous other Maine communities in which he has lived.

Carrie is a loner, ousted by her peers at her school, who eventually uses her special talent to gain revenge on the classmates who treated her so badly.

That the book is about Maine high school life is no coincidence for King wrote his first book while in high school himself. His first rejection, along with a letter that perhaps he should try another field of endeavor, came that same year.

A person who has always been interested in the sociology of high school, King says he is considering remaining in his job as a teacher, even though he feels teaching has its definite disadvantages. Like his first job, once graduated from the University of Maine, working in a Bangor laundry, King says that teaching often takes up time he'd rather spend writing.

"We might travel a bit," he says, "just to see places we'd normally never have time for." He admits, however, that no amount of travel would allow him to write about a place as comfortably as he can write about Maine.

King's impressions of Maine are not those the tourist sees. Instead, he says, his characters are the millworkers who throw beer cans from cars. *Carrie* was first written to be in Massachusetts, but Doubleday asked him to change it because the action was "a bit greasy" for Massachusetts. King said his editor didn't think that characters drinking beer instead of smoking pot and driving old rust-bucket cars on back country roads quite fit the Massachusetts image.

From his New York City office, King's editor also didn't believe you could still buy dime root beers or that high schools still had senior proms, but King convinced him these things shouldn't be changed.

"I went back to Lisbon Falls last week and bought a root beer at the fruit store for a dime," he said, and on the senior prom he quipped, "they don't exist anymore? I'm chaperoning one this Friday night. Tabby even bought a new dress."

King said he wrote the first draft of the book last summer, taking about three months to do it. He spent a week on the first five pages and was about to dump the idea until his wife read the pages, and urged him to continue. The book is now 70,000 words and spans about a month in Carrie's life "with flashbacks to infancy."

Sitting in the kitchen of his modest Sanford Street, Bangor apartment, King has not changed much since his own high school days. He has always been a writer. At Maine, he wrote a weekly column called "King's Garbage Truck," so named because he would write about anything that was around waiting to be discarded.

A former editor of the *Maine Campus*, the university newspaper, remembers that "King was always late. We would be pulling our hair out at deadline. With five minutes or so to go Steve would come in and sit down at a typewriter and produce two flawless pages of copy. He carries stories in his head the way most people carry change in their pockets."

Five of his students at Hampden Academy have asked his advice on novels they are writing and he is encouraging them as best he can, which is one of the reasons he hasn't decided to quit teaching despite his new-found fortune.

Doubleday has sold the paperback rights to the book for $400,000 and has two offers from movie companies. King, now working on another book, says he plans to write all summer. Other than that, he says nothing is definite except a few trips to New York to "check with the publisher and wrap up the details and maybe take in a ball game while we're there."

With Connie Footman

Carrie is expected to be a household word around Durham and Lisbon Falls soon with the recent publication of Steve King's book, by Doubleday Publishing Houses in New York.

King, who is a Maine native, lived in several sections of the country until he was about 10 years old, when his mother returned to Maine and settled to raise her two sons in a modest farmhouse on a dirt road in the west section of Durham known as "Methodist Corner." King had been spending summers in Durham with an aunt since he was a very young boy, and according to his aunt, he showed great interest in writing as early as the age of six. She says she cannot remember him ever just sitting idle, he was always writing. At the time the Kings returned to Maine, Durham was one of the few towns still using one-room schools with all eight grades in the same room. The author received his fifth and sixth grade education in the one-room schoolhouse at West Durham. The structure still stands today, near his former home.

His teacher at the time, fondly remembers him as a smart, friendly, outgoing boy who was continually writing stories and plays. She described his writing as well beyond his years and age level, and says he particularly enjoyed writing "space stories."

As a boy, he attended the small 200-plus-year-old Methodist Church next door to his home, later taught vacation Bible School classes, and when he was a teenager, he would occasionally preach a Sunday sermon to the small group of parishioners who attended the church. Membership was so small that they could not afford to pay a minister, and they depended upon a lay preacher most of the time, and a few times a year a guest minister would come in and conduct services. However, many persons thought King's sermons were just as good, if not better than any the ministers gave.

By the time he completed the eighth grade, Durham's one-room schoolhouses were a thing of the past, as the town had constructed a modern centrally located school. However, Durham had no high school, so the town paid tuition costs for the young people to go to whatever high school they preferred as long as they provided their own transportation. King chose to attend nearby Lisbon High School in Lisbon Falls because it was the nearest. Getting to school whatever way he could sometimes with a prearranged ride, hitchhiking, or whatever, many times he would remain after school and would miss all the regular cars going his way and would end up making the six mile trek home on foot.

This did not discourage him, he did well at high school and his interest in writing only seemed to grow, in fact, he wrote his first novel while still in high school. He was graduated in 1966 and went to the University of Maine, Orono, where he majored in English. During his college career, he wrote a column in the *Maine Campus*, a newspaper for the University of Maine, titled "King's Garbage Truck," for two and a half years.

He was graduated in 1970 with a Bachelor of Science Degree and reportedly told friends and family he was "tired of school." He then went to work for about a year in a Bangor laundry which he later admits is about as close to the bottom of the ladder as one can get.

He accepted a contract to teach English at Hampden Academy in the fall of 1971. During these years he had written three books that were rejected before his success with *Carrie*. He says he could pinpoint no real inspiration for the book, that it was from his experiences at high school, and it was a story that, in his words, "Just happened to pan." The book tells the story of Carrie, a high school girl residing in the fictional town of Chamberlain, Maine, who is a loner, and not accepted by her fellow students and of her special talent for getting back at them.

About a year ago the publishers sold the paperback rights to the novel, and residents in the general area have been watching and waiting for the book to appear locally ever since, anxious to read a book by a local boy everybody knew. Film rights for the novel have already been sold.

King has since given up teaching school and is devoting full time to his writing career, and in an interview he said his second novel *Jerusa-*

lem's Lot has been accepted and will be published by Doubleday in August, 1975. When asked what the story was about, he said, "I'm not supposed to talk about it, my publishers want it this way." *Carrie* is on the bookstands now in some of the larger cities, and is expected to be in most area bookstores this week.

He and his wife, the former Tabitha Spruce of Old Town, and their two children Naomi, 4, and Joe, 2, reside in Windham, near Sebago Lake. He says he likes the area, and intends to do a little fishing before long. King has come a long way since his days at the one room schoolhouse with a potbellied stove and no indoor plumbing, and is expected to "Put Durham on the map," according to one of his admirers.

With Emmett Meara

It's a long way from teaching English at Hampden Academy to selling 5 million copies of three books, all of which have been sold to the movies. But Stephen King, 29, has made that stupendous jump in only four years.

From a trailer park in Hampden, King has gone in that space of time to a comfortable house on a Bridgton lake, with a dusty but new Cadillac in the drive. Just the sale of *Carrie* to Hollywood brought in $40,000 alone (plus a percentage of the $5 million gross) or almost 10 years salary at the school.

King found his niche when he sold an abbreviated version of the bestselling *Carrie* to a men's magazine for a measly $200. "Those checks kept us eating then," laughed his very pregnant wife Tabitha, a poet in her own right.

King said when he read the published version, he realized that the plot—a teenage girl cursed with telekinetic powers—was too good for the men's magazine short story. He developed the plot into a full length novel, which has horrified readers and moviegoers all over the world. King said the novel is now selling 3,000 copies a day in London.

'Salem's Lot, set in a small Maine town, as is *Carrie*, sold "only" 19,000 in hardcover editions before breaking away for 2.5 million sales in paperback. *Carrie* sold 13,000 in hardcover and a million in paperback.

The new book, *The Shining*, about a child who can see into the future, has topped the others in hardcover sales with 47,000 and has yet to go into paperback.

Why do people plunk down money to be horrified? King has his own private theory that "people aren't really afraid of vampires, what they are afraid of is their own death. . . or the oil bill. When they are reading and watching my stories, they are not afraid of the oil bill, I'll tell you."

The release people get from watching a horror film "is sort of narcotic," King said which frees people from their normal tensions.

A trifle defensive perhaps, King denied that anyone who writes such works is a "sicky" as some of his letter-writing fans have charged. "I just laugh at them," but he admitted that anyone who writes such works, from Poe to Alfred Hitchcock, has "an abnormal twist to them. But we all have a little of that." King said. Otherwise, why are we all buying his books, he asked.

King said he writes, "What I want to and not what I think will sell."

While defending the horror scenes in his own works, King said that gore can be excessive, like in the movie *The Texas Chainsaw Massacre*. "That went too far," he said.

"When I go into a horror scene, I take my own good taste with me," King said. Some passages he put in *'Salem's Lot* King would like to have back. "Those were a little gory. I wrote them when I was tired," he said.

Although both *'Salem's Lot* and *Carrie* are set in small towns in Maine which are eventually destroyed, King denied that this is any reaction against his roots. King grew up in Pownal and his wife in Old Town.

He watched the screening of *Carrie* with apprehension because he had no control over the movie production, the author said. "It's a pretty good movie," he said. "But the book is better."

The major difference between life in Hampden and Bridgton, King said, is "We don't have to worry about money anymore."

With Robert W. Wells

King got into the horror field only after he tried other kinds of novels that couldn't find a publisher.

"The earliest writing I can remember doing is when I was stuck in bed with the flu and starting copying Tom Swift books into a tablet, changing the stories as I went along. Once you get a taste of that kind of power, you're lost forever.

"I started collecting rejection slips when I was 12. I sold my first story when I was 19 to the *Magazine of Strange Stories* for $35. It was edited by Robert Lowndes. It's now defunct and Lowndes, who's about 80, is editor of *Sexology*.

"I wrote a novel at 16. I wrote another that was a little better at 19 and another at 20. When I was 22, I wrote one that nearly got published.

"Finally, I wrote *Carrie*, the first in the occult field. I'd done a lot of short stories by then and most that sold were horror stories. I started *Carrie* as a short story, but then it crossed my mind that there ought to be a longer fuse before the explosion and the next thing I knew it had grown into a novel.

"That was after *Rosemary's Baby* but before *The Exorcist*, which really opened up the field. I didn't expect much of *Carrie*. I thought who'd want to read a book about a poor little girl with menstrual problems? I couldn't believe I was writing it."

King, who will be 33 years old next Sunday, was teaching high school English at $6,000 a year in 1973. Now movie and paperback rights bring in millions.

Has wealth changed his life? Not much, he said.

"I was born in Portland and raised there, except for a period in Indiana and a while in Milwaukee. We lived here when I was 4. My father had left two years before. We were evicted from our apartment here after the babysitter fell asleep and my brother crawled out on the roof.

"We were living in what amounted to a tenement in Bangor with two kids when the paperback rights for *Carrie* went for $400,000. The hardcover only sold 13,000 copies, but the paperback did quite well.

"Luckily, the $400,000 didn't come all at once in small, unmarked bills. We could make the transition gradually, like a diver coming to the surface stage by stage so he won't get the bends. It wasn't like a rock star who goes from being broke one day to having a Rolls and a mansion the next. I don't think the money's changed us as much as it might have."

King said he, his wife and their three children, aged 3, 8, and 10, live in a "nice Victorian house with turrets, gables and horrible heating bills," have a summer place and cars that run. His wife, who recently sold her first novel, is from Old town. They met at the University of Maine when both were students.

"Long before I had any success, I had put down roots in Maine. At one point, we tried living in Colorado, but I kept thinking I'd like to see the ocean—and I don't even like the ocean that much. I only thought about it when I was out there."

It is King's theory that horror stories and movies become more popular during periods of anxiety such as the 1930s or now. That may be a partial explanation of the success of such books as his new one, but there's an added factor worth noting.

"Fantasy is to the human mind what salt is to the diet," King said. "If you don't use imagination, imagination will use you.

"*Carrie* dealt with telekinesis. But I've never tried to write hard-core science fiction. I got Cs and Bs in biology and chemistry.

"Besides, I'm more interested in what's going on in this world than someplace else."

King's 3-year-old, Owen, has figured out his father's life pretty well.

"Around the house, he knows I'm daddy. When I leave on a trip like this, he says, I'm going off to be Stephen King."

CHAPTER TWO

†

EARLY YEARS

†

With Charlotte Phelan (1979)

Writing a few years ago about his work, Stephen King, the horror story specialist, found himself feeling guilty when he compared his financial fortunes with those of another novelist. This was David Madden, whose *Bijou* was among those books King admired "most in the world."

King went on to say, "Madden worked on *Bijou* for six years and made $15,000. I worked on '*Salem's Lot* for about eight months (three months first draft; three months second draft: two months third draft) and stand to make nearly half a million dollars if all falls together."

He hastened to add in this piece in the *New York Times Book Review*, "This is before taxes, in case any potential kidnappers happen to read *The Times*."

There is more than a touch of irony here, and it actually has little to do with the length of time it took to write '*Salem's Lot*, a chilling New England tale inhabited by voracious vampires. It goes back to the early 1970s, when King was a teacher at a high school in his native Maine.

He was still a young man, but he was married and had children, so he was moonlighting in an industrial laundry, "earning money to keep my wife and kids and myself fed," as he said in telephone chat the other day.

King noticed an older woman who also worked at the laundry and began studying her and her aura of strangeness. The woman soon became the prototype of the mother of Carrie, the title character in his first novel.

It was *Carrie* then, a novel that evolved from an imaginative characterization of a co-worker in an industrial laundry, that got readers hooked

on Stephen King's particular brand of fiction; *Carrie* that made publishers and others want to pay King as much as $500,000 for his second
eerie effort, and even more for those that were to follow.

Indeed it was the re-issue of *Night Shift* in paperback that occasioned
the call from King, who is spending this year as a writer-in-residence at
the University of Maine. Talk, however, ranged over his other work as
well, and with his preoccupation—or is it obsession?—with his chilling, macabre genre.

"For some reason, nobody asks writers in the quote normal unquote
fields of literary endeavor why they have chosen their particular area. If
you met Joseph Heller at a cocktail party, would you ask him why he
chose the Air Force for *Catch-22*?

"Another question I get is, 'Are you ever going to write something
serious?' My answer is: 'Everything I do is serious.'"

Meanwhile, he has been highly sensitive to the reviews of *The Stand*,
which is on the bestseller lists:

"I think very long books, one like this that weighs 2 pounds, are a
personal affront to reviewers with all the other books they have to read."

With Charles L. Grant

Q: Let's start with *Carrie*, your first published novel. How did you come
to create it?

KING: I don't remember. That's the truth. I was publishing stories in
Cavalier at the time. Just before I got married in 1970, I sold a story to
them, and another, from then on I could sell them almost anything. I
tried to sell them a story about a corpse that came back to life, but Nye
Willden, the editor, said the corpse would have moldered away after a
hundred years. I thought that was a really nasty quibble.

Then, as I started to publish more, some woman said, "You write all
those macho things, but you can't write about women. You're scared of
women." I said, "I'm not scared of women. I could write about them if I
wanted to."

So I got an idea for a short story about this incident in a girls' shower
room, and the girl would be telekinetic. The other girls would pelt her
with sanitary napkins when she got her period. The period would release

the right hormones and she would rain down destruction on them. (I have to admit, though, that this hormone thing wasn't very clear in my mind.) Anyway, I did the shower scene, but I hated it and threw it away. My wife fished it out of the wastebasket and read it. She said, "I think this is pretty good. Would you go on with it?" So I did. And I really got sadistic about it. I said, "I can't have her rain destruction on them yet; they've got to *do* more to her." So they did more, and they did more—and finally it wasn't a short story, it was a novel. But I can't remember the real kernel, where the idea came from.

Q: How about Carrie herself? Where did *she* come from?

KING: She was based on a couple of real people—who, of course, weren't telekinetic. You meet kids like this when you teach school. Somehow they don't fit in, they're out of any peer group, and everybody turns on them. One of the girls was a kid I went to school with, and the other was a student of mine.

The one I went to school with was a very peculiar girl who came from a very peculiar family. Her mother wasn't a religious nut like the mother in *Carrie*; she was a game nut, a sweepstakes nut who subscribed to magazines for people who entered contests. And she won things—weird things. She won a year's supply of BeBop pencils, but the big thing she won was Jack Benny's old Maxwell. They had it out in the front yard for years, with weeds growing up around it. They didn't know what to do with it.

This girl had one change of clothes for the entire school year, and all the other kids made fun of her. I have very clear memory of the day she came to school with a new outfit she'd bought herself. She was a plain-looking country girl, but she'd changed the black skirt and white blouse—which was all anybody had ever seen her in—for a bright-colored checked blouse with puffed sleeves and a skirt that was fashionable at the time. And everybody made *worse* fun of her because nobody wanted to see her change the mold. Later she married a man who was a weather forecaster on top of Mt. Washington—a very strange man, a man as peculiar as she was. She had three kids and then hung herself one summer.

Q: Did she look like Sissy Spacek?

KING: No. She looked like Carrie.

Q: Not many authors are fortunate enough to have a film made of their first novel—much less one directed by Brain DePalma that turns out to be a big hit. It's a shame, though, that the movie didn't do more with the destruction scenes at the end.

KING: Well, Paul Monash produced the film, and he almost didn't get it produced at all. When he started off, he'd bought the film rights for a song. I think he went to Twentieth Century first, tried Paramount, and finally got this deal with United Artists. But they wouldn't go a penny more than two million. And for two million, they just couldn't destroy the town the way Carrie did in the novel.

There's *something* of it in the film, though. After Carrie leaves the prom, just before those people run the pickup truck at her, you see a fire truck screaming through the night, presumably to the school. In the book there were fire trucks from five or six towns, not just one. But that's my one fire truck from *Carrie*. I treasure that.

Q: Your next book was 'Salem's Lot, a modern-day vampire novel. Had you written about vampires before?

KING: Yes, among the stories I'd submitted to *Cavalier* was one I thought had a really nice twist. It was about a vampire who's a coal miner—so he can more or less be on the job all the time, since he's underground where it's always dark. There's a cave-in, and this vampire drinks all his mates' blood while they wait for the others to dig them out. Of course, when he goes out into the sun, he sort of evaporates.

Q: But 'Salem's Lot was considerably more ambitious. You were dealing with an entire town, not just a group of miners. What made you think, with all the vampire films and books around, that you could get away with it?

KING: There was no reason in the world to think that I could. But I wanted to do it because I wanted to play off *Dracula*. Whether or not I could get away with it never really entered my mind, because at the time I was writing it, I hadn't even sold *Carrie*. I was halfway through 'Salem's Lot when Doubleday bought *Carrie* for the princely sum of twenty-five hundred dollars. When I'd started 'Salem's Lot, my wife and I were talking about what it would be like to have Dracula in a present-day small town, and what would happen. And I ran into the most bizarre problems with that. I wanted all the traditional trappings. For instance, according to tradition, you kill a vampire by driving a stake through its heart—which assumes that if you destroy the heart the vampire is destroyed. But today, when they do an autopsy on somebody, they take all that out. You're eviscerated. So I sort of slid over that.

Anyway, the book was accepted for publication, but there were cold feet for a while. "Maybe this isn't the book to go with," people were saying. "Aren't you afraid you'll be typed as a horror story writer?" I said, "My God, I've been writing horror stories since I was ten years old." I'd done other stuff, but the stuff that came through with some force was the horror.

So when people say, "Do you write this kind of stuff for the money?" I say, "No, I was always writing this kind of stuff." The money found *me*, and I wouldn't want to kick it out. Anybody who throws money out the door has got to be nuts.

Q: You don't do it for the money, then?

KING: I do it because I love it. It's what I do.

Q: Is that a question frequently asked?

KING: Yes, people are always asking why you write those things, which I think is a question that can't be answered. The mind is like a table, and it's on a tilt; you put a marble on it and it rolls in a different direction from mine. Some people collect stamps, and they have interesting stamps. The same with coins. I doubt that anyone goes to Louis L'Amour and asks him why he writes western stories. He does, and they accept it. But they always ask horror writers things like that.

The other question everyone asks is, why do people *read* horror stories—which presupposes the whole idea that things like that are morbid and unhealthy.

Q: How healthy are *you*?

KING: I decline to answer that! I like to scare people, and people like to be scared. That's all there is to it.

Q: You make scaring people sound like fun.

KING: Yeah, that's the whole idea. It's a funhouse sort of thing. I'm the fluorescent ghost—or actually, I'm more like a stage manager or a puppeteer. I'm running the ghost, which is more fun than being the ghost. I know where all the trapdoors are that people are going to fall into.

Q: How do you feel when you spring the trapdoors on your own characters? Do you get any satisfaction from killing people off in your fiction?

KING: Well, it's murder by proxy, for one thing. You get this feeling of tremendous power, being able to jerk a character right out of a story.

Q: Do you ever feel bad when you like a character and you realize that he or she has to go—and in a particularly bloody way?

KING: Yes, sometimes. But there are also times when I'm glad to see characters go. Like Susan Norton in 'Salem's Lot. I began to have serious problems about that character, because I'd conceived of her as being a really independent Maine girl. I started to say to myself: "This girl is twenty-three years old and out of school—yet she's still living with her parents and not working." Belatedly I realized that I had to get her out of that situation, and it wasn't very long before I decided, "Well, I'll kill her off." It gave me great satisfaction to get rid of her. And I also thought that the reader's reaction would be: If Susan Norton can go, anybody can go. Nobody is protected.

Q: Which makes the book even scarier.

KING: Right. I want to scare the shit out of you if I can. That's what I'm there to do. I like to go for the jugular.

Q: Do you ever get *too* horrific?

KING: Well, there was a lot of stuff edited out of 'Salem's Lot that the editors thought was too strong. I stood by and let it happen; I wasn't in the position I am now. Still, I never want to be in the position where I can refuse editorial advice. One of the things I've found out is that a lot of editors know what they're doing. Someday, though, I want to do a definitive Lot and put it all back in.

For example, Dracula is supposed to be able to control the lower animals, like rats and wolves and things like that. And in the original draft of 'Salem's Lot I had all the rats leaving the town dump at the end and going to the basement of the boarding house to guard the vampire. In the published version of the book, the doctor is impaled on knives; in the original draft he went downstairs and the rats got him. They were running in his ears and down his clothes and in his mouth and everything else.

Q: It's been said that the literature of "terror" inspires a sense of cosmic awe, whereas mere "horror" just revolts us. Would you say the scene you just described is terror? Or horror?

KING: I don't want to make that distinction between what's terror and what's horror, what's frightening and what's revolting. A little revulsion is good for the soul.

Q: An awful lot of readers must think so, too. The book did well, didn't it?

KING: *'Salem's Lot* sold more than three million copies in paperback. As to who bought it, it's hard to say. I mean, the mail I got on *Carrie* came from a lot of young girls and boys who felt ugly and could identify with a character like that. But the letters on *'Salem's Lot* came from everybody. And most of them were favorable.

Q: Your next book, *The Shining*, sold even better; over four million copies so far, and it's still selling. One of the strongest elements is probably the setting itself, that massive old hotel isolated in the Rockies. How'd you come up with such a place?

KING: Oh, it's a real place. We were there, my wife and I. We were on a trip, a vacation, and we stopped at this hotel; and as I wandered around those long halls and empty rooms, I knew I had to do something with it. Once I got the idea about the boy, Danny, being telepathic, it all came together. Don't ask me how.

Q: Well, however it came together, it certainly was effective. When you're writing this sort of thing, don't you ever just plain scare yourself?

KING: Occasionally. The scene in *The Shining* where the woman in the bathtub gets out and goes for the little boy didn't really scare me initially. I thought I had a good scene when I first wrote it, but a funny thing happened when I was rewriting the book. As I worked, I found myself thinking, "In about eight days I'll be rewriting the bathtub scene." Then it was, "In five days I'll be rewriting the bathtub scene." And then it was, "Today—the bathtub scene!" And I really got tense and nervous about doing it because when you write, you live your story, and no reader ever has a reaction as tight about your book as your own.

Q: Maybe that scene works so well because Danny just gets a glimpse of what's in the tub.

KING: Yeah, I like that kind of stuff—the way he hears that thump when something comes to greet him, the way that knob starts to go back and forth...Boy, things like that really get to me. In the movies they drive me crazy!

Q: But you write them anyway.

KING: Sure. If it drives me crazy, maybe it'll drive the reader crazy, too.

Q: The bathtub scene was also a highlight of the movie—though Stanley Kubrick handled it differently. How did you feel about his version of *The Shining*?

KING: There are some parts of it that I liked, and some parts that I didn't like at all. If you add it all up, it comes out to a zero. Kubrick said he wanted to make a horror movie, but I don't think he knew what that was. What he ended up with was just a domestic tragedy.

Q: I must be somewhat unsettling to have your work interpreted by a stranger. Does it bother you when a movie isn't faithful to your book?

KING: I love the movies. I love to go to good horror movies. As for my own books, well, you have to make a basic decision: do you want to sell to the movies or not? What it comes down to is, you have to take a "worst case" attitude—if they screw this up, how am I going to feel? I talked that over with myself, and what I came up with was: I don't care if they destroy it, if they make a terrible movie out of this book, because *they can't destroy the book*. The book stands. I'm a book person. Movies are very nice, but they're not high art the way I think books are high art. Sometimes a perfect book becomes a terrible movie. My favorite example of that is *The Day of the Dolphin*; I thought it was a lovely book, but Mike Nichols just didn't do it right. As far as I'm concerned, whatever they do to the movie, I still have the book. I wrote the book and I'm happy with it.

Q: How do you feel when other people *aren't* happy with it especially the critics?

KING: I hate bad reviews. That's standard. They hurt, that's the thing; they hurt. For example, the Sunday *Times* review of *The Shining* was terrible. The guy really ran the book through a Mixmaster. To show you how sensitive I am, I'll immediately follow this by saying that the review in the daily *Times* was better. Though even in the daily review, Richard Lingeman couldn't avoid that Forrest Ackerman approach, a lot of puns and things. I don't know if you'd call them cheap shots, exactly, but they kind of poke fun at the whole horror field.

The thing about this field—if you visualize American Literature as a town, then the horror writer's across the tracks on the poor side of town, and that's where the "nice" people won't go. On the other hand, it's never been ghettoized like science fiction or mysteries, because you see horror sold more or less as mainstream fiction. I don't know if it's because horror has an element of allegory or what, but it's never been put into that kind of ghetto, even in the days of Fritz Leiber's *Conjure Wife*.

Q: Why do you suppose that's true?

KING: I don't know. I have no idea. But I do know that when you look at the reviews. . . well, take *Burnt Offerings*, for example. It didn't get very good reviews, yet I thought it was an excellent book.

Q: You're someone who's well-read in the field. What other writers have influenced you?

KING: Ray Bradbury was an influence. I read *The October Country*, and I've never forgotten the effect of great stories like "The Jar" and "The Crowd." But the first one that really hit me was Robert Bloch. I picked up his Belmont collection, *Yours Truly, Jack the Ripper*, and that really made an impression. I also like Jack Finney, because he deals so well with ordinary life. He's very good at evoking the humdrum, and then introducing that little skew that goes off into the unknown, adding those other elements little by little. I think this kind of story works best.

And then there's William Sloane. *The Edge of Running Water* reminds me in some ways of Arthur Machen. Machen said something once that I've never forgotten: that true evil is when a rose begins to sing. I'm not sure I understand perfectly what he meant, but the feeling of the statement is so clear! I read H.P. Lovecraft, of course, when I was young. I went through a stage when I was ordering his books from Arkham House, and they published a big collection of novellas, *At the Mountains of Madness*, that really got to me. I have my favorite Lovecraft stories that will stand out and last forever, but the man's style is a real roadblock. I think he appeals to you when you're younger and can accept that rococo style.

I love Charles Beaumont, too. And I think that Richard Matheson is fantastic. When he's at his best, he has no peer. Some of the stories he's done are classics. "Duel" is beautiful. He's another writer who goes for the jugular. He doesn't play around, no games; he goes right for the effect he's after. He did a story called "Mute" that's a personal favorite of mine.

Q: Who do you like among the newer writers?

KING: Peter Straub is one of the best. I know I'm chewing off a big bite here, but I think *Ghost Story* is one of the best gothic horror novels of the past century. And then there's *Shadowland*, his new book. It's really spooky, really something.

I also like Ramsey Campbell and Dennis Etchison; and James Herbert's books have a lot of raw vitality, a lot of really powerful things that just grab you by the throat and don't let go. Some of the early things by John Farris I like; you can't do much better than the opening sequences in *All Heads Turn When the Hunt Goes By*. Just close your eyes and picture that scene in the chapel, when the bride takes hold of the ceremonial sword.

But there's a lot of garbage out there, too. I think some writers are doing the usual thing, getting on the bandwagon while the getting is good. It'll work out in the end; they'll fall by the wayside, I hope, and the good ones will last.

And there are some who just don't get me—at least the way I think I *should* be gotten by a horror story. I don't like Robert Aickman, for instance, because I admit I don't know what he's about. I feel like I'm lost in there. I also don't get off on stories like Brian Lumley's "Cthulhu" stuff or the Lin Carter types. Their stuff just doesn't work for me; it's too much like too many things that have already been written by guys who've been dead for a hundred years.

Another thing that disturbs me, that I think a lot of people have taken advantage of in the genre, are novels—and they're usually the novels that I don't like—about children as objects of horror, objects of fear.

Q: But aren't children treated that way in your own books, when you consider what terrible powers they have? There's Carrie, who wrecks a whole community, and Charlie, the little girl in your new book, *Firestarter*, who can start fires with her mind. . . .

KING: Yes, but Carrie isn't what I think of as bad. By the time she's done all that stuff—destroys the town and hurts all those people—she's crazy; she's lost her mind, she's not responsible for what she's doing. And Charlie, in *Firestarter*, is a kid who's been through a hell of a lot. She's mad, and she hits back just like a kid will hit back—only she has something more.

I have, of course, written stories where children are downright evil. There's a story called "Suffer the Little Children," for instance, that wasn't in my *Night Shift* collection because it's a lot like a Stanley Ellin story, which I wasn't aware of when I wrote it. It's about a schoolteacher who finds out that all her children are monsters. She leads them down to the mimeograph room one by one and murders her entire class. She looks out the corner of her eye, see, and these sweet little faces are turning into these grotesque, bulbous-eyed things that are coming to get her. And I've written a couple of others like that on the "evil children" idea. . . . But mostly I see children as either victims or as forces of good.

Q: You don't, then, have the ambivalence toward children that Ray Bradbury seemed to have in his early stories—stories like "The Small Assassin," in which an infant murders his parents.

KING: No. I think children are lovely people. They're innocent, sweet, honorable, and all those things. I know that's a romantic ideal, but to me they seem good.

Q: How do you account for all the monstrous kids that populate books and movies today? There's *The Exorcist, The Omen, The Changeling, It's Alive*. . . .

KING: My own feeling about this is that almost all horror stories mirror specific areas of free-forming anxieties. And that sounds like a mouthful, a lot of intellectual bullshit, but what I mean is, when you read a horror novel or see a horror film, you make a connection with the things you're afraid of in your own life. Why was *The Exorcist* the hit that it was? I tend to think it's because it came at the height of the youth revolution, that hallucinogenic experience we were all going through. I mean, kids were coming home and saying, "Nixon's a war pig," and the parents were saying, *"What* did you say?" And the kids were growing their hair long. Even now, people forget how terrible it was when boys let their hair grow long; they took a lot of shit for something like that. Like in Bangor—boy, it was bad news! So *The Exorcist* comes along and what happens? You have a nice middle-class girl who's respectful to her mother and outgoing and friendly and all the things that parents want their children to be—and she turns into this foul-talking, ugly, straggly-haired, screaming, killing monster. And it seems to me that, symbolically, there's a very satisfactory parallel to what happened to the kids in the Sixties.

Same way with those bug movies in the Fifties: *Them, The Beginning of the End, Rodan.* . . . What were people afraid of in those days. The Cold War, the Atomic Bomb. We were on the edge of doomsday, not just another world war but the end of the world. And all those monsters?—it was radioactivity. They all came out of White Sand Proving Ground or some atoll in the Pacific.

I admit that slobbering, 1950s-type monsters are fun to work with. I've done it, too, in "The Mist," that short novel in *Dark Forces.*

Q: It's clear that horror can reflect society's current fears, but how about our more personal fears? It's been suggested, for example, that all horror fiction has a strong sexual element. Do you thing this is true?

KING: Yes, but I don't think sex has been dealt with the way it needs to be, or the way it could be. Horror stories appeal to teenagers, usually boys, who are very doubtful about their own sexual potency, what it is that they're supposed to do. Boys at that age know, according to tradition, that they'll be the sexual aggressors, and they're very doubtful about how to go about it. I think that the horror story serves as an outlet or a catharsis for these deep-seated fears that are really about sex. That all sounds very Freudian, but people like Howard, Lovecraft, Poe—they all had their problems.

Q: Isn't there some common denominator here? Some appeal that goes deeper than just current concerns or even sexual fears?

KING: Well, on another level, all this stuff is only a rehearsal for our own death. That's the deep reason people read it. In fact, one of the reasons the field is so open to criticism is because it deals with morbidity, because it deals with mortality. That Faulkner story, "A Rose for Emily" —which is really a horror story—is the most morbid thing I can think of. The way the house starts to stink, and the men from the town put quicklime around it to take away the smell because they assume a sewer main has broken—Faulkner's very careful about how he says this—and the way the smell disappears because the flesh has gotten past the stage where it's ripe. . . . Her lover's body was up in her bed. We really don't know what she was doing with it, if she was sleeping with it, but there's that hint of necrophilia there.

Q: Could this rehearsal for our death be, somehow, an attempt to *reassure* ourselves about death? To make us more comfortable with it?

KING: That's what Stanley Kubrick says: it doesn't matter whether the supernatural forces are good or evil; all that matters is that they exist. It means that after this life, there's more.

Q: And that, of course, is a comforting thought. Do you yourself believe in the hereafter?

KING: Yes.

Q: In what sense?

KING: Well, I believe in God, but I don't think any of us has a line on Him, on what God is like. All of us may get a big surprise. We may expire on our deathbed and rise through dark clouds to whatever hereafter there is and find out that God is Mickey Mouse.

Q: Do you regard yourself, then, as a Christian?

KING: I don't think so—but I don't know. I think there's real possibility that Christ may have been divine, but I don't think it's been proven. How can you prove a thing like that? Of course, you have to take it on faith. In fact, the whole tenet of Christianity is that you have to take these things on faith. Well, that's fine. If you can reject your intellect enough to have faith, that's fine.

Q: Yet even a skeptic might somehow find a certain religious element in most horror fiction.

KING: Yes, a lot of books deal in religious terms, even when they don't deal with standard religions. I think most of Lovecraft has religious overtones, in the sense that people in his stories worship various good and evil gods, with set rituals for calling them forth. There's a kind of doctrine in his fiction. There's even a Bible, the *Necronomicon*.

But even more than that, there's a great revival of mystical ideas today. Look at the society in which we're living, with all manner of technological horrors. Just take the difference between now and the time Bram Stoker wrote *Dracula*, when all the heroes were technological men. Seward put his diaries on a phonograph, which was very cool for his day. Van Helsing was a surgeon, gave transfusions, was even a psychologist, I think. Stoker was very taken by all this, the idea that technology was the wave of the future, the savior of mankind. But look at it now: fluorocarbons, cancer scares, pollution in the water, all this stuff. People are beginning to see that maybe technology is its own dead end. And so they've come to see mysticism as a possible alternative route.

Q: Some people have seen mystical overtones in your fourth novel, *The Stand*. In fact, it's been called a Christian allegory.

KING: Well, *The Stand* starts with a plague that wipes out most of the world's population, and it develops into a titanic struggle that Christianity figures in. But it's not about God, like some of the reviews have claimed. Stuart Redman isn't Christ, and the Dark Man isn't the Devil. It's the same with *'Salem's Lot*—Christianity is there, but it isn't the most important thing. The important thing is that we are dealing with two elemental forces—White and Black—and I really do believe in the White force. Children are part of that force, which is why I write about them the way I do. There are a lot of horror writers who deal with this struggle, but they tend to concentrate on the Black. But the other force is there, too; it's just a lot tougher to deal with. Look at Tolkien and *The Lord of the Rings*; he's much better at evoking the horror and dread of Mordor and the Dark Lord than he is at doing Gandalf.

Q: What you're saying is that the Black, at least logically, presupposes the White. If there are werewolves, there are also probably good fairies.

KING: Yes. But werewolves, of course, are a lot more fun.

Q: Maybe they're more fun because they appeal to the savage in us all—the thing that sneaks out and reminds us of what we've repressed.

KING: Yeah! Oh yeah. That David Keller story, "The Thing in the Cellar," is a classic example of that idea. That's what's so marvelous about the horror story. It's a kind of interface between the conscious and the subconscious, where you can go off in fifty different directions.

Q: With the possibility of going off in so many directions, you still manage to keep to just one. What kind of discipline do you impose on yourself in order to maintain such a prolific output? Is it true you try to write a set number of pages every day of the year?

KING: Yes, every day but Christmas and my birthday. I work on what's important to me in the morning, for three hours. Usually, in the afternoon, I have what call my "toy truck," a story that might develop or might not, but meanwhile it's fun to work on. Sometimes it's a story and sometimes it's a novel that might germinate. I begin to pile up some pages, and eventually it'll get shifted over to the morning.

Q: It looks, then, as if you intend to stay in the field.

KING: Sure. Of course. I don't feel the urge to change. I don't always intend to do horror, but somehow things almost always head that way. If they don't, I'm not going to fight it. You go where you feel you have to go. Writing is like that. You can't always tell yourself you're going to write one particular thing and that's that. You get the story, and the story takes hold, and away you go.

With Richard Wolinsky and Lawrence Davidson

Q: Your early work was in some of the Doc Lowndes magazines.

KING: Yeah, he was one of the guys that I knew about who was publishing the sort of stuff I wanted to do. I'd been submitting all along to *Fantasy & Science Fiction* and to *Fantastic* and to places like that, but Doc Lowndes gave me the first real encouragement. I also got some from the fellow who was editing *Fantasy & Science Fiction* at that time. Avram Davidson, that's who it was. It was Avram Davidson. But Lowndes—I sent him a story which later appeared in *F&SF*—oddly enough, it was rejected there by somebody—and it was called "Night of the Tiger," and he sent me a letter back and said I think it's a good piece but it's too long, because they were doing a lot of reprints then. So I sent him some other stuff and then finally he published my first two short stories there, and I understand that now he's the editor of *Sexology* and he must be really old. It's kind of funny.

Q: Did he give you a lot of feedback on your stories?

KING: Yes he did. One of the things that he did that I thought was useful was on "Night of the Tiger" he blue-penciled the story and he had surrounded phrases and things. He'd say "this phrase is hackwork," "this phrase is trite," or whatever it was, and he was pointing this stuff out, and I thought I was, you know, at that point Maine's answer to Shakespeare, and it was good to have things put in perspective, and he was good at that. I suspect that he was the last of the really great pulp editors.

Q: He's also unfortunately very underrated. A lot of people don't realize the impact that he had and that he was capable of keeping magazines going with basically no money at all.

KING: Yeah. Well, he bought a third story called "The Float," which he never ran because the magazines went out of business. And neither of the stories, the first two stories, have ever been anthologized. The first one I wouldn't want to see anthologized. That was called "The Glass Floor" and the second one was a better story and was called "The Reaper's Image," and that was a pretty good story. I stand by that one, but the first one, he was very kind to have published it all.

I went on writing short stories and I discovered the men's magazines as a market. What's odd about it is that I discovered the great key in the early Seventies right through to Seventy-five, and that was that they were not interested basically in porno fiction. I'd never read any fiction in the men's magazines. I rarely bought them at all, but when I did, it certainly was not to read their fiction and enlightening articles. I wanted to look at naked ladies. And I read some of this fiction and I was really surprised because they were publishing westerns, they were publishing science fiction, they were publishing everything but sex, and women were even not mostly in the stories at all. So I published a lot of stories in *Cavalier* and *Dude* and *Gent*. I published one in *Adam* that I wish was not under my real name, but it was, 'cause that's a real sleezo magazine.

So basically I did that and it kept bread on the table and the phone in the house 'cause we had two kids then and I was teaching school and we were really poor. But I stand by most of those stories and most of them are in *Night Shift*. There are two or three that are not, but most of them are. And, you know, I'm not the only writer in the history of the world that wrote for money instead of art but sometimes the two of them come together. There's no reason why they have to be exclusive.

Q: Did you come by the idea of writing horror, or primarily horror-related stories haphazardly, or was there some kind of rhyme or reason to it?

KING: There was no real rhyme or reason to it. I don't think that— first of all, I think that writers are made instead of born. I think that there are a lot of people beyond the number of people that become writers who have the talent to become writers but people underrate the amount of determination and work it takes to hone to the ability where you're good enough to be read in a kind of mass market way. So I think that writers are made and not born. But what you choose to write about is buried so deeply inside it's like lodestones inside you and sooner or later you come near something that you're supposed to be doing with your life and it's like a magnet. It attracts. It's like if you take a nine year old boy and he's just sort of walking around, not doing too much and maybe his mother takes him to a ballet, and he looks at that and says "that's fantastic." No reason why. And then all of a sudden he says "I want to be a ballet dancer when I grow up."

Q: What was the earliest horror thing that really attracted your attention when you were growing up?

KING: The first thing that I can remember, and I must have been no more than three at this time, was creeping out of my bedroom at night and hiding inside the darkened dining room while there were people in the living room listening to an adaptation of Ray Bradbury's "Mars Is Heaven" on *Dimension X*. This is the one where they get up there and all their dead relatives are there and they say, gee come on up and sit on the porch. We'll make you lemonade, afterwards we're gonna have some hamburgers and listen to the Yankees and they have the Yankee game and all the dead Yankees are playing and they're having a great time and they go to bed that night and this one guy wises up and he wakes up and he goes into the bedroom and their faces are changing and running and turning yellow and they got knives and they're stabbing all the astronauts. Which is what the Indians should have done. That's the first thing I remember and then I went back and slept with my brother that night I was so scared.

The second thing I remember is going to the Drive-In and seeing

Creature from the Black Lagoon. And just sitting there and watching and the thing that really got to me was the creature from the black lagoon was walling them up in the lagoon. He put sticks and things so that they couldn't get out again, and it's the reaction that people get to the works of Poe when they're older but I was only, like, four years old. He was walling them up. And I said, "I wanna do that! I'm really scared. I want to make people as scared as I am."

Q: When you got a little bit older, did you begin reading science fiction?

KING: Yes, I read a lot of science fiction. But something has happened to science fiction that I don't understand now. And I can't really say what it is. But it's taken a kind of sociological turn that I don't fully follow. I date my drawing away from science fiction to the time when Robert Silverberg started to do his really serious work and from that point on I think that he was a kind of, not a trend-maker, but he's kind of a seminal writer in modern science fiction and to me when somebody says Silverberg, I say early Silverberg or late. Because the later Silverberg, that's where I date people like Thomas Disch, Larry Niven, a lot of the people that I don't fully follow. Kate Wilhelm. Kate Wilhelm wrote a wonderful horror novel in the early sixties called *The Clone*. That was wonderful.

Q: The other primary element, besides horror, and I guess it's in line with horror, that occurs in all your fiction is telekinesis, psychic stuff— primarily *Carrie*, and I guess *The Dead Zone. The Stand* is a little different. I want to get into that a little later. Was there any interest in that from, let's say, a level of "gee, wouldn't it nice to be psychic," or "I am psychic," rather than merely as a tool to create horror.

KING: No. It's always been sort of a tool but not to create horror. More to create the situation. Because I tend to see people's lives as this nice fabric that's full of holes. We walk along through our lives and those holes are there and you can fall into one anytime. Like, you can go out and cross the street and some guy could come along who was drunk out of his mind and kill you dead and we don't think about that because we got this sort of selective perception, this tunnel vision that keeps us from thinking about it. You see what I mean?

As far as the horror and the psychic go, I see them as two sides of the same street. The psychic stuff to me is more realistic only because most people believe there is such a thing as telepathy. You know you catch a thought from time to time. Although it doesn't seem to be a controllable function whereas the other side of the street, the real horror, the stuff like

'Salem's Lot or *The Shining*, to me that is saying "Let's take people that are real people and put them in the context of a situation that's so incredible it's beyond belief and let them see what they do." And also, "let me see if I can make the reader believe it." And for me it's the game, to take the people, put them in the situation the way that you'd put lab rats in a different environment and see what happens. But the basic object in view is always to engage the reader, which is what the suspense novel is supposed to do and that's what the horror novel is. It's the difference between methadone and heroin to me. It's the real stuff.

Q: What strikes me in line with that is the juxtaposition in your books of the mundane, America as we know it—*The Stand* is very full of that, where everyday life goes on, and it kind of gets shot, and you do that to a lesser degree in the other books—and I guess you intend to make all that detail counterpoint to the horror.

KING: Not only counterpoint to horror but to try and give the situation enough reality so that people will be taken into the story because when you take a story of horror there's a seam that runs through it. It doesn't matter who the writer is. No matter how finely you sew, the seam always shows up. And my idea is that somehow you have to take the reader across that and still make them believe in the story. The reader will say, all right, I'll suspend my disbelief but to a certain point, that's okay, but beyond that if the story is not working on the realistic level it won't work on any other level either.

Q: Is that one of your reasons for bringing in a lot of real characters into *The Dead Zone*, like Jimmy Carter for instance?

KING: The book spans the Seventies. It starts in October of 1970 with Nixon president and Vietnam going on and it ends—the last real event that's mentioned is the Jonestown thing where all the people committed suicide, and my idea was let's bring as many real people into the story that would have actually existed in that period as possible. I try not to bring in just Jimmy Carter, who Johnny Smith shakes hands with in New Hampshire during the primary, but also Cassie Mackin, who was a correspondent on the Nightly News on NBC at that time, and a guy named George Herman who was a correspondent for CBS at the same time. And to bring in the little things as well. One of the ways that Johnny Smith knows that he's been out for four and a half years in his coma is because the doctor has a Flair pen and they weren't in general distribution in 1970. . . .

Q: The *New York Times* liked that one.

KING: Yeah, yeah.

Q: Did you actually do any research to figure out exactly what did and didn't exist?

KING: I did some. Oddly enough, one of things that I didn't remember and I had to look up was who died when because one of the things that Johnny says he's done when he comes out of the coma is to get a pile of *Newsweeks* and go through the obituaries to see who died and like Janis Joplin died, Jimi Hendrix died.

Q: In *Night Shift* you talk a lot about horror stories. What do you think makes a good horror story?

KING: Well, it has to appeal to fears that are general. That's the major thing. It has to appeal to the fear of death, the fear of closed in spaces, the fear of something so radically different from humanity as we know it that people simply recoil in horror, like spiders or rats or something like that—but it has to be something that is recognizable. To me, the big thing about Lovecraft is that what he continually seems to say is it's so horrible that if I describe it to you it will drive you insane, so I won't describe it to you. And to me that's like saying, "Wow, something happened and it was really sexy—Oh, my God was it sexy. Oh! If you knew you would just probably run out on the street raving, but I can't tell you what it was 'cause I don't want you to do that." It's tantalizing without actually going the extra step. Which leaves the reader to eventually say to himself, "Well, Lovecraft was saying this because he simply was bluffing and he didn't know what it was that was horrible." So I think that you have to go the step and say what it is and you risk—and I've been criticized on this, too—that when the horror is finally revealed, it's not as horrible as you thought it was. But that's always the case and that's why the horror novel always ultimately fails. Because when you describe what it is you throw light on it. It's like a little kid in his room and he sees the shadow on the wall and he says "Oh my god it's Jack the Ripper," right, and then his mother turns on the light and the shadow is the shadow of a box of toys or a pile of books or something.

Q: It seems that it's more the shock—that moment of ambiguity—that's the most important thing.

KING: Yeah, but I'm not that intellectual about it. You know, terror is the best of emotions, the best of the low emotions. That's what Poe said, and he's right and if I can get terror I will and if not, I'll go to horror, and if I can't succeed on the level of horror, I'll try to gross people out. That's one of the things about the literature that I believe the most strongly, is that you go with the effect. If you're not willing to go for the throat, you ought not to be in the business.

Q: In *Dead Zone*, you seem to veer a little bit away from horror and more toward suspense. I'm not sure if those moments in *Dead Zone* where John Smith sees what the future is going to be are horror necessarily. So much is just setting up the next step, which is, What is he going to do?

KING: Yeah. But what I really think is that effect follows story. Story does not follow effect. That is, you can't sit down and say I'm gonna write a horror novel now. What will I write about? All you have to say is I got an idea for a story and then you write it down and see what kind of an effect it has. I will not deliberately sit down and say "Okay, people like *Carrie*, *'Salem's Lot*, *The Shining*, so the next book will be horror." I'm going to write what I need to write because if you don't that's when you start to lie.

Q: At the end of *The Stand*, there's a resolution, and the same with *Dead Zone*. Do you know where you're going or at that moment, when you're writing it, did you make that decision?

KING: You know what the climax is gonna be, but you don't know what's going to happen. You see what I mean. You know that you're going toward that place and you know who is going to be there, generally speaking, but you don't really know what the characters are going to do, for sure.

Let me give you an example. This book that I'm just working on. I've gotten finally to the climax of the book, to that final scene. I knew from the beginning that—well, I don't want to give away the plot of the book—but there's a fellow involved who's done a really terrible thing and he realizes after it's too late that what he's done has set a chain of events in motion. There are just terrible things from beyond the grave that he's let loose with the best of possible intentions and I knew it was going to come down finally to a confrontation between himself and these forces, but I thought that the man's wife and children would be safely away, and as it turned out, his wife came back. She did that on her own. I didn't make her come back, I didn't say she would come back. She just ran back. Because characters get away sometimes and they start to go on their own and all you can do is hope that they go in a place that won't make the book too uncomfortable for you. You don't always know what's going to happen.

Q: In *The Stand*, did you anticipate what the stand would be?

KING: I did, comfortably before the end of the book, but I wasn't sure what the stand was going to be until I was about three quarters of the way through the book.

Q: Who is Randall Flagg?

KING: Randall Flagg to me is everything that I know of in the last twenty years that's really bad, or maybe even since Hitler. He's mostly Charlie Starkweather who I was afraid of when I was a kid. I read the stories about Charlie Starkweather and his killing spree and I was really terrified by what he was doing. He's partially Charles Manson and he's partially Charles Whitman, the Texas tower killer, and Richard Speck and all these people. The thing that impresses over and over again is these people are really stupid and that something goes into them, whether it's the devil or Satan or whatever it is, it goes into them and then these people get caught and that thing flies away and you have someone who says, "Well, I don't know what I did, Jeez, I don't know." "Did you do it?" "Yeah, I did it." "But why did you do it?" "I don't know. I don't know why I did it."

Because they don't, see? Something got into 'em. It's like Lyndon Johnson when he was running the war in Vietnam. That man was possessed of the devil. Satan was in that man and then he came on TV and he said, "I'm not going to run for re-election." It was in '68, and I saw the devil go out of that man and he just turned into this old guy. Somebody interviewed him shortly before he died, and she said somthing like "Lyndon, why did you do that? You knew that you couldn't win cover there without using nuclear weapons." He was in bed. He had his gall bladder out and he was dying of congestive heart failure, or something. He had the sheet pulled up to his chin and she said "Why did you do that?" He said, "I don't know." Just like that. 'Cause it was out of him. See, it gets into you. And that's what's in Randall Flagg, and toward the end of *The Stand* it leaves him. Whatever it is, it's leaving him, a little at a time, and he's just nobody.

Q: Do you believe in the devil?

KING: I have a view of the devil. I do, but my view of what he is is so complex that I don't think that I could express it in words.

Q: Do you believe in an absolute good and an absolute evil?

KING: Next question, please.

Q: What kind of research did you do on assassins?

KING: I didn't do any. Nothing that isn't common knowledge.

Q: What kind of research did you do on psychics?

KING: I read about psychics. Psychics kind of fascinate me. People like Hurkos and Edgar Cayce and people like that. I tend to believe that a lot of what goes on in the psychic world—well, let's put it this way, that most of it is either the work of knowing charlatans or people who are being misled by their own needs, their own psychological make-up. But some of it defies that easy explanation, so I'm an agnostic who leans toward belief.

Q: You've had movies made of three of your novels. . . .

KING: But I've only seen one.

Q: You've only seen *Carrie*. . . . What did you think of it?

KING: I liked *Carrie*. I thought *Carrie* was good. You've put it in context particularly if you've read a lot in this field, the fantasy field. Back in the days of the silents, they made a picture out of A. A. Merritt's *Seven Footprints to Satan* and it's written in one of Forry Ackerman's books that when Merritt saw it he wept. And that would be a standard reaction, I think, among most writers of fantasy whose books have been adapted for the films. Look at what happened to Zelazny's *Damnation Alley*, for instance. There are other examples as well. But I think that I was treated well in *Carrie* the way that, for instance, Fritz Leiber was treated well in *Burn, Witch, Burn*.

I'm hopeful for the other two. *'Salem's Lot* is going to be a miniseries on CBS and I'm hoping it will be good. I've read the script, and the script is good. The stars are good, but still, it's TV, and it makes me nervous. And, of course, Kubrick's doing *The Shining*. I hope for good things.

Q: What was your reaction when you found out that it was Kubrick doing *The Shining*?

KING: I didn't have one. The man's gotta do something.

Q: My feeling was that Kubrick is one of the greatest American directors.

KING: Well, I think that too. I think he's a genius and there are only about three in the business where most directors have good visual eyes and they're intellectually pinheads. And Kubrick is not that. He's not a pinhead, but also I don't have any reaction to him doing the book, primarily because I don't believe he has any real reaction to my work. It's a question of having read the book and saying "We can do certain things with this."

It's been so long, too. You know, I got to be a big hit with my friends. I would just casually toss it at a cocktail party. "By the way, Kubrick's doing my new book and . . ." "Oh. Really?" I was quite a hit there for a while, but two years have gone by and people say now "Is it ever gonna come? Yeah, where is it?"

Q: What do you think is the greatest horror movie of all time?

KING: Let me give you about five names. I think that *The Texas Chainsaw Massacre* is one of them. And I think *Night of the Living Dead* is probably one of them. And *Freaks* by Todd Browning is probably one of them. *The Cat People* by Val Lewton. The original *Invasion of the Body Snatchers*. And I'm leaving some out. *Psycho, Frenzy, Dementia 13*, which was Francis Coppola's first picture.

Q: What about *Alien?*

KING: I think *Alien's* very good, but I don't think it's one of the best of all time. It might be, with the cut 11 minutes restored. *The Haunting*, yeah. That's another one.

Q: What about books, other than yours?

KING: The best horror novel I've read in about . . . well, I liked Peter Straub's *Ghost Story* very much. That's a good one. But the best horror novel that I've read in the last three years is Anne Rivers Siddons's book, *The House Next Door.*

With Bhob Stewart

Q: Have you done any TV/radio interviews with people who have never read a single word you've written?

KING: Yes. I don't get angry. It's fun to watch them fumble around for any kind of a decent question when they haven't read anything that you've done. The bad part of it is that you answer the same question over and over again: "Why do you write this stuff?" Not very interesting questions after you've answered them for the fortieth time.

Q: What do you think of Fritz Leiber's *Our Lady of Darkness*, J. Ramsey Campbell's *The Doll Who Ate His Mother* and *Breakthrough* by Ken Grimwood?

KING: I thought *Our Lady of Darkness* was probably the second or third best fantasy novel by Fritz Leiber that I'd ever read. And I think it's the best thing he's done easily since *Conjure Wife*. I thought the middle was very static. About 40 or 50 pages take place in the old sorcerer's house in San Francisco. The central metaphor of the book, when he talks about the city as organism, I think is very vivid and very alive. The first long section of the book where he walks out to this hill and sees the Pale Brown Thing waving from *his* window: that's a shocker. That could stand by itself. *Breakthrough* by Grimwood I have on my shelf, but I haven't read. In *The Doll Who Ate His Mother* Ramsey Campbell is consistently pointing at the bridge between horror and fantasy as ghetto fiction; it's a kind of New Wave breakthrough for fiction. I think that it's a tremendously exciting book. I don't think it's the best book he can produce because I don't think he feels totally comfortable with a novel yet. But I thought the climax in that cellar was the best part of the book. People talk about how Campbell didn't know how to end this book and so the ending is very disappointing. I think they missed the entire point of the ritual aspect of that because it's really Lovecraftian. I think that's wonderful. To me, who the cannibal was is the least important aspect of the book. The most important aspect is what caused it in the first place: this kind of spellcasting with all those dolls in the basement. I think it's a terrible title, *The Doll Who Ate His Mother*, but a fantastic book. His new one has just been sold to America; it's a long, long novel.

Q: There's a new Roald Dahl anthology series, *Tales of the Unexpected*. Do you remember Dahl's superb *Way Out* TV series?

KING: *Way Out*? Yes. I liked the one where Barry Sullivan or whoever had the retouching fluid to make his face younger—and his wife spilled it all over him. His face was smooth on one side. Remember that?

Q: No, but it reminds me of the E.C. story "Drawn and Quartered" about the voodoo artist who dies in a subway accident at the moment a bottle of turpentine is spilled over his self-portrait. Did you ever do any comic book stories?

KING: No. When I was really on my uppers, before *Carrie* sold, I submitted several ideas to *Creepy* when, I think, Marv Wolfman was editor. I stopped reading it for a while. They started to do a lot of reprints and I got rather pissed. Just dropped it.

Q: What were the titles of the fanzines you wrote for?

KING: I wrote for a magazine called *Tales of Suspense* edited by Marv

Wolfman. The story that I did was reprinted in his magazine and was originally done by a fan from Alabama named Mike Garret who had a magazine of his own. Originally it was a story called "I Was a Teenage Graverobber." The title really stank. The story was a lot better than the title. Wolfman retitled it "In a Halfworld of Terror" which kind of caught the feeling of the story.

Q: Was that straight text or a comic book story?

KING: It was straight text, and they illustrated it with three or four comic illustrations—different ones for each of the magazines. That was the only fan story I ever did. One of the things I think has been good for me—really, really good—is that I stayed out, mostly by luck, of that circle of fanzines and fans that club together. They do the same thing that the literary bohemians do in Greenwich Village when they all go down at the Lion's Head and drink a lot of beer and piss out their novel ideas. These fans, a lot of them, don't realize how destructive it is to any aspirations that they have for writing. They get together and talk about "Gee! How wonderful this movie was" or "how wonderful the last story was by Fritz Leiber" or whatever. They're pissing away anything that they might be doing on their own. I've got no animus against the fan magazines. Whenever anyone sends me one, I always read it cover to cover. But I'm glad, for myself, that I stayed out of that.

Q: Your first four books were sold without an agent.

KING: First five. *The Dead Zone* is the first where the deal was done by an agent.

Q: Before that, you did several novels that never sold?

KING: Yeah. I did one called. . . trying to go back to the very beginning . . . It's very dusty in that part of my mind. What the hell was the name of that? I cannot remember. Isn't that funny? I've just come up totally blank. *Getting It On.* I did a book called *Getting It On.* And *Babylon Here*—which was just a very strange surreal book. It wasn't very good. I did a race riot novel, *Sword of the Darkness*, that was just terrible. After that I started to get it together; I did *Carrie* and *Salem's Lot*, and the other stuff came right along.

Q: These first books were submitted to and rejected by a number of publishers?

KING: Two were, and one of them just seemed Dead On Arrival. It's never been seen by anybody but me. It's just tucked away in a drawer. The race riot novel is fun to read. It's embarrassing as far as the human motivations go. It's a long book. It's exciting, I think, but it's not believable.

Q: How did you manage without an agent?

KING: The actual progression was I had *Getting It On*—which I did think was good. I decided to go to Doubleday because Doubleday is a publishing mill, and I thought I'd have a better chance at a place where they were publishing a lot of fiction. I wrote a letter. I said, "I've got this book that's a psychological suspense novel in its tone." It reminded me a little bit of *The Parallax View*, this little novel they had done that became a movie later on. My letter went to the editor of *The Parallax View* who was out with some kind of sickness—influenza or something. So that went to Bill Thompson who later edited all of those books—*Carrie* through *The Stand*—and he had seconded *The Parallax View* for publication. He read my letter, and he wrote me a letter: "Send the book along." He was really impressed with it, and he tried very hard to get it published through Doubleday and couldn't. He then jobbed it around to some other publishers and almost lost his job when they found out. After that he dropped me a line every now and then, saying, "Are you doing anything now?" And I'd say, "I'm trying." We corresponded back and forth. When *Carrie* got done, I didn't think it was a very commercial book or a very saleable book, but I sent it to him so he'd know I was doing something. I was really surprised when he bought it. That's how I ended up with Doubleday, a very paternalistic outfit. I heard one member of the top brass once say he'd like to get every agent in New York and blow their knees off with a shotgun. It's that kind of an outfit. I stayed with them, and they did decently by me, I would say.

With George Christian

Q: What kind of kid were you, what were you afraid of?

KING: Well, as a kid I was afraid of the things that children are always afraid of. Of not being accepted by my peers. Although I think I was, pretty well. I was afraid of the dark. I liked to go to the monster movies, but after the monster movie was over and I was *alone*, you know, I'd think: what if that thing comes and gets me? I'd say that all in all they were pretty natural fears.

I had a big imagination. When you're a kid, you're not in control of that. You know, it's like giving a little kid a great big V-8 automobile and saying, "Now drive this."

The thing is God doesn't make any allowances for that. You have to grow into your imagination. Your imagination doesn't grow with you. I'm convinced that it's innate. And it may even be stronger when you're a kid.

Ghosts. Boogies. I was afraid that my mother would die and we would be orphans. You name it, all the things I suppose all children are afraid of. My father deserted the family when I was two. My brother was four. And so my mother worked a lot of jobs and we didn't see her a lot. There was a succession of babysitters. Stuff of that nature.

Q: How did you cope with childhood terrors?

KING: I pulled the covers up over my head. I dealt with them the way anybody deals with them, you know. I had a night light. My mother was very understanding about that. I told her I needed to see to go to sleep. I think she understood, exactly what it was I was talking about.

The only other thing you do with your fears is you live through 'em. I was convinced as a kid that I would die before I was 20 years old. Because there was a lot of violent radio when I was a kid. You know, radio programs like *The Inner Sanctum* and *The Swinging Door* and *I Love a Mystery, Dimension X*, I used to listen to all of those.

Somebody on your block would have a TV and you'd drop by to watch *Your Hit Parade, Highway Patrol* with Broderick Crawford or some of that stuff. You know, death came cheap. And I was convinced I would be walking home from school one day and somebody would just grab me and that would be the end.

You learn just to exist with your fears. Which is what we do as grownups. We just have a much smaller circle of fears because we block the rest of them out. Very efficiently. Part of what growing up is that systematic quenching of one's imagination.

If you see imagination as a bunch of candles on a candelabra, then for every year we grow up we put another one out. As kids I think we're wide open. Kids believe in Santa Claus. They have no trouble swallowing that at all. You tell a kid about the devil and the kid says: "What's the devil?" You say: "Well, he's a demon with a forked tail and he's got cloven hooves and he lives at the center of the earth in a hot place called hell." The kid says: "Does he really? He's bad?" And the mother and father say: "That's right, he's bad, and if *you're* bad, you'll go down to hell and you'll burn there for eternity." And the kid accepts that but he'll say: "What's eternity?" And you say: "Forever and ever."

It works.

Q: Would you say that by denying fear we deny imagination?

KING: Yes! Because that's the price we *pay.* It's like that fairy tale about the mermaid that wanted to be a woman. And the fairy godfather or whatever said: "Well, you get rid of your tail and we'll give you feet but every step you take on land will be like walking on the blades of knives." And she said *okay.* It's got two edges. It can swing out and do wonderful things and create marvels. But it can cut you as well.

A lot of it has to do with what you let out of the cage you can't necessarily put back in.

Q: When one denies fear, what happens to it?

KING: Well, the *fashionable* thing to say is that those fears become sublimated. They become part of the subconscious. And that those fears come out in other ways. And to some extent I think that's true. But on the other hand I think that children have a better grasp, for instance, on the experience of dying—maybe up to the age of 10—than we do as adults. It isn't something we concern ourselves with. We have other things. We have the job. We have the family. We have a wife. We don't spend a lot of time concerned with those things. I think that if you don't think about these things that after a time they atrophy and they die quite naturally.

I don't think that we sublimate all our fears. There are fears I think we *do* sublimate. There are various sexual fears. There are fears that we may do violence to people. There may even be for a lot of people fears that we're losing our grip on the world. Those fears we do sublimate.

Q: Is part of the appeal of your books that you help people surface these things?

KING: I like to think it is. I think that this is the idea of catharsis, which is something that people who deal with horror have used—the first time I read the word was in defense of the horror story by Ray Bradbury, when I was no more than 10.

There's an article in *Harper's* this month that deals with my work. Where the fellow takes the thesis that this is some sort of religious experience in a generation that's lost any kind of spiritual thing.

Q: A wish for something supernatural?

KING: Yeah, the idea that this is bigger than all of us. But the whole point is that it's akin to how many angels can dance on the head of a pin. Catharsis is a very old idea, it goes back to the Greeks. The point I guess I'm trying to make is that there's an element of horror in any dramatic situation that's created.

Certainly Ahab in *Moby Dick* is a creature of horror, as is the whale.

It doesn't have to be supernatural to be horrible.

Q: How did *Dracula* affect you?

KING: I think I was about 11 when I first read it. Got it out of the adult section of the library. That was my first adult book. And I read it at night in bed. I expected to be scared out of my wits, and I really *wasn't*. I was transported by the excitement, by the *adventure* of it. And that's why people label me as a horror novelist. If I had to take any label other than just novelist I'd say I'm an adventure writer.

You know, because to me all of these things are adventures. *Dracula* certainly is. The first five chapters are wonderful. Jonathan Harker is cooped up in this castle, and what I liked about that, what I responded to both as a child and as an adult, was that he's terrified of Dracula but he's also terribly brave. I think this bravery in the face of horror is one of the things that people respond to in my work. I don't think that people just want to see a kind of supernatural car crash.

Q: Is the measure of a good horror novel that its characters confront their own fears?

KING: Yeah. We see them facing up to the worst things in their lives in various ways. And in the most successful horror novels I think that they measure up to those fears rather nobly. Rosemary in *Rosemary's Baby* is very brave and very resourceful. I've never forgiven Ira Levin for not allowing her to get away, for the coven to get her baby. I know the baby was the devil and had little horns and little golden eyes, but it should have been up to her to deal with it.

Q: How do you deal with nightmares?

KING: You don't *deal* with that. You just experience it and hope that it won't happen again. I guess that I spent some sleepless nights. I thought about them a lot. I can remember some of them today. But you can't *deal* with that.

Q: How have you preserved this magical childlike gift for terror?

KING: Because I've cultivated it, that's all. I've always written the stuff and writing keeps it alive. You tend to see things in a little wider way or from a different angle.

I did the Mike Wallace radio show in New York at the CBS building. We went in and the electric eye had a case of the hiccups. The door was one of these doors where you'd step on the pad and the door would slide open. And this door was jerking back and forth, not closing or opening all the way.

And my feeling about that is that somebody else would look at that and say: Oh that door has the hiccups. Whereas a little kid would walk up to that door and might very well shrink away from even going near it. And say: "It wants to eat me, it's alive!" Because they're broader, they see things from a different perspective.

And in that sense I'm childlike. I looked at it and I thought, gee, that's make a good story if that thing came alive and somebody walked up to it and CHUNG! Which is a very childish sort of fantasy.

People respond to this. It doesn't really die. It atrophies and lies dormant. And if you can show them that different perspective that's what I get paid to do. It's like exercising a muscle, rather than letting it go slack, if you continue to exercise. Now I've gone slack in other ways. I've got kind of a beer belly and that sort of thing. But I'll tell you a funny thing. There are writers who *look* like children. They've used this facility so much for so long that they literally look like children.

Ray Bradbury is 60 years old and he has the face of a child. You see it in the eyes a lot of the time. Isaac Singer has the eyes of a child in that old face. They look out of that old face and they've very young.

That's why people pay writers and artists. That's the only reason we're around. We're excess baggage. My God! I can't even fix a pipe in my house when it freezes. I am a dickey bird on the back of civilization.

I have no skill that improves the quality of life in a physical sense at all. The only thing I can do is say: "Look here, this is the way you didn't look at it before. It's just a cloud to you, but look at it, doesn't it look like an elephant?" Somebody says: "Boy! it *does* look like an elephant!" And for that people pay because they've lost all of it themselves.

You know, I'm like a person who makes eyeglasses for the mind.

CHAPTER THREE

✝

A BRAND NAME IS BORN

✝

With Jerry Harkavy (1979)

Be careful this Halloween! That tall trick-or-treater behind the witch's mask may be none other than America's premier horror writer.

Stephen King, whose latest novel, *The Dead Zone*, is soaring on the bestseller lists, will be stalking the back roads of rural Maine this Wednesday night, wearing a pullover mask of a toothsome witch with gleaming orange eyes.

While lovers prefer Valentine's Day and patriots yearn for the Fourth of July, it comes as no surprise that King's favorite holiday is Halloween.

"It is the day when the door is unlatched, when evil holds sway," says the 31-year-old master of the macabre.

"It's a day to acknowledge the idea that most people live in a very small lighted space, surrounded by all of the darkness of the unknown. Maybe a crash out of the tunnel vision for a little bit and regard that darkness. What are the shapes moving around in it?"

When the sun goes down, King, his wife Tabitha and their three children will be out trick-or-treating.

"This is Uncle Creepy. He glows in the dark," says King, showing off the fiendish mask selected by his 7-year-old son, Joe. Daughter Naomi, 9, will dress as the evil Snow Queen of fairy tale fame, while Owen, 2½, will portray the ever-popular Frankenstein.

Despite King's enthusiasm for Halloween, he laments that its spirit has been devalued over the years, much the way candy bars passed out to children have shrunk in size.

"Halloween is just another case of a serious holiday that's become secularized," he said. "There's been a conscious demystification of the holiday, just in the time since I was a kid. And it's done on purpose—there's a real feeling that Halloween has got to be stamped out."

To King, Halloween is a day to acknowledge dark forces at work in the world. But this isn't easy, he says, when people no longer believe in the supernatural and won't give credence to things they can't perceive with their own senses.

It's hard to dwell on evil spirits, he admits, when parents focus their concern on more mundane possibilities—the apple with the razor blade, the treat laced with LSD, or traffic safety.

King, whose novels—*Carrie*, *'Salem's Lot*, *The Shining*, *The Stand* —and short stories feature vampires, psychics and things that go bump in the night, says it's become much harder for today's youngsters to get a good scare.

He pins the blame on child psychologists, who say it's wrong to frighten children, and mass merchandisers, who created cereal-box and cartoon-show monsters that border on the benign.

What to do then, to get back in touch with the true spirit of Halloween?

The real aficionados, says King, should wait until 10 or 11 p.m., then go off to a graveyard, "sit down for a while and talk about spirits."

For the less ambitious, he suggests simply turning down the lights, telling ghosts stories and exploring the darkness.

"There's too many electric bulbs...on Halloween, every power company in the world should pull their switches."

With Bill Munster

Q: Did you write "The Mangler" and "Gray Matter" as a sort of comic relief or were you seriously writing them as horror stories?

KING: I didn't have tongue-in-cheek—they were written as "straight" horror stories.

Q: In many of your short stories like "Trucks," "Graveyard Shift," and

"Gray Matter," you leave the ending open. Is this to make the reader use his or her imagination or so that you could continue the story at a later date?

KING: There comes a point where the story is over. It may seem that it's left up to the reader's imagination, but I think in a good story all the sign posts are there, and unless you are a lazy reader, you know where the author is going.

Q: What do you consider your best work thus far?

KING: That's a hard question—I think *IT*, an unpublished manuscript I recently finished, may be my best work to date. It won't be published for a couple of years yet, not until I do a re-write.

Q: You stated that you plan to leave the horror genre of literature so that you won't be classed specifically as a writer of horror. Do you feel that you will be as successful in a different genre and do you expect your following to continue reading a non-horror story?

KING: I don't recall every stating that I would leave the horror genre, and I'd be interested to know where you heard that. I love the genre, and while I may occasionally depart from it, I'll never entirely leave it. I have no set plan of design for the future—I write what seems right, what occurs.

Q: In your recent works, such as *The Stand* and *Cujo*, you seem to be growing away from a more Victorian class of horror towards one that deals with more familiar topics, i.e., the switch from vampires to atomic explosions and rabid dogs. Could this be because you find many of the older devices utilized by horror to be worn out and trite?

KING: The fact that the more familiar horror topics such as vampires, werewolves, ghosts are overworked and threadbare is not entirely the reason I've stayed away from them somewhat. I think they can still be great if you can come up with a fresh approach I tried a werewolf novel set on a college campus, but had to abandon it. Just couldn't breathe life into it.

Q: Several of your short stories serve as a basis for novels that you later went on to write. For example, "Jerusalem's Lot" and "One for the Road" served as an introduction to *'Salem's Lot*; "Night Surf" was the underlying theme for *The Stand*; "The Boogeyman" provided a scene for *Cujo*. Was this purely accidental or did you intend to develop these short stories into novel length?

KING: With "Night Surf" I knew the book was there, I just wasn't ready to write it (I was about nineteen when I wrote that story). Many of those stories were written for the money, and I sensed that they could be novels; examples would be "The Bogeyman" and "Gray Matter."

Q: There seems to be in most of your stories an English teacher, an academic setting, or a writer. *Carrie* spills havoc onto a high school; "Sometimes They Come Back" has Jim Norman, an English teacher, fighting against demons; *Firestarter* begins on a college campus; *The Dead Zone* provides a high school teacher with a splitting headache; and a writer in '*Salem's Lot* must fend off a village of vampires. Having served as an English teacher yourself, are you vicariously living out your own fantasies?

KING: No, I'm not living out my fantasies, just using what I know. I've been student and teacher both, and know the routine, which makes what I write more convincing. In my next book, *Different Seasons*, there is a section called "Apt Pupil" which deals with grade fixing, and my experience as a teacher came in handy for that.

Q: Having written so many visually interesting stories, would you ever consider hosting a TV-show of your material on a weekly basis?

KING: I have been offered a series seven times, by various networks. I have turned the offers down, partly because it's not a good time for such a project for me personally, and partly because I feel to do horror well, you have to have some freedom, which television doesn't give you because of the restrictions imposed by "standards and practice" laws, which is basically censorship.

Q: When you sit down to write a story, do you outline it first or do you plunge right into the story?

KING: I plunge right in, but only after months of thought and turning it over in my head.

Q: Horror films today seem to have the attitude that to scare an audience all that's needed is tons of gore and a tap-'em-on-the-shoulder-and-yell-BOO! Do you feel that films that employ a startle and repulse philosophy are doing justice to the genre of horror?

KING: I don't think gore is necessarily bad—it can be used well, as in *Psycho*. There have been some badly made horror movies lately, because they were made by people who don't care about the genre.

Q: In *Danse Macabre* you state that the early *Twilight Zone*, *Tales from the Crypt*, and films such as *Them*, *The Thing* and other related horror movies influenced your writing. What modern day movies, TV-shows or magazines influence your writing today?

KING: Not too many shows, movies or magazines influence me today, because I think you reach a point where you are not so easily influenced. I just read some Charles Dickens though, and found it heavily influenced my work.

With Pat Cadigan, Marty Ketchum and Arnie Fenner

KING: I did two screenplays just this year. I joked to people about it, although by the time I was finished I didn't feel like it was much of a joke. I was calling it *King's Double Feature*. I did *Cujo* and I gave myself two days off and then I did *The Dead Zone*. When I finished I felt like an editor for *Reader's Digest Condensed Books*.

I think that that experience more than anything else showed me there's creativity involved in writing the original screenplay. But in taking your own work and trying to transfer it to that medium, it isn't an *anti*-creative act, but it isn't creative either. It's just trying to take out everything that you can from your original work in order to fit a mold.

Q: *Creepshow* will premiere October 29th. What are your feelings about the film?

KING: I feel good about it. On the other hand, anybody who is on the inside of a film has this tendency to feel good about it. I don't know, maybe there's a possibility that your creative judgment warps after a certain point. It's like, what haunts me is I think that Gore Vidal and everybody else involved with *Myra Breckenridge* probably sat around and said, "Yep, this is probably the greatest movie since *The Great Train Robbery*, since Chaplin." And then the thing came out and it was absolutely dreadful. In that sense, you can't accept my word for whether it's good or bad. All I can say is that I like it and feel satisfied with it. It's been previewed in a version that's substantially longer than the one that's finally going to play and the audience just tears up the seats. They go crazy.

Q: How do you like being an actor?

KING: I'm not very crazy about it, really. It's hard. The deal with the make-up—this is a story about a guy who turns *green*—he just *grows*, man! So at first they had broken this thing down into five separate make-up stages. The first stage is just Jordy Verrill who clumps around in his bib overalls; he's just a guy. Then there were some blisters that they put on with some kind of polyurethane material—it's very shiny—and injected with a green fluid through a hypo. That was Okay. Then there was growth starting on the arms, chest and head. And there was a prosthetic tongue; I wore that around a lot. That was *fun*. I would go over to this mall that was next to where I was staying and stick out my tongue at clerks and things. They'd go, "Yaahh! Jesus!"

By the end it was like full make-up all the time and it would be four or five hours sitting in a chair while they'd put greenery on with airplane glue—sometimes—and sometimes with surgeon's glue. And you'd wait for it to be over and the only way you could console yourself was to say, "Well, Boris Karloff: six hours, seven hours getting into make-up as the Mummy." But even that aside, you sit around waiting to be called and you sit and you wait and with all that greenery on you can't even go the bathroom without help. Literally. You can't unzip your fly or anything else. To spend those long periods and wait for something to happen can be wearing. And then when it happens there are those cases where it has to be *right* or everything gets screwed up and you're costing somebody a lot of money. The first shot of the episode that I was in involved a matte shot where Jordy watches the meteor come down from space. It was simply something where I looked at the sky and moved on cue so that later when it was scratched on the matte it would look like I was tracking the fall of the meteor. The sky had to be just right and we only had time for two takes. If they hadn't gotten it I could have cost somebody $10,000 just by having the wrong expression. I don't like to be responsible for that sort of thing.

Q: How active is your role in the productions of *Firestarter* and *The Dead Zone?*

KING: Well, I did the screenplay for *The Dead Zone.* It's a Dino de Laurentiis production. I like the screenplay very much. *He* had problems with my version so right now it's sitting in limbo. I think he'd like to bring somebody in and get a revision done on it. I'm not sure why but, then, that's why I can't do the revision because I can't understand why he wants further changes.

John Carpenter's going to do *Firestarter.* Bill Lancaster did the screenplay—he's the guy who did *The Thing.* It's a pretty good screenplay. The weird thing is that they turn Rainbird into a woman; the big Indian is a woman in this version. It doesn't work very well until the very end of the screenplay when it *does* work. There's something very terrible about the character—I guess maybe it's the flip side of Rainbird instead of a kind of Oedipal sexual attraction between the Indian and the little girl. That was never overt in the book, but it was there. I was aware of it.

What you get in the movie translation is this hideous maternal thing where the little girl is sort of drawn to trust this scientist who has had her mother killed so they can dissect her pituitary gland after they complete the cycle of their experiments. But in a lot of ways I think it lacks punch and they may change things back to be closer to the original. Carpenter has a few problems with Lancaster's screenplay. We talked them over and I suggested some things he could do. But honestly, the problems that Carpenter had didn't strike me as terribly problematical. I thought the screenplay was pretty good. It's workable.

Q: *Different Seasons* has just been released in hardback. In the book's afterword you commented that you'd written each of the four stories after having finished a novel. Since only one of the four is a horror story, I was wondering if you were using the short stories as a change of pace. Were they a way to purge yourself of the novels?

KING: Sort of. The other thing was that all of these stories were my bedtime stories. If you're writing a novel, that doesn't mean that the idea machine stops. You still get ideas and a lot of times you get really glum about it because you have a good idea and you say, "Fantastic! I'm gonna write this right now!" and this little voice says, "No, you can't! You're in the middle of *The Stand* and you won't be done for a year!" Oh *shit*! So what I do, a lot of times what I've always done, really—is instead of counting sheep when I go to bed I'll let a story start to unroll. It's a little bit like watching a movie; like going to sleep in front of a television set.

A lot of times there'll be six or seven of these things you run though in the course of a novel. A lot of them never seem worth writing down. Or you've told the story so completely to yourself that there's nothing left to find out. But in the cases of the *Different Seasons* stories, they were just sort of there and the impetus was there to finish them up. With the exception of "The Breathing Method," which is the horror story. And what happened with that was that it just really did get too long to be published anywhere as short fiction, but it was nowhere near long enough to stand on its own. But in another sense, except for the prison break story, they're all sort of horror stories. The worst one isn't the supernatural one: I think it's "Apt Pupil" about this old guy and a boy. That's a *dreadful* story. Unghh! Nasty.

Q: With your enormous popularity and with all of your books high on the bestseller list why did you decide to go the small press route with *The Dark Tower*? Why Donald Grant instead of Viking?

KING: I think it's a book that's got a small audience; a naturally small audience. It's a weird book to start with. Very strange. It's not complete. That's the other thing. It's really the opening; it's like part one of a novel. It's like having *Lord Foul's Bane* without having *The Illearth War* and *The Power That Preserves*. It's just the start. Also because it's what I think of as being hard fantasy in the sense of—I'm trying to think of some of these writers—people like Karl Edward Wagner and those guys do hard fantasy. It isn't the sort of thing I've done ordinarily that's accessible to people who are not used to reading say Tanith Lee or C.J. Cherryh. I guess that's why.

But also because Don asked me and because I'm, you know, sort of a fan myself and fans like to have something that nobody else has. With a book like *Different Seasons*—how can you collect a first edition of *Different Seasons*? The first edition is 140,000 copies. I mean, really. That's absurd. So with *The Dark Tower: The Gunslinger* there are 10,000 copies in the trade edition and there are 500 that Michael Whelan and I signed. And that's *it*. There isn't going to be a paperback, there isn't going to be a second edition. You've either got one or you don't. To me that sort of makes it a legitimate collector's edition. It has a bigger print run, granted, than anything H.P. Lovecraft ever had in hardcover, but still there are a lot of people that like it, I hear.

Q: There's a popular rumor floating around that you have a novel on the stands now that was written under a pseudonym. The book is *The Running Man* by Richard Bachman and Signet has supposedly confirmed the rumor. Are you Bachman?

KING: No, that's not me. I know who Dick Bachman is though. I've heard the rumor. They have Bachman's books filed under my name at the Bangor Public Library and there a *lot* of people who think I'm Dick Bachman. I went to school with Dicky Bachman and that isn't his real name. He lives over in New Hampshire and *that* boy is crazy! [laughter] That boy is absolutely crazy. And sooner or later this will get back to him and he'll come to Bangor and he'll kill *me*, that's all.

Several times I've gotten his mail and several times he's gotten mine. He's at Signet because of me and when the editors got shuffled things might have gotten confused. Maybe that's how it got all screwed up and the rumor started.

But I am not—*not*—Richard Bachman.

Q: *Cujo* and *Danse Macabre* are now in paperback. *Different Seasons* is out in hardcover and the *Creepshow* comic adaptation is on the stands. What will be your next book?

KING: There's a novel coming out called *Christine* in May. It's a great big long book and it's the first horror novel I've done, I think, since *The Shining*. I think I've only done two: *'Salem's Lot* and *The Shining* and now *Christine* is a real horror novel. That's all I'm going to say about it. Except it's scary. It's fun, too. It's maybe not my best book—it's kind of like a high school confidential. It's great from that angle.

Q: Your books have sold something like 40 million copies, there are four movies based on your work and more on the way. You seem pretty much the same since we first met, but I have to ask *the* dumb question. Has success spoiled Stephen King?

KING: Yes. Yes, it has. It has. I've turned into an utter shit in the last year and a half. [laughter] I couldn't help it!

With David Sherman

Q: At this point, you've got to be utterly sick to death of interviews. Is there any one question that will make you run away screaming if you hear it again?

KING: No. Not yet. Twelve years from now. . . . The interviews that I dread are, "I'm going to ask you a lot of questions you've never heard before." You know somehow, at that point, that they're going to ask you *all* the questions you've heard before.

Q: You're going to be asked again if you're dissatisfied with the film version of *The Shining*.

KING: Where do you get your ideas, right?

Q: I think they've done you to death on that one. I understand you had an autograph session this afternoon. A magazine or television interview, such as this one, is generally done in a reasonably controlled environment. But with an autograph session, you're pretty much thrust into the hands of your adoring public. Does that ever become a little frightening? Don't you worry that a couple of hundred of the faithful are going to bolt the line because they all want to hug you and shake your hand and tell you how much they love your books, until they wind up crushing you against a wall?

KING: Yeah. You think about. . . it's like *The Day of the Locust*. You know, the one where they eat the guy up or something. But what really happens—the scariest autograph party that I ever did was the first one where *a lot* of people came. It was a Dalton in South Portland. And nobody there was prepared. I had an idea that there might be a lot of people, and this thing was around Christmas time.

Q: Which book was it for?

KING: It was for *Firestarter*. Nominally. But at this period, people were bringing everything, and it was before the time when I started asking book store personnel, "Would you limit the number of copies you let a person ask to be signed? And then if they have more books, tell 'em they can get in the back of the line again." And none of 'em want to do that. So, what happened was, there was no crowd control at all, and the crowd collapsed inward, around the table. At first, there's a kind of charisma, about writers, that maybe film stars or rock stars don't have. There was an open circle, and it grew smaller, and smaller, and smaller. And I started to feel like an Edgar Allan Poe character, buried alive. Only I was buried in people, instead of earth. I thought, "You've got to write your way out of this." The way you'd dig yourself out of the ground. Then about 10 minutes later, when I heard the first lady scream, somewhere in the crowd—she's screaming, "You're stepping on my feet! You're stepping on my feet!" I started to think, "You've got to write your way out of this and not panic!" The air was getting bad in this little pocket, as people in the back pressed people forward. So that was really the worst.

The session last night was great. They had about 12 rent-a-cops, because they're all over the place at Christmas time. Tabby, my wife, said they were really sort of into it, getting people to come forward five-by-five.

Q: What about all the letters you must receive—you must get an awful lot of "input" from your readers, whether you want it or not. Does that kind of "feedback" influence you at all, and, if so, how?

KING: There's a lot of criticism, and I acted upon *all* the constructive criticism in *Danse Macabre*. I collated the letters, I kept a file. We answer everything that comes in. We used to answer everything personally. When I saw "we", I mean that the secretary would know what to do. She's like a horse that's been down this road four or five times, and knows how to find the barn. We'd respond specifically to every letter. There was no form; there was a skeleton that was in the memory typewriter. But this year, we did finally have to go to a form response, which I wrote, and I hate it, and the form card says that I hate it. We keep a file of everybody who's ever written. We don't want to sell them ginzu knives or anything like that. But it's nice to have, so you know who wants to be your pen pal, and when you can stop writing back to them. We've got a card file now that covers one whole wall. Literally thousands of 'em.

Q: What percentage are from the lunatic fringe? Crazies who want to provide you with a descriptive list of 14 new ways to mangle a human body?

KING: The lunatic fringe is less than one percent. It's a rare week when we find one. We just sort of all gather together and exclaim over it. Most of the letter writers look to be from people who are, I would say, just middle-to-upper class people. Women outnumber men, but not by much. There's a lot of fan mail that comes in—it isn't the majority, but a lot of it—that comes in these sort of labored, almost scrawled things in pencil, from people who obviously don't read much or write much. And those would say about the same thing; they say, I don't read much, but I love what you do.

Q: It must be gratifying to know that your work is affecting people like that.

KING: Well, it's nice, because they go on from there. They all go on from there. They find something they can touch from there. It gives them confidence, like going over a beginner's ski jump. Now, a couple of years ago, *Time* magazine did a piece in conjunction with *Different Seasons*, called "The Master of Post-Literate Prose." That was me.

Q: I recall reading that. It was not the kindest article.

KING: No. It was real... it was real heavy. And it depressed me for weeks afterward. But, you know, what really depressed me was the tone. The tone wasn't particularly angry, it was sort of sad. It was this guy saying, well, okay, the Visigoths are in the crumbled remains of Rome, and they're pissing on the curiae and the steps of the Senate. And what he was talking about were these people who aren't very bright, who are reading these books, and I thought, "My God, this guy, I wonder if he knows how elitist all this shit sounds."

Q: You should have sent him a one-sentence response which read, "Better they should watch *Love Boat*?"

KING: Yeah, I know. Well, it makes them uneasy. They would be happier, I think. We're talking about "they", and who I mean by "they", generally speaking, are the self-appointed guardians of literature, who a lot of times, turn out to be critics. Not always. But they're the people who really feel it would be better for my readers to watch television, because they're corrupting the word pool.

Q: Nevertheless you've gone beyond the point of being a popular author. Being Stephen King in 1983 is like being a one-man Beatles. In a society that supposedly doesn't read—as we've just discussed—that's incredible. How have you come to terms with being a cultural phenomenon?

KING: Well, I don't see it in wide terms. Because if I did, then I might start to draw some conclusions. I might even, let's say, admit that what you say is true. If I answer this, I'm not admitting that what you say is true. I'm just saying that I see things in terms of what's going on in my own life, from day to day and week to week, and I respond to it on that level. And the most difficult thing is that you begin to be separated from what started it, which is your work. You discover, little by little, that if you are a cultural phenomenon, or if you're a celebrity—and I don't know if I'm a cultural phenomenon, but I *know* I'm a celebrity—but in America, that's like. . . hot dogs. It doesn't really mean anything in a wider sense. Orson Bean is a celebrity. Charles Nelson Reilly is a celebrity. I watched this guy on *Hollywood Squares* for about seven years, and one day, my kid said to me, "But what does he *do*?" And I said, "I don't *know*." I don't know what Charles Nelson Reilly *did*.

Q: Nor do I. He's a likeable enough fellow. . . but what *is* his job?

KING: Yeah. He's funny. But what did he say when he was a kid? I want to be on TV game shows?

Q: Maybe he's an articulate bus driver from Gary, Indiana, who Johnny Carson took a liking to.

KING: Right. Charo. That sort of thing. . . So, you know, what I try to do is save enough so that I can write, and divorce what I write from everything that's going on around me.

Q: You're on the inside looking out.

KING: Yeah.

Q: I ride a crowded commuter train to New York every day, and one night I noticed that fully half the passengers—young, old, male, female, black, white—were reading one Stephen King book or another. That's pretty damn impressive.

KING: They ride the subways! My people, in the dark!

Q: I have to admit, I couldn't help fantasizing about what it would be like to be Stephen King. How something like that would make me feel.

KING: What happens, though, that's bad, is that a kind of caution sets in. I don't mean in your work, but in your life. You wonder why people are talking to you. You know what I mean? You discover, little by little, that everybody was right; that a lot of people will come on to you, and it turns out that there's a bottom line that they want something. And so, it makes it tougher. And the worst thing, man, is if I'm in a mall—and I'm not going to do a signing, I'm just walking around—you start to hear this whisper: "That's Stephen King!" That's what paranoid people start to hear just before the men in the white coats take them away. Except that it's really happening unless I'm dreaming all this.

Q: Remaining anonymous in public must be particularly difficult, given the fact that you're a rather. . . large and distinctive-looking gentleman.

KING: Yeah.

Q: You didn't help your own cause by appearing in *Creepshow*, either.

KING: No. No . . .

Q: So if they haven't caught your photo on a dust jacket, they're still going to know about what you look like.

KING: Even people who can't read.

Q: That's right.

KING: That's the sort of thing, again, where you say, either I'm gonna do this because I wanna do this, or I'm becoming a prisoner of whatever I am.

Q: You couldn't back out of it now even if you wanted to.

KING: I guess so.

Q: Do you worry that there will eventually be a kind of "backlash" against you because of your success? You're known to be a big baseball fan, so you must've heard the old saying, "Rooting for the Yankees is like rooting for U.S. Steel." Do you think there will come a point where people will say, "Buying a Stephen King book is like rooting for U.S. Steel?"

KING: Right. Yeah, I do. I think that it's already set in to a large extent. I used to be able to get good reviews in sort of "counterculture" papers like the *Boston Phoenix.* Now, this thing's started in. *The Village Voice* did a review on *Danse Macabre* that was a fury of indignation, with a caricature of me, looking like a large, overweight weasel, grinding dollars out of his typewriter. You start off, and you're writing in a counter-medium, or counter-genre, anyway—the horror genre—and people whisper your name. Like David Cronenberg. With *Rabid*, and stuff like that, people would say, "Have you seen this thing?" When John Carpenter was just starting out, my friend Peter Straub had a friend who was in New York, and he said, "I want to take you down to 42nd Street." And this guy said, "I don't want to go down there! I'll get mugged! I'll get robbed!" And Peter says, "Yeah, there's this *great* film, called *Assault on Precinct 13*. You gotta see it!" And that's what happens. Then, after a while, you become David Cronenberg of *The Dead Zone* or John Carpenter of *Christine*. Or Stephen King. Everybody knows about you. And again, that elitist thing sets in. There's this small coterie of critics, or readers, or whatever, who can no longer say, "Here's something that you don't know about." When people talk about books, it's nice to be able to say, "Well, I've read this book, *'Salem's Lot*. Have you heard of it?" "Oh, no, I've never heard of that." It's like a cache. So it happens, like it happened with *Pet Sematary*. Walden and Dalton weren't going to order very many. They'd simply heard: He's doing two books this year, this is a piece of shit. The only way you can combat that is to try and get better. If you continue to get better, then all you do is hold your place in line.

Q: It's been suggested that, in addition to the literary merit of your work, that part of your success can be attributed to your books appearing in the right place at the right time, meaning American of the 1970s and '80s. Do you feel there's any validity to this, or would your books have been comparably popular had they been published, say, 20 years ago?

KING: Don't know. I have a tendency to suspect they wouldn't have been. But—okay, this sounds really conceited—class usually tells. It doesn't *always* tell. But if you're doing good work, if you're doing work that people can relate to. . . I'll tell you what might've happened to me if I'd been publishing, let's say, in the mid Fifties. I think if I had been publishing 20 years ago, if I had started in the mid Sixties, I would have become a fairly popular writer. If I had been publishing in the mid Fifties I would have been John D. MacDonald. I would have been somebody that 20 million working men knew about, and carried in their back pockets to work, or in their lunch pails to read on their lunch hour or their coffee break. You know, the little Gold Medals, stuff like that. That's where Richard Matheson published. That's where he published *The Shrinking Man*, and where he published *I Am Legend*. Books which have been filmed since then and gone through God knows how many languages and how many copies. I think that's where I would have been.

I don't think I could've gotten a hardcover house in hell to look at my stuff if it hadn't been for *The Exorcist* and some of those others.

Q: Whatever shape the stories themselves may take, your books all have one common thread, and that's the examination of fear. Given your enormous popularity, and the response to the recent TV-movie *The Day After*, which exploited one of our society's most dread fears, do you perceive a sort of mass-masochism in this country? Why do we love to stick these pins in ourselves?

KING: Yes. We really do like that. One of the reasons I've been so successful is that I was brought up by a woman who worried all the time. She'd say, "Put on your rubbers, Stevie, you'll get a cold. You're gonna get pneumonia and die." You couldn't go swimming in public pools because of polio and stuff like that. We're a nation of worriers. We worry about cancer. You go to a newsstand and every magazine that isn't a skin magazine has got an article on cancer. And the skin magazines have got articles on herpes and AIDS. We worry about our health. We worry about whether or not we've got enough money. If we've got a lot of money, we worry about what it's doing to our family. We worry about the after-life, we worry about the Russians, we worry about the Chinese, we worry about South America. We worry that the President's going to die, and we worry about what's going to happen if he fulfills his term in office. And the reason that we do all this worrying is that it's a luxury we can afford. We happen to be the richest nation on earth. We're the best educated nation on earth. We have everything.

You know, it's easy to worry about your fucking est or your Rolf or something else when your stomach's full. But if you're a Biafran, you have a tendency to worry about whether or not your kids are gonna die.

Q: You can't stop to contemplate niceties when you have to clear a forest.

KING: That's right. So it's a luxury of civilized people who have a lot of time on their hands, and can sit around picking their scabs. I mean, I've been in England, and watched the TV news: they have news all the time there. Any time of the day. It's like rock 'n' roll music over here. Somebody's always broadcasting news in this terrible monotone, this English/educated/monotonal voice. Over there, what they talk about on the news is what's going on in England. They talk about their soccer matches, they worry about their bread strikes and everything else. You know, 80 percent of the news is what I would call local news, because England is a country that could fit in our Midwest. Am I right?

Q: With room to spare.

KING: And America is this huge country. There are things going on everywhere. People are swallowing frogs, seeing UFOs, they're shooting each other in the street. And 80 percent of our news is about things that are going on in Krakow and things that are going on in El Salvador. Because we just don't have enough to worry about at home. It's like, expectations expand to fulfill income, and worry expands to fulfill the time that you have to worry in. So I think that the books that I write either feed that or tap it. And I suspect that they probably tap it, but, in the end, the result's the same. People feel that they're reading about themselves, and I'm mirroring something that's in their own hearts.

Q: Is reading a Stephen King book in 1983 therefore any different that building a fallout shelter in 1957?

KING: Well, it's getting ready for 1984.

Q: Do you ever find yourself growing attached to the characters in your books, to the point where you want to spare them from harm, even though the plot might logically dictate otherwise. Specifically, I have Johnny Smith of *The Dead Zone* in mind. I recently saw the movie—which I thought was quite good—and the book remains one of my very favorite Stephen King novels.

KING: Yeah. You want to spare them harm. I was real sad when the little boy died in *Cujo*, in the book. I was asked if I could revive him for the re-draft; at the publishing company they didn't want him to die. And I said no, that it would be a lie to say that he was alive. The movie people came along and said, "What do you think about if the kid lived?" And I said fine, because movies are not books, and what they do doesn't bother me. I thought it would be fun to see what happened if he *did* live. Even though I knew that it wasn't real. That would be make-believe. The kid really died. Anybody who reads the book and sees the movie, or sees the movie and reads the book knows: the kid really died. So, you want to spare them sometimes. But, on the other hand, the plot is the boss. The characters are not the boss. Sometimes people survive that you didn't expect to survive. There's a little girl in *Pet Sematary* who lives. Nobody else lives. And there's no rhyme or reason for it. There'd be more justification in that story—in the sense of a final tying up of loose ends—if she died, too. But that isn't the way life is.

Q: *The Dead Zone* is not so much unpleasant or discomforting as it is sad, almost overwhelmingly so. There's a feeling of imminent doom right from the beginning. I thought the movie captured it well.

KING: Yeah.

Q: Johnny Smith is a genuinely tragic character. The ending of the book is especially moving. It's enough to make you cry.

KING: Good. That's good. I'm not afraid of that spiraling down into a very unpleasant conclusion. Partly because I think life sometimes does that, and also because I was really impressed by the American naturalists and the British naturalists when I was in high school and in college. People like Thomas Hardy, Theodore Dreiser and Frank Norris. Even people like Raymond Chandler seemed very naturalistic to me. They all say the same thing: Things are not ever going to get any better, and if you want to see how things go, just think about what's going to happen to you. Sooner or later, you're gonna lose control of your kidneys, and that's very sad.

But, on the other hand, what always happens for me—with a book— is that you frame the idea of the book or the "what if," and little by little, characters will take shape. Generally as a result of a secondary decision about the plot.

In the case of *The Dead Zone*, it was simply what if a man was able to have this ability to see the future. What if you were to explore that idea in the book, if he was just an ordinary guy that could really do it? The secondary thing was the visualization of this guy taking a test paper from a student, and saying, "You gotta go home right away. Your house is burning down." That never actually appears in the book, but it set the thing of him as a teacher; there were some other decisions that were made, and then it was time to pick the book up and begin to go. And as the circumstances themselves developed, I felt this web begin to form around him. I never felt any urge to introduce an artificial element that would allow him to tear free of that web, and escape what was building up. So I let that happen and I watched to see what would happen to the man himself. Finally, the conclusion that I had was that he was going to die, and leave this girl Sarah alone. And she was going to be unhappy, but we all live with unhappiness, and it generally doesn't kill any of us. She'd have her cry in the graveyard, and she'd go back to her husband, and her baby, and pick up her life. Her life would be a little bit less; it certainly wouldn't have been the life that God intended.

Q: It was the book's final scene, where Sarah goes to Johnny's grave, that I found so emotional. Yet it was eliminated from the movie completely. I suppose that was due to David Cronenberg's directoral needs. . . .

KING: I think it was mostly Dino De Laurentiis's need to have a 98-minute film. There was a little bit more in the rough cut that I saw, but it all seemed very pointless. It didn't include the graveyard, or anything like that. She goes back to the fair, which is still there . . . and she looks around and it ends there. It all seemed very pointless to me. I like it better the way it is. But it disturbs me that, of all the babies in New Hampshire, it turns out to be Sarah's own baby that Stillson happens to grab. A lot of the plot choices reflect an obsession in Hollywood that everything has to support everything else, like a house of cards.

Q: Perhaps Cronenberg, or De Laurentiis, or Debra Hill, or whoever had the final say was concerned that a graveyard scene would remind people of the last scene in *Carrie*.

KING: That's an idea. I'd never thought of that. I'll bet they discussed that.

Q: They were probably afraid that if Johnny didn't climb out of the ground as a slobbering zombie that the audience would be disappointed.

KING: Yeah. I bet that's the truth, yeah.

Q: I thought Christopher Walken was about as right for Johnny as any mainstream Hollywood actor I can think of. Did you have approval over his casting, or were you simply told, Walken is going to be Johnny Smith, and that's it?

KING: No, I had approval, actually. At least that's my memory of it. Dino called me up, and we had discussed the actor I wanted—and I pitched him very hard—my choice was Bill Murray. Dino thought it was a good idea. And it didn't work, that's all. He had a commitment, or he was on vacation. . . something like that. But, anyway, Bill Murray couldn't do it. So, we talked over some other guys, and he mentioned some names, and I didn't mention anybody else, because I couldn't think of anybody right off. He called me up on the phone, and he said, "Stephen, what would you think of Christopher Walken?" And I said, "He'd be great."

Q: Walken is rather haunted looking to begin with.

KING: I've met him a couple of time. He always seemed either a little bit sad to me or a little disinterested; a little bit disconnected from the proceedings.

Q: Possibly because he grew up in the same part of Queens as I did.

KING: Maybe. That could do it to anybody.

Q: Thanks, pal!

KING: But my reaction to him was that it would either be a great choice, or he just wouldn't be able to handle it at all. Because he can seem real cold, and if you're going to feel *sorry* that Johnny died or anything, you have to feel this kind of lost warmth as well. I think that Walken's great when he smiles. He looks sort of goony, but he's great. He never smiled in *Deer Hunter.*

Q: He didn't have much to smile about in that picture.

KING: Yeah.

Q: I'm sorry that Cronenberg and Company couldn't have found a way to include the scene where Johnny shakes hands with Jimmy Carter. That scene exemplifies one of the aspects of your writing that I enjoy most. Johnny picks up the Secret Service man's disjointed and panicked associations with the Wallace shooting. That Secret Service man is an insignificant character in the context of the story, yet, for that moment, we don't just feel that we know him, we feel that we *are* him. How are you able to accomplish this? Is it insight, or professional technique?

KING: Well, I never thought that scene worked. I worked on it, and I did it a couple of times. Finally, I dropped it. I put in a scene where he talks to somebody in a shopping center. I can't remember which candidate it was. I think it was Sargent Shriver, who was running that year. I tried to do something with the assassination idea there, by him making some sort of a movement to his pocket. And I was persuaded—actually by my wife—to put the Carter scene back in. I always thought it seemed a little bit lame. But the Secret Service man—it worked! For me, yeah. Carter himself. . . maybe because politicians don't seem real, even when they *are* real.

Q: Similarly, you are able to put the reader inside the mind of a dog, and it seems perfectly natural. Kojak, the dog in *The Stand*, was just as three-dimensional as any of the human characters. How can you make a dog's perceptions believable? Does it come naturally?

KING: Ah. . . yeah. Everything does. Including the bad stuff. So what I do, and what's always worked for me, is that I think: this is the way the dog would think of it. You've got to sling your eyes way down low, and think of what you'd see if you were down there. You've got to think about what you know about dogs; about their sense of smell, about their innate ability to tell time, all that sort of thing. Then you write something like, "He knew THE BOY would get back soon." Then you go right on ahead, and when you get about halfway up the page, you can look at it, out of the typewriter. And I've always known that—if it was good or bad, if it was going to work or not. That's all I know. The same thing is true of things like word choice. You'll look at it. I can't tell when it's in my head. There are things where I knew it's a crapshoot, and it probably isn't going to work. So I put it down anyway and look at it. You can always take it out if it doesn't work.

Q: Speaking of *The Stand*, who would you cast to play the leads, Stu Redman and Randall Flagg?

KING: Oh...for Randall Flagg, I think Armand Assante. For Stu Redman...I don't know. I really don't know. Somebody who looks a little bit like Clint Eastwood, but maybe 20 years ago. But I don't exactly know who that is. Maybe the best guy would be David Keith.

Q: Too young.

KING: He might be a little bit too young. I don't know.

Q: I was thinking about David Carradine as Flagg. He's gaunt and demented enough.

KING: Yeah. Armand Assante is very short, but man, he looks so *bad*.

Q: He looks too healthy to be the devil.

KING: How about Richard Pryor?

Q: I never thought of that. That's an interesting angle.

KING: He'd be okay. Richard Pryor would be great. He'd be real funny, but he could look oh so real, throwin' that woman off the balcony.

Q: And Trash Can Man; got to be Anthony James.

KING: Steve King for Tom Cullen. That's what I think.

Q: Oh, come on.

KING: I think I'd be great.

Q: Okay. Fine. I'll play Lloyd. How's that? We'll be all set.

KING: Okay.

Q: I just finished reading *Cycle of the Werewolf.*

KING: Ah!

Q: I enjoyed the hell out of it.

KING: I enjoyed it, too. I wish that it could have been either more or less, in terms of the book project, because it sorta got out of hand there. It seems thin to me, for the price.

Q: Can you give us a quick Stephen King preview for 1984?

KING: *The Talisman*. That's the book with Peter Straub. The movie of *Firestarter* comes out in May.

Let's see...there's those two things. I'm planning to do a limited run of a novel I wrote for my children, called *The Napkins*. It's a book-length comic, almost like a fairy tale. And the bad guy in that book is Randall Flagg. His name's changed a little bit, but his last name's the same—Flagg. It's him! He turned up in this other book. In this other *world*.

Q: Making his triumphant return.

KING: He's the court magician, of course.

Q: I get a kick out of your cross-references. Characters and places and events from one book or story have a way of popping up in other books or stories. Do you do that for your own amusement, or to see if the readers are paying attention?

KING: They show up sometimes! If you're gonna go back—as I have several times—to Castle Rock, Maine, which is a town I feel like I know a little bit. . . I like that town. I know where a lot of stuff is in that town. I don't have any maps. I don't have all the names categorized, but I like that town. Carbine Street, all those streets.

And if you go back. . . Frank Dodd was *there*; people sometimes mention him. In Castle Rock, they talk a *lot* about that dog, that Cujo, and what happened to the Cambers, because that's the biggest thing that happened to them in years.

There are several people now who are beginning to say—are you ready for this?

Q: Yeah. . .

KING: That something's *wrong* with the town. Because it's a little town, and too much has happened there in the last 10 years. And there are two or three different people—fairly young kids, in high school—who are beginning to speculate: What if it isn't a real town? What if somebody *made it up*?

That somebody is me! They're talking about *me*! In *my* town!

Q: Well, you know how to take care of *them*.

KING: Yeah!

Q: Say, how far is Castle Rock from Jerusalem's Lot?

KING: Mmm. . . 'bout 65 miles.

With Randy Lofficier

Q: *Christine* doesn't seem to fit into your usual fictional universe of New England towns like Castle Rock or 'Salem's Lot.

KING: No, it doesn't, although there is some reference made to the fact that Arnie Cunningham, on some of his fireworks runs for Will Darnell, goes through the town of Stovington, Vermont, which is where Jack Torrance from *The Shining* taught and where the plague center was in *The Stand*. *Christine* takes place in Pittsburgh, which is far from the New England setting of the other stories. Most of the books I've written have been located either in Maine or in Colorado.

Q: There is a picture of you with a Plymouth Fury on the book's dust jacket. Do you yourself own a Christine?

KING: No, that car actually was loaned to us by a Pennsylvania outfit that handles vintage cars for movies. They ran the car over the New Jersey line, just like in a Springsteen song, and we did the photograph session almost like a rock 'n' roll album cover. The photographer, Andy Unangst, liked the car so much that he bought it.

Q: Why did you pick a 1958 Fury as your subject?

KING: Because they're almost totally forgotten. They were the most mundane Fifties car that I could remember. I didn't want a car that already had a legend attached to it, like the Fifties Thunderbird, the Ford Galaxy, etc. You know how these things grow. Some of the Chevrolets, for example, were supposed to have been legendary door-suckers. On the other hand, nobody ever talked about the Plymouth products, and I thought, "Well . . ." Besides, Lee Iacocca gave me a million bucks!

Seriously, I don't know how Chrysler feels about *Christine*, any more than I know how the Ford Company feels about *Cujo* in which a woman is stranded in a Pinto. But they should feel happy, because it's a pretty lively car and it lasts a long time. It's like a Timex watch—it takes a licking and goes on ticking.

Q: It's difficult to tell from reading the book whether Christine is evil herself, or whether Roland Le Bay, the car's first owner, makes her evil. What do you see as the source of the evil?

KING: That's one of the questions which the movie people started to wrestle with. Was it Le Bay or was it the car? I understand that their answer is that it was the car. In fact, it may be—and I'm just guessing—that Le Bay isn't anywhere near as sinister as he is in the book. In the book, there is the suggestion that it's probably Le Bay, rather than the car.

When the film people came to me, I said, "Look, this is your decision. You decide what you're going to do with the story." But later I was told that in the opening sequence, when the car rolls off the assembly line, one of the workmen is dead behind the wheel. This would suggest that the car was bad from the beginning.

Q: You seem to bring up the Fifties a lot in your work, and show a great deal of nostalgia for that time.

KING: Sure. I grew up in the Fifties. That's my generation. There's been a fair amount of that from writers who I would say are now the "establishment." When I started writing, with *Carrie*, I was twenty-four or twenty-five. I was a kid. Since then, ten years have gone by, and 1947 has become a very respectable birth year for writers. There are a lot of us who actually developed our understanding of life in the Fifties and who grew to be, if not adults, at least thinking human beings. I've got a lot of good memories from the Fifties. Somebody once said that life is the rise of consciousness. For me, rock 'n' roll was the rise of consciousness. It was like a big sun bursting over my life. That's when I really started to live—and that was brought on by the music of the Fifties.

Q: Do you have any more macabre memories of the Fifties?

KING: No, I don't. All the macabre things that I can remember, and that come out of reality rather than from something I made up, started with the Kennedy assassination in 1963. I don't have any bad memories of the Fifties. Everything was asleep. There was stuff going on, there was uneasiness about the bomb, but on the whole, I'd have to say that people in the Fifties were pretty loose.

Q: Was it the E.C. comics you read then that spawned the horror in your work?

KING: Some of them had to, sure. Those comics really grossed me out when I was a kid, and they also fired my imagination. Those are the two different ways in which they've influenced me. The gross-out business isn't nearly as important to me as just sort of flipping people out, so that they say, "Jeez! This car's running by itself!" You see, *Christine* is an outrageous kind of riff on one chord. I mean, this car's out there running by itself and getting younger! It's actually going back in time. An audience can relate to a certain degree to something like a haunted house, *The Amityville Horror*, traditional horrors like ghosts, vampires, and things like that. But you give them a car, or any inanimate object, and you're suggesting something that is either along the pulpy lines of the E.C. comics, or else obviously symbolic—a symbol for the techno-logical age, or for the end of innocence, considering the part a car plays in adolescence and growing up. When you give them something like that, you're really starting to take a risk. But that's also where the excitement is. If you can make somebody go along with that concept, that's really wonderful.

Q: Do you consciously try to give your work a subliminal content?

KING: No, never subliminal. I think it should be out there where anybody can see it. I don't believe in the idea that a symbol or theme should be coded so that only college graduates can read it. The only thing that type of self-conscious literature is good for is for people to dissect it and use it to get graduate degrees or write doctoral theses. Theme and symbol are very strong and valid parts of literature, and there's no reason not to put them right out front.

Q: Why was *Christine* written using two different narrative styles, Denny's first-person narrative for the opening and closing parts and third-person narrative for the middle?

KING: Because I got in a box. That's really the only reason. It almost killed the book. It sat on a shelf for a long time while I walked around in sort of a daze and said, "You know, this is really cute. How did you do this?" It was like when you paint a floor and you end up in a corner saying, "Aw, heck, look what I did! There's no door at this end of the room!" Dennis was supposed to tell the whole story. But then he got in a football accident and was in the hospital while things were going on that he couldn't see. For a long time I tried to narrate the second part in terms of what he was hearing hearsay evidence, almost like depositions —but that didn't work. I tried to do it a number of different ways, and finally I said, "Let's cut through it. The only way to do this is to do it in the third person." I tried to leave enough clues so that when the reader comes out of it he'll feel that it's almost like Dennis pulling a Truman Capote, writing a non fiction novel. I think it's still a first-person narration, and if you read the second part over, you'll see it. It's just masked, like reportage.

Q: Do you plan on doing a *Christine II*, with the car coming back across the country?

KING: God, I don't want to go through that again! Once was enough! All I can think of is, if the parts were recycled, you'd end up with this sort of homicidal Cuisinart, or something like that. That would be kind of nice.

CHAPTER FOUR

†

GOING HOLLYWOOD

†

With Peter S. Perakos *(1978)*

Q: How did your fascination with the horror genre come about?

KING: My "fascination with the horror genre" began with the E.C. comics of the early Fifties—my generation's *National Enquirer*—and with the horror movies of the Fifties, most notably *The Creature from the Black Lagoon, Invasion of the Body Snatchers* (I look forward to the coming remake with an odd mixture of dread and anticipation), *The Brain from Planet Arous* (which starred John Agar and was, in some way I've never been able to figure out, the basis for my novel *Carrie*), and later the AIP creatures features, which remain interesting to me because the best of them (although none of them was really very good) involved teenagers and took off into horror from such mundane settings.

Q: Which writers have influenced you the most?

KING: In terms of reading, the early Bradbury played a part (although I did not discover him until my teens), the early Bloch, and a number of Forties paperback editions of Lovecraft that I found in an aunt's attic. Lovecraft struck me with the most force, and I still think, that for all his shortcomings, he is the best writer of horror fiction that America has yet produced.

Q: I was also thinking of Poe, and perhaps Oscar Wilde?

KING: Neither Poe nor Wilde influenced me particularly. Other than the horror/supernatural writers I've already mentioned, I would say Thomas Hardy, John D. MacDonald, and most importantly James M. Cain.

Q: Do commercial considerations play a part in your writing?

KING: Sure, I'm a commercial writer. I'd like to get filthy rich and own a yacht. But I write only to please myself, and to entertain myself. For me, my books are home movies.

Q: Would you say there is a statement, or a point of view, common to your work? By statement I mean, if you excuse the term, "message."

KING: The point of view in my works, the "pitch of concern," to put it a slightly different way, has been fairly constant in everything I've written over the last ten years or so, and probably won't change much in the future—it is the dead opposite of the writers most of us read in college, the "literary" writers, if you like (my definition of a "literary writer": a novelist of whom no one ever asks, "Yes, but when are you going to do something serious?"). People like Doris Lessing, John Updike, Joyce Carol Oates, people like that. They do books about extraordinary people in ordinary situations, while I'm more fetched by the exact opposite... ordinary people in a pressure-cooker, in a crunch situation. Preferably one where events have skewed from the unusual to the unnatural to the out-and-out unbelievable. It is, maybe, a *Twilight Zone* school of writing, but Serling and company weren't there first. A guy named Jack Finney was...the guy who originally wrote *Invasion of the Body Snatchers* on which Siegel's film was based. I hope Finney makes a million dollars on the movie tie-in this fall; he deserves it. They should have paid him a royalty on all those *Twilight Zone* stories like "The Monsters Are Due On Maple Street."

Q: Religion, Christianity—for its embodiment you created Margaret White who is really the stereotypical religious fanatic. Are your feelings towards Christianity predominantly negative, or is your apparent anathema restricted to fundamentalism?

KING: My feelings toward Christianity are neutral—I believe in God, but not necessarily in organized religion...although I will qualify this by saying that, as a kid brought up in the mostly-lukewarm atmosphere of Methodism, I was always fascinated by the trappings and solemnity of Catholicism. Coincidentally (or maybe not) the only girl I was ever serious about in college is a Catholic, and the woman that I married is a Catholic —of the lapsed variety. The power of the Catholic Church plays an important part in *'Salem's Lot* partly because it felt so natural and right.

Q: Why is it in your work, and in most works of the supernatural, the greater power belongs to evil, or the demonic, or the devil, while good or God is more or less passive?

KING: In my own books, the power of God doesn't play a passive part at all. (Call it the power of White, if you prefer; sometimes I do, although the White concept is more pagan than Christian). . . . Good wins out over evil in *'Salem's Lot* and *The Shining*, and at least earns a draw in *Carrie*. Anyhow, this whole question is very central to my new book, *The Stand*, and I direct your attention to that.

By the way, I also reject your contention that in *most* works of the supernatural, the power belongs to evil—short-run power, maybe, but check your *Dracula*, or (again) Finney's *Body Snatchers*, and a good many others (M. R. James, Coleridge, William Hope Hodgson, Bradbury's *Something Wicked This Way Comes*. . . :).

Q: Do you consider yourself to be a religious person?

KING: I'm religious in terms of the White, but I don't go to church. God and the devil—the White and Black forces—proceed from the *inside*—that's where the power comes from. Churches make morals, which, I suppose, is useful. . . . So is Tupperware, in its way.

Q: How would you respond to the comment that the lack of spirituality in society is a turning away from God, and consequently any alternative, which might deal with evil or the devil, is necessarily popular?

KING: I don't think there's any lack of spirituality in today's society; I think there is a lack of focus because so many of the organized religions have begun to crumble in the latter half of the 20th century. . . the Catholics are the most extreme case in point, of course, but the same is true all the way from Islam to Methodism. To some degree you can blame this on technology, but the other focus for spirituality these days is the fact that technology is gradually making itself obsolete—witness the wounded, what-did-we-ever-do-to-anybody attitude of many hard-core SF fans and writers. (The defense Niven and Pournelle make of nuclear reactors in *Lucifer's Hammer* is bitterly laughable.) The same splendid technology that has pushed back the frontiers of "God's province" so rapidly since 1900 is also the technology that has given us the fluorocarbon spray can, CBW, and the threat of nuclear holocaust. Besides, people's spiritual lives always seem to fall into turmoil and the literature of the supernatural always becomes more prevalent (and more interesting) as the end of the century approaches. I don't know why it's so, but it is. . . you find your rationalists in the middle of the century, and your real good wars.

Q: A major source of evil, indeed the primary source in *Carrie* is human, not supernatural—her psychotic mother, sadistic teenagers.

Even the Overlook's terror in *The Shining* has a human origin, the monsters who lived and died in the hotel. What is your definition of evil?

KING: My definition of evil is "the conscious will to do harm."

Q: Then, do you feel that you are creating allegory in your novels?

KING: Yes, my novels are sometimes allegorical in nature (or in effect), but—and I think Ray Bradbury would agree with this—for some reason I don't understand (although he may), almost all long-form horror fiction has a tendency to reverberate and to *become* allegorical. I think that's the main reason that neither horror novels nor films have ever been placed in a "genre" ghetto.

Q: What did you think of Brian DePalma's *Carrie*?

KING: I liked DePalma's film of *Carrie* quite a bit. The attitude of the film was different from my book; I tended to view the events straight-on, humorlessly, in a straight point-to-point progression (you have to remember that the genesis of *Carrie* was no more than a short story idea), while I think DePalma saw a chance to make a movie that was a satirical view of high school life in general and high school peer-groups in particular. A perfectly viable point of view. Sissy Spacek was excellent, but right behind her—in a smaller part than it should have been—was John Travolta. He played the part of Billy Nolan the way I wish I'd written it, half-funny and half-crazy.

I don't have any real quibbles. I think that DePalma is a worthy pretender to Hitchcock's throne. . . certainly he is as peculiar as Hitchcock.

Q: In a review of *Carrie* (and perhaps applicable to your book as well) Janet Maslin comments in *Newsweek*: "Combining gothic horror, offhand misogyny, and an air of studied triviality, *Carrie* is DePalma's most enjoyable movie and also his silliest. . . alternating between the elegant and the asinine. . . ."

KING: I think that Ms. Maslin's comments on the film in her review are off the mark—or, to be a bit irreverent, I think she's full of shit. The movie—and the book—is not about "triviality" or "misogyny" but in-groups and out-groups, The Wheels and The Outcasts. The gothic horror part is okay, but that, of course, is DePalma's homage to Hitchcock's *Psycho*, which seems a bit studied and overdone for my taste (Bates High School, for instance).

Q: You might be consoled by the knowledge that Ms. Maslin no longer writes for *Newsweek*. *The Shining*—is it your most ambitious work?

KING: I think *The Shining* is the most ambitious novel I've published to date, but the one which follows this October, *The Stand*, is a bit more ambitious... certainly I worked harder on it, although to whatever ultimate critical result yet remains to be seen.

Q: Kubrick has a unique view, ostensibly Freudian, of the relationship of man to society. Are your views compatible?

KING: Please believe me: *nobody* has a Freudian view of the relationship of man to his society. Not you, not me, not Kubrick, nobody. The whole concept is abysmally silly. And as a moviegoer, I don't give tin whistle what a director *thinks*; I want to know what he *sees*. Most directors have good visual and dramatic instincts (most good directors, anyway), but in intellectual terms, they are pinheads, by and large. Nothing wrong in that; who wants a film director who's a utility infielder? Let them do their job, enjoy their work, but for Christ's sake, let's not see Freudianisms in the work of any film director. The only director who seems to have any psychological point of view at all is Ingmar Bergman and his is Jungian, which is the next thing to saying "instinctual." Can you imagine Bergman doing *The Shining*? That would be interesting.

Q: Despite your assertion that Kubrick does not have a Freudian viewpoint, it is rumored that he attempted to write and modify the script under the guidance of a psychiatrist. Kubrick has changed several elements of the novel, including your apocalyptic ending.

KING: From the beginning, when I first talked to Kubrick some months ago, he wanted to change the ending. He asked me for my opinion on Halloran becoming possessed, and then finishing the job that Torrance started, killing Danny, Wendy, and lastly himself. Then the scene would shift to the spring, with a new caretaker and his family arriving. However, the audience would see Jack, Wendy, and Danny in an idyllic family scene—as ghosts—sitting together, laughing and talking. And I saw a parallel between this peaceful ending at the end of the picture and the end of *2001* where the astronaut is transported to the Louis XIV bedroom. To me, the two endings seemed to tie together.

Q: The ending of *2001* is a cosmic rebirth. Your description of Kubrick's proposed ending for *The Shining* seems to show that what is after-or-beyond life is something which is neither terrifying nor horrific, but pastoral, mystical.

KING: The impression I got from our conversation is that Kubrick *does not* believe in life after death. Yet, he thought that any vein of the supernatural story (whether it is horrifying, or whether it is pleasant) is inherently *optimistic* because it points towards the possible survival of the spirit. And I told him that's all very good as a philosophy, but when an audience is brought face to face with the slaughter of characters that they care about, then they will cry for your head once they go out of the theater. But Kubrick has modified his original ideas extensively, so I don't expect to see this ending in the final film.

I also want to comment on the omission of the topiary animals. It's very funny to me that he chose a hedge maze, because my original concept *was* to create a hedge maze. And the reason that I rejected the idea in favor of the topiary animals was because of an old Richard Carlson film, *The Maze*. The story was about a maze, of course, but in the middle of the maze was a pond. And in the middle of the pond, on a lily pad, was *grandfather* who was a *frog*. Every night, grandpa turned into a frog and so they had to put him into the pond. To me, that was *ludicrous*. So I abandoned the idea of a hedge.

Q: It is disappointing—the alleged effects problems notwithstanding— that the hedge animals have been dropped.

KING: I never really though that the topiary animals would make it to the film, anyway. The director would face a dual risk, the first being that the effect would not look real. The second risk, is that even if the effect *does* look real, the audience might laugh. These are problems facing the filmmaker, problems I didn't have to contend with writing the novel.

Q: There is a great deal of graphic horror in *The Shining*—actually in all your works. Do you feel this makes them difficult to adapt as films?

KING: Yes, violence is *dynamite*. It's a dangerous package to handle. It is all too easy to let violence dominate. A lot of good directors have floundered on that particular rock. And that's one of the reasons I like Don Siegel, because he handles violence well. I would have preferred Siegel to direct *The Shining*, or perhaps *'Salem's Lot*. I believe he would be very successful directing *'Salem's Lot*.

Q: What do you think of the casting for *The Shining*? Does it fit with the characteristic of your work: ordinary people in extraordinary circumstances?

KING: I'm a little afraid of Jack Nicholson as Jack Torrance in that context because he is *not* an ordinary man. So far as I know, he's *never* played an ordinary man and I'm not sure that he can. I would have rather seen Michael Moriarty or Martin Sheen portray Torrance. But these actors are not supposed to be "bankable"—Hollywood loves the word.

Q: What do you think about Shelley Duvall cast in the part of Wendy Torrance?

KING: That's an example of absolutely grotesque casting. . . . But Kubrick is certainly an inventive, thinking director. He is one of the three or four greatest directors of our day, maybe of all time. However, I think he is indulgent, terribly indulgent. *Clockwork Orange* just doesn't hold up today. Some of his other films do. (It's amazing that *any* film does. A statement of genius is the ability of a film to hold up ten years from now.) I think *Dr. Strangelove* and *2001: A Space Odyssey* do. And *Barry Lyndon* will. But even if his film of *The Shining* is an artistic failure, it will probably be a commercial success. . . . And even if it's a failure, it will be an interesting failure. . . . Anyway, you have to realize I'm only talking as an interested observer. I'm not a participant.

Q: What about the possibility of you directing several of the stories in *Night Shift* for Milton Subotsky?

KING: Subotsky has six of the stories in *Night Shift*; he offered me both the chance to screenwrite and to direct. I'd like to direct very much, but I'm scared of that—not the conceptualization or visualization, but trying to control a big crew, all of whom have forgotten more about movie-making than I'll ever know. Also, I'm primarily a writer. I declined the chance to direct—reluctantly—and just for now.

Q: What is the status of bringing '*Salem's Lot* to the screen?

KING: CBS is interested in adapting '*Salem's Lot* as a "Novel For Television," but the Standards and Practices people, the censorship bureau, have raised fifty or sixty objections, creating a problem which I feel is insurmountable. But, that's okay. Warner Bros. bought it; they paid for it. So, in a way, it's the best of both possible worlds, as I'd rather not see it made at all.

Q: Can you tell us anything about your script for 20th Century-Fox and NBC?

KING: I've adapted three of the stories in *Night Shift*. Those are "I Know What You Need," "Battleground," and "Strawberry Spring." The film is being produced by a production company which is called, appropriately, The Production Company. The producers are Mike Wise and Frank Leavy. They like the screenplay. And if it were five years ago, I could confidently say that the movie would be immediately produced and on the air by next March. But I can't say that because the climate of TV production is now so tight towards anything that has to do with horror or violence. "Strawberry Spring," which is a latter day Jack The Ripper story, is of course violent. NBC Standards and Practices called me and said, "We can't have this lunatic running around stabbing people to death." And I said, "Well, that kind of shoots the story down, doesn't it?" And NBC replied, "Oh, no! Stabbing is out, but he can *strangle* them." So, either they're afraid of showing blood or alluding to ritual penetration.

Q: What is the possibility of your new novel, *The Stand*, being developed for filming?

KING: *The Stand* will be shown around Hollywood. And if the book is very, *very* successful, it might be sold. But I don't think, because of its complexity, that it will ever be sold.

Q: Finally, how do you feel about your novels and stories being transformed, by others of varying capabilities, into films?

KING: I am pleased that all the people involved are very good in what they're doing. But, ultimately, they *can't* mutilate anything that I wrote because the writing will stand on its own, one way or another.

With David Chute

Q: Your first contact with horror stories was through the movies?

KING: Yeah, it was. As a kid I saw things like *Curse of the Demon* and *The Creature From the Black Lagoon*, a lot of the early American-International pictures. *The Night of the Living Dead* really took me back, because there it was all over again. It was made in black and white; that alone was a tremendous step backwards, and I loved it.

Q: In an article you wrote for *Oui* magazine you mentioned *Invasion of the Body Snatchers* as an influence on 'Salem's Lot. Did *Night of the Living Dead* come into it also?

KING: There is one scene in 'Salem's Lot that is drawn directly from *Night of the Living Dead*, and that's the scene when Susan gets the stake put through her heart. There's a scene in *Night of the Living Dead* where this little girl kills her mother with a garden trowel, and there's an effect with the shadows, with a light bulb swinging back and forth. That's a very powerful image and for me it was the idea of a flashlight jittering around making shadows.

But actually, *Invasion of the Body Snatchers* had a much greater effect. The thing that had stayed in my mind was the situation at the end, where Kevin McCarthy and Dana Wynter are the last two humans in town; all the other townspeople have been replaced by pods, and they're closing in. I just thought that was so romantic, two against this whole town, and that's pretty well reflected in '*Salem's Lot*. There's a feeling of paranoia that's the same—one a product of the McCarthy period and the other of the Watergate era—of never knowing who might not be "one of them," even though they still *look* just the same.

Q: Clearly your books have something in them which lends itself to adaptation, which catches the imagination of movie people.

KING: I think you can point to certain writers—and it's no reflection on whether they're good or bad—whose works are very adaptable. Richard Matheson has written a book called *I Am Legend* which has been made into three different movies. . . .

Q: There was one with Vincent Price: *The Last Man on Earth*.

KING: Right, that's the one I liked best; in black and white, shot in Spain, with these wonderful scenes of Price throwing bodies into this big dump. Then there was *The Omega Man* with Charleton Heston, and I think there was one more at some point. But anyway, it's him; Matheson. Every novel he's written has been made into a film. Some authors write things which must appeal to the directorial eye, that's all I can think of. I think there aren't very many novelists in this country under forty who are writing novels; they've all writing movies. It isn't anything as simple as the canard of writing dialogue and stage direction, but of seeing things in image after image, which is what good movies do.

Q: You've said that when you begin your books it isn't in terms of mental pictures, but of an idea. You mentioned meeting an intensely religious woman in a laundromat before writing *Carrie* and wondering what her children would be like.

KING: Yes, but you know that's too easy. You have to say that because people ask "Where did you get the idea for *Carrie?*" Which is a *destructive* question, because immediately you're forced to say something that sounds rational. There has to be direct cause and effect or people aren't satisfied. The woman in the laundromat came into it, but what I really saw was Carrie walking from the high school—I didn't see a prom or anything like that—and destroying everything in this town as she went. . . .

Q: Which is very "cinematic" but never made it onto the screen.

KING: They didn't have enough money! They had two million dollars, which just wasn't enough. And to me that's what *Carrie* really centers on. The book was hard to write, because the first three quarters of it seemed to me to be all a build-up to the destruction of the town.

Q: When Pauline Kael was reviewing *Carrie* she described the plot as "beautiful"; the symmetry, the way the motif of blood is used.

KING: She described the novel itself as "an unassuming potboiler." I started out to write her a letter about that and ask her why she said it. I was convinced someone had *told* her the book was an unassuming potboiler, and that she hadn't read it. But she would immediately have said, "Of *course* I read it; I thought it was an unassuming potboiler!" There's no way she's going to say, "No, I hadn't read it, I just called it that."

Q: You've said that the reviews of *Carrie* ascribed to Brian DePalma some things that came directly from the book.

KING: Pauline Kael says in her review that one of the good things about the film is that it discovers the junk heart of America. I understand why she says that about the film; but on the other hand I also believe that there was a good portion of that in the book itself. You don't write a novel that could be subtitled "High School Confidential" without the thought foremost in your mind that there is a junk, kitschy part of America that's very compelling and that's fun to play with.

To sort of backtrack a little bit: Brian DePalma was quoted in one of the Washington, D.C., papers as saying, "You see the kind of strains a young director has to work under; this is the kind of shit they hand me, and I have to do something with it." That was the tone of his comment. My own feeling was that that was an impolitic thing to say, whatever his opinion of the book. I thought a lot of the reason the movie succeeded was that DePalma had a strong plot skeleton to work with for the first time. *Carrie* owes a lot to Hitchcock, it's an homage to *Psycho*, but a lot of the motivation from the book is there. Some of the things he took from the book I think he just took for granted, some of the virtues of construction. I liked *Obsession* but it's full of all sorts of motivational flaws, and I don't think *Carrie* has that problem. So I resent DePalma's saying that. But there's no question or any doubt that he did a masterful job with *Carrie*. It's a great film by almost any standards. And I can say that, because I didn't have any part in making the film.

Q: How does an author come to sell a book to the movies? Did you have an agent who sought out a movie deal?

KING: No, I was never agented. Doubleday has a department that deals simply with movie agents, and it was all done there. In the case of *Carrie* they had a lot of prepublication interest from the movies. We had three or four offers and finally settled on Paul Monash—not because he had any financing, but because I respected his work. I liked *Butch Cassidy* and I liked *Slaughterhouse Five,* and most of all I liked *The Friends of Eddie Coyle*—it never got nominated for awards or anything, but I thought it was tremendous cinema. So Monash bought *Carrie.*

Now, you know, they buy options, these people, like you or I would buy a loaf of bread, mostly because if it doesn't work out they can take a tax loss. Monash paid forty-five grand for a year's option, and it looked for a while as if he wouldn't get financing at all. Finally he went to United Artists, where he did get financing, but on a very limited basis. It's weird: everybody did well out of *Carrie.* Now Monash is head of long-form at CBS.

With *'Salem's Lot,* Warner Brothers optioned it and Stirling Silliphant got his hands on it; he was writing and producing it. Warner's was having a lot of problems with him. It just wasn't working out. I have his original screenplay around someplace, and it's not very good. Warner's option was running out and people were lined up, you know, if they dropped it. We really wanted them to drop it, but they just didn't. They may make it or they may decide to take a tax loss. It would be too bad; I think it would make a nice picture.

Q: What exactly bothered you about Silliphant's script?

KING:Q: I thought it was dead on the page, and that's a hard thing to explain. The transposition was pretty good of the major incidents in the book. But his method of solving the problem of length and the number of characters was to combine, and it didn't seem to work very well. The combinations of traits weren't believable. He combined the teacher and the priest, for instance; the priest also taught classes at the school. It was *just* a solution to the mechanical problem, and there didn't seem to be any real inspiration, as if a lot of the spark he had earlier as a screenwriter was gone.

Q: There was mention of a possible 'Salem's Lot mini-series for TV, which would make the problem less acute, perhaps.

KING: Well, the people we would have sold it to if Warner's had dropped their option, were Lorimar, and they would have done it as eight hours for TV. You lose something, but you gain something, too. There's a scene in the book where the woman, Sandy McDougall, tries to feed her dead baby back to life; she slams him into the high chair and says, "Eat it, damn it!" You couldn't do that on TV; it's too intense for TV. But on the other hand, you wouldn't have to worry about losing all the characters, and I'd like to keep everybody in.

Q: When you sold Carrie, did you retain any control at all over the adaptation?

KING: I don't think there was a way in the world that I could have gotten any control. What's happened has been a steady progression. With Carrie, they didn't want me involved with the project at all, and I didn't really want to be involved. It's funny: I correspond with Lawrence Cohen, who did the screenplay. I thought he did a tremendous screenplay, and I wrote Cohen a letter telling him this. He was a little knocked over, because usually what they get from writers is "Jesus Christ, you butchered my baby!" Which was the way I did feel about Silliphant's script.

With 'Salem's Lot, I could have gotten more control for less money, and I chose more money and less control, because I was working on a lot of other stuff.

The Shining was purchased by an outfit called Producer's Circle, bankrolled by Johnson & Johnson Band-Aid money. With that one, under contract, I had a screenplay and a rewrite. I did a screenplay for it, and while I was working on it, Producer's Circle just turned around and sold the book to Warner Brothers, who had Stanley Kubrick in mind. Kubrick said he wanted to do it. What Producer's Circle did, in effect, was serve as an agent; they took a commission by reselling the book at a profit. At that point my rights lapsed. I could have been a tough guy about it and demanded my rewrite, but at that point it would have meant doing what Erica Jong did with Fear of Flying and just making a real prick out of myself. I don't want to be involved in anybody's project who doesn't want to be involved with me. So Kubrick's got it, and he wants to do everything; he wants to produce and direct and write it, which is the way he works.

Q: How much do you know about what he plans to do with it?

KING: Well, you hear rumors, but they don't mean much. My agent says that he once went to a film symposium where Kubrick spoke—this was just after *2001*—and someone asked him what else there was that he wanted to do. And Kubrick said that his one great unrealized ambition was to make the most frightening movie that had ever been filmed. I've also heard, from two other sources, that he's planning a black comedy, a send-up of the whole horror genre. I suppose those two things are not completely exclusive of each other, so I'll just wait and see.

I had a talk with Kubrick on the phone, we talked about an hour, and he was asking me—and he seemed to be seriously soliciting my opinion —about his plan to end the film. I won't tell you exactly what his plan is, but you imagine the worst thing that could happen, beyond what happens in the book, and that's what he has in mind. He asked me if I thought audiences would accept it. My answer was that, no, I didn't think they would, considering that there's a child involved. But my God, the man's a genius, I think, so I'm not going to stand in his way. If anybody can bring it off, Kubrick can; he can do *Dr. Strangelove*. I mean, shit, if he can make a joke out of the end of the world!

Q: A number of people detected an element of parody in the film of *Carrie* as well.

KING: Oh, yes! And it's there for the taking in the book. DePalma just did this tremendous satire of those high school peer groups. I mean, shit, those two—Bill Nolan and Christine Hargenson—who dump the blood on Carrie, are hilarious in that business. Travolta is very, very funny. As a matter of fact, since you asked before, the only time that I protested during the making of *Carrie* was when Paul Monash wanted Travolta to sing a theme song over the credits. I heard about this when Larry Cohen called me up, and he was sort of screaming about it. At that time Travolta had a hit record on the radio, "Gonna Let Her In"—he can carry a tune, if you stretch your imagination; it's a very thin little voice. So I called up Monash, and I said, "You know, Travolta is playing the *heavy* in this picture, and you want him to sing this love song over the credits, to the girl he's dumping pig's blood on?" And he said, "Well, how about the Bee Gees?" and I said "No, I *really* don't think so." I didn't descend to calling him "Paul Baby," but. . . . Well, nepotism reigns supreme out there, that's all I can figure. Monash is married to a lady named Merritt Malloy, and she's also a lyricist. She did three songs for the movie, which Brian DePalma very wisely buried. They're doing the songs at the prom, and the nicest one is played when Carrie and Tommy are dancing; they're talking over the song, so you can *just* hear it in the background.

As I said, DePalma handled the movie superbly; this business with the songs is just one example. His latest picture, *The Fury*, is from a book by John Farris. A lot of people came to me after *The Fury* came out and said, "John Farris ripped off *Carrie*." I don't think that's true; I read *The Fury* and liked it, but the similarity is there. I couldn't understand why DePalma would want to do *Carrie* all over again.

Q: I wanted to ask about particular changes that were made for *Carrie* on film. How about the change of setting, from Maine to Southern California, did that matter?

KING: I don't think it did, because the setting was never very clear in my own mind. When I wrote the book I set it in Massachusetts, around Andover or Boxford, one of the suburban towns outlying from Boston. That was before I had any idea the book was going to get published, because I never really thought it would. When it turned out that the book was going to get published I changed the setting to Maine, just because Maine's home and I thought people up here would like it.

Q: I had the impression that Carrie's mother had been turned from almost a left-over New England Puritan, as she is in the book, into a born-again Christian, with a slight Southern accent, as if to smooth over the problem.

KING: Yes, I didn't care for the Southern accent, that was a little bit too much for me; it sounded as if any minute she was going to jump up there on PTL Club and start testifying! But, the thing that *really* sets my teeth on edge every time, is when Carrie is pulling her mother down off the wall, and there's this *popping* sound. Awful!

Q: What about the hand coming out of the ground, which isn't in the book?

KING: That was DePalma's idea. It was cheaper than burning a whole town, and it works, it's really scary. Your defenses are all down. The thing about horror movies, the reason people laugh at them so often, is because their defenses are up; everybody's ready to defensively turn that shock into something funny. DePalma catches you at the end with your mind half out in the street. Men scream, and men *never* scream in horror movies, because there's supposed to be this macho thing. When was the last time *you* screamed at a horror movie?

Q: At the end of *Carrie*! . . . I'd like to see Spielberg do '*Salem's Lot*.

KING: Yeah, I've thought about that a lot. I'd like to see either Spielberg or Don Siegal do it. The other person I've mentioned consistently is John Boorman. I don't give a shit about *Exorcist II*; anybody can stub their toe once, and it doesn't change the fact that he did *Deliverance* and *Point Blank*.

Q: What, in general, is your impression of the attitude movie people have toward authors they're adapting? They don't think of you as a collaborator, by any chance?

KING: They don't have any real feeling for books. I think that this guy Jerzy Kosinski is a total asshole in a lot of ways, and I think Erica Jong and a lot of other people who holler bloody murder are assholes. I didn't even have much sympathy for Ken Kesey, because I don't like writers who go along until the movie is all made, and *then* complain. But Kosinski is right about one thing; when movie people buy a book it ceases being a book and becomes something called "a property." Kosinski says that when people call up and say, "Now, about this property," he says "Oh, you must want a real estate agent," and hangs up. They just see it as a loaf of bread or a turkey to be carved up—and that's often just what comes out, too—a turkey.

Q: What could an author do to protect his work from being carved up in the first place?

KING: Well, the major thing you can do is take less up front and try to get some kind of artistic control over the project. And that doesn't mean that you have to be a real son of a bitch about it. Most writers aren't; there are a few writers who give all of us the reputation of being real SOBs about having our work put on the screen. Most writers are delighted to have movies made out of their books. We all view it with some trepidation, because we see some of the abortions that get made. But if you take a little bit less money and just exercise some control over the final result—the kind of control I think Joseph Wambaugh would have been wise to exercise over *The Choirboys*. And if they make a bad movie out of your book, any writer should be able to understand that the movie is not the book and that the two things are not interchangeable. I don't think a book can be raped.

Q: One thing I wondered was whether you visualize your characters in terms of actors who might play them.

KING: It's a funny thing. When I wrote '*Salem's Lot* I always visualized Ben Mears as Ben Gazzara. I don't really describe the characters that I write about because I don't think you have to. If they seem like real people to the readers they will put their own faces on them. All I really say about Ben Mears is that his hair was sort of black and almost greasy. Then we were talking about the movie and somebody said, "But Gazzara is too old," and I saw him in some gangster picture a while later and, by God, he *is* too old. I guess if I could have my pick of anyone I'd say Martin Sheen.

Q: I pictured Straker, in *'Salem's Lot,* as Donald Pleasence.

KING: Yeah, so did I!

Q: Aha, good. And what about Sissy Spacek?

KING: I thought she was great for the part, and I had thought so when she was first mentioned. There were a lot of people who were doubtful, because Carrie is described in the book as being sort of chunky. But I thought Spacek would be all right because she's a girl who can look plain, and then, in other lights, she can look quite glamorous. When I heard about the casting I had just seen a TV movie called *Katherine,* and Spacek was just great in it. On the other hand, I think there are other actresses who could have played Carrie White. Mackenzie Phillips could have done it; she was actually the person who was in my mind.

Q: Are you moving toward writing directly for the screen, or maybe even producing yourself?

KING: Boy, yeah. I've got so many things that I'm working on that I'm afraid to take anything else on. On the other hand, I've had ABC after me for two years now, and it gets to be that they're holding out a bigger and bigger carrot each time. At first it was, "Have you thought about a made-for-TV movie." I said, "It's a great idea, but I really have a lot to do." The next thing was, "Have you ever thought about adaptations in long form?" I wrote back and said, "Well, it's interesting, but all of the books have been optioned already." After that I got a letter, "Have you thought about *creating* something for television in long form? Eight to ten hours, like *Roots,* from Monday to Friday!" And my immediate reaction was like, "Wow, *yeah!*" And they said, "Well, then come *down* and let's *talk* about it." Finally, I went down. I had three ideas that weren't working out as books, and I presented them. One they liked very much, and they started talking about budgets and twelve hours of TV on consecutive nights, and I got a little bit scared. It seemed like the sort of thing that you could get into and suddenly find yourself in California surrounded by tequila bottles. I said, "Look, I think that maybe I'd better just sell you the idea for a song." "Oh no, we want *you*, we want the name," or whatever. So, nothing happened for a while, and then we were in England; they wrote and said, "How'd you like to do a series of one-hour horror-suspense things, and you could introduce each one as host, like Rod Serling." And I had to say that I didn't think I could *do* that. They said, "Well, keep us in mind," and that's where things stand right now. I mean, God, it's really a tempting idea.

I've written a number of screenplays, and some of them are pretty good, but I think I'm still really a beginner. I did a screenplay based on "Children of the Corn" from *Night Shift*. I did it not because I thought a movie would come of it, but mostly because I needed some practice. I had gotten a book on writing screenplays, because I wanted some examples to read, to see how it was done. I'm working on a screenplay now, off and on. It's a story about the owner of a radio station in western Maine. He fires all his disc jockeys and imports this computer radio thing. It's one of these automated radio voices, with this syrupy, totally mechanical voice, totally divorced from any real human being. One of the deejays commits suicide, and after that the machine starts to take over. It's saying things like, "And now the latest from, and *blah*, *blah*, *blah* and fuck you, you're going to die; I'm going to kill you." I'm having a good time writing it.

Q: You have adapted Ray Bradbury's novel *Something Wicked This Way Comes*, and your own *The Shining*. Which was more difficult?

KING: I think the Bradbury was easier, because I felt more divorced from the source material. I loved the book, and I think that of all the screenplays I've done, that was the best. But in spite of loving it I was a little divorced from it, where I wasn't with my own book. Another difference was that I had a screenplay by contract on *The Shining*. You can say that a contract is wonderful because it means that you're going to eat, but it's also a chain around your neck. You *must* do it, it's like getting a homework assignment. It's the greatest single advantage of being a freelance writer down the drain!

Q: How mechanical can you be about the process of adapting *The Shining*, obvious things like getting the conflicts in Torrance onto the screen without being able to put his thoughts in. How do you translate those things?

KING: They didn't want a lot of flashbacks, which would have been the obvious way. I did it by playing up some of the physical mannerisms, as he began to get more and more uptight, always wiping his lips or getting very nervous and jumpy about things. The two flashbacks they agreed to were to the time when he broke his son's arm, and a couple of conversations about the way things had been. What would have been shown if they had used my screenplay, was Jack and Wendy taking the boy out of the hospital with his arm in a cast. I thought that it all worked out fairly well. What Kubrick will do with it I don't know, whether he'll use flashbacks or not.

Q: I don't know quite how to put this. You have this thing, this object, that has been created in one medium—it already exists and you've thought the whole story through in one medium—and then rather than writing something new you have to take this old one and turn it into something else, to slice away. . . .

KING: That was the beauty of it, I didn't have to slice *anything* out of it. I'll tell you what it was like: you know that sliced bologna that you get at the supermarket? Imagine that package of bologna with five slices in it; what I did was just peel off the top two slices, and they were my screenplay. The rest of it was all underneath, it was all what they thought. The place where that came up most clearly was in the first chapter of Part Three—"Up On the Roof"—with the wasps' nest. It's a long chapter, and Jack goes into thinking about all this business, about his self-destructive drinking and so on. What happened in the screenplay was, he's working on the roof, the wasps sting him, he goes down the ladder and gets the bug bomb, takes it back up and sprays it in the wasps' nest. And that's it. Twenty-three pages in the book boiled down into one page of script. It was fun. There were other things it was possible to do later, when things get surreal; to work certain past events in as visions or hallucinations. You just try to find alternatives.

With Chris Palmer

"Hey! That's my guy!" said Stephen King gleefully as he sat watching a preview screening of 'Salem's Lot, a four-hour, two-part TV movie based on the novel he wrote about vampires taking over a small Maine town. "It's pretty good." King said after all four cassettes had run through the machinery at Bangor's CBS affiliate, WABI.

It was the first time King and his wife Tabitha had seen the Warner Brothers production of the gothic horror story. Watching them, while they were watching it, was delightful. King is a fellow with a wit surpassed only by his imagination.

A Maine native who now lives in Center Lovell, King was generally pleased with the TV treatment of 'Salem's Lot, though he pointed out several differences between his book and the TV-movie. Some of the discrepancies are minor—like the timing of the killing of one of the vampires—while some of them are major.

"There are fewer characters in the movie than in my book," King commented. "And there is more in the book about Ben's experiences with the house. I think if they had had six hours, they could have done my book."

The biggest plot difference between 'Salem's Lot the book and 'Salem's Lot the TV show is one that is largely symbolic. "The book chronicles the decay of a small town." King explained. "The vampires represent the life blood being drained away." The town, a major entity in the book, does not measure as prominently in the TV-movie.

"The major difference," King continued, "is that they have turned the focus away from outright horror to suspense. Suspense is okay, but it's not the same as horror. Suspense is diluted horror." The reason for this dilution, he said, is that television is "down on violence," and can't accommodate the bloodiness of a Stephen King novel. "You can take Kool-Aid and pour in six gallons of water and it's still red, but it's not the same."

King has a point. The television version of 'Salem's Lot is not as scary as the book. The acting is adequate, but nothing special. David Soul (of Starsky & Hutch fame) plays Mears. James Mason is Straker, the antique dealer and front man for the head vampire; Bonnie Bedelia is Susan Norton, Mears's love interest; and Lance Kerwin (James at 16) is the boy hero, Mark Petrie.

"I think the casting is good," King said. "I'm not the kind of writer who has a strong visualization of my characters." The only character he didn't especially like was Parkins Gillespie, the town constable, whom he pictured as thin and lithe. In the movie he is played by beefy Kenneth McMillan.

After the screening, when King was discussing the show, he said, "I do wish that when actors play Maine people they would stop trying to do that Maine accent. You just can't do it."

"As for the town, the producers changed its name. —It was Jerusalem's Lot in the book, abbreviated to 'Salem's Lot—and positioned it somewhere in Maine where it simply couldn't be. In one scene, Ben and Susan are taking off to the movies in Bangor. In another, the body of a young boy is taken to a Cumberland morgue. Cumberland and Bangor can't both be that close to 'Salem's Lot.

"Don't these people have maps?" King fumed when he noticed the error. Earlier, when the cameras flashed down the main street, King quipped, "I'm sorry, but that doesn't look like Maine. Well, maybe a little like Ellsworth."

Another objection King had was to the make-up job on the chief vampire, Barlow, portrayed by Reggie Nalder. In the CBS show, the bald menace is an odd shade of translucent green, with Mr. Spock ears, yellow eyes and fangs in the front rather than on the sides of this mouth. King contends that the same make-up has been used before, and that it shows a "bankruptcy of imagination" on the part of the producers to copy previous work.

The young novelist, whose other books include *Carrie, The Shining* and *The Stand*, all of which either have been or will be made into motion pictures, retained no artistic control over the *'Salem's Lot* project.

"Considering the medium, they did a real good job," he summarized. "TV is death to horror. When it went to TV a lot of people moaned and I was one of the moaners."

With Tom Wood

As guest of honor at the Kubla Khanate science fiction convention King was the main attraction and he was beaming over *The Shining*, directed by Stanley Kubrick and starring Jack Nicholson and Shelley Duvall.

"He wants to hurt people. He wants to make a movie that people will be afraid to go see. And they'll go see it anyway. I think he's going to try to make a picture so scary that it'll make *Alien* look like *Romper Room*.

"It's going to be so scary that people will have to leave the theatre." King said he had only seen bits and pieces of the movie, but understands it might have an "X" rating.

"When I heard that, I was delighted because it meant to me that Kubrick was really gonna go out and get the audience."

To give some idea of the intensity involved, King described one scene of the movie in detail.

"The hero is a fellow named Jack Torrance and he's had various problems and he and his family have gone up to be caretakers at this hotel. While he's working on a novel, things start to happen. . . and the wife would like to go and the boy would like to go because he knows things are going to get terrible after awhile. The one thing that holds her there is that her husband is working productively for the first time, really, since they've been married. She can hear steam coming out of the typewriter—*clackety, clackety, clackety*—all day long.

"She's forbidden to look at the manuscript. . . and finally, she can't help herself. She thumbs into the middle of it and written from top to bottom and side to side with no margins anywhere over and over again is the phrase '*All work and no play makes Jack a dull boy.*'

"She's looking at it and her eyes sort of widen with horror. A shadow falls over her and it's. . . it's Nicholson and he's saying 'Do you like it? It's good, isn't it?' And he's got an axe in his hand.

"And this is the sort of thing he is going to do, except it's going to go on two hours and 15 minutes."

The Shining is the third novel King has had adapted to film. *Carrie* was made into a movie by Brian DePalma in 1976 and *'Salem's Lot* was a mini-series on television this past fall.

"CBS is supposed to be doing a *'Salem's Lot* series in January, a takeoff from the movie. I intend to be in Costa Rica when that happens. I'm not into that."

King said that doesn't mean to imply he is dissatisfied with the screen treatment of his works.

"I've gotten off pretty lucky. I'm doing the screenplay for *The Stand* and am hip-deep in that and a couple of other projects. But whenever anybody points to the movie and says how bad they are compared to the book, I answer, 'But look how bad it could have been.'"

With David Chute

"Well, the most obvious thing is that it isn't what *anybody* expected. It certainly isn't what *I* expected." Stephen King is mulling over the

$18-million movie that Stanley Kubrick has fashioned from the third of his best-selling horror novels, *The Shining*. The novelist appears rather taken aback by it, uncertain whether to hail or carp.

"I had been telling interviewers for months beforehand," King continues, "that what I thought Kubrick wanted to do is hurt people. I had visions of heart-attack patients being loaded into ambulances. But apparently that *isn't* what he wanted, because certainly there are missed opportunities to scare the shit out of the audience. The question I really have is, did Kubrick *know* what he wanted? Or put it another way; did he know how to *get* what he wanted? Everything we were told beforehand suggested that Kubrick wanted to make a commercial picture in the wake of *Barry Lyndon*. And if that's true, it opens the possibility that he tried to make one, and then discovered that he didn't know how."

King sits flopped back in a plastic-mesh deck chair on the porch of the incongruously modernistic home secreted in the woods down a rolling, lumpy road in western Maine. He isn't having much luck staying hidden in what he calls his "hermetically sealed environment" these days. He had returned from Pittsburgh only the day before, after visiting the set of the upcoming *Knightriders*, and the director-to-be of two King screenplays, *Dawn of the Dead*'s George Romero.

The Dead Zone was a number-one best-seller, King's first, and it might even be the first number-one best-seller ever to contain a reference to the Ramones—and a favorable one at that! According to King, "Ramones songs like 'Rockaway Beach' and 'Sheena Is a Punk Rocker' are my idea of what the music should do." No small point, this, since all of King's novels have drawn on rock for images and epigraphs. The title of *The Stand*, for example, derives from the Drifters' chestnut "Stand By Me." And in an upcoming novel called *Christine*, "rock itself becomes an ominous, crepitating force that just keeps getting louder and louder until it overwhelms" the central character. "As a writer," King says, "what's important to me is not getting scared and sliding off to one side at the critical moment. And the best of rock goes straight to the heart. It goes in and gets out."

For King, the connection between rock and horror seems largely one of tone and temperament. "The dedication to my next novel, *Firestarter*, is to Shirley Jackson, 'who never had to raise her voice.' When I write a book, I may say to myself that I'm going to speak in a low, rational tone, but I always end up screaming. I can't seem to help it. I'm just jumping up and down, hollering my guts out. Which is what someone like Mick Jagger does." But King also notes that the most recent novel by his friend Peter Straub, *Ghost Story*, has been his most successful because of a change of attitude. "Peter said that '*Salem's Lot* made him realize that this sort of material isn't supposed to be quiet, that horror was best when it had a big, operatic effect."

If one thing is clear from the film version of *The Shining*, it's that Stanley Kubrick is no rock 'n' roller. "I think that the movie is brilliant," King says, "And at the same time I wanted *more*. I thought Kubrick dealt with things sometimes in a way that was almost prissy. Somebody was telling me that he lives in a glass dome, that he's kind of germicidal. I wonder if he's ever seen *Dawn of the Dead* or if he's ever seen *Alien*? If he's ever had a conversation with himself about primal terror? What I'm talking about is just going out and getting the reader or the viewer by the throat and *never* letting go. Not playing games and not playing the *artiste*. Because horror has its own artistry, in that never-let-up sort of feeling. That's what's wrong with *The Shining*, basically; it's a film by a man who thinks too much.

"I'll tell you, *The Shining* is much more of an Edwardian ghost story than what we've come to think of as a horror movie: something like *Halloween* or *The Fog*. And, on that level, it's fairly effective. I think it might appeal to the same crowd who like *The Amityville Horror*, a much older crowd than you usually see at horror movies. *Amityville* wasn't really frightening; what it was, was sort of *interesting*, like that Raymond Moody thing, *Life After Life*. *The Shining* is not a personally threatening movie, either, not like *Dawn of the Dead*; you can't go to a movie like that without feeling personally assaulted by the images."

But, I protest, I *did* feel assaulted at *The Shining*; by the editing rhythms and the nerve-racking music and the frantic tracking movements down endless corridors, with the camera three inches off the ground: the movie made me feel liked a rat scurrying through a maze.

"Well, okay," King agrees. "But most people aren't going to feel that way. They'll go for the story, and if the camera movements work, they'll work subliminally. And actually, it's on the story level that the movie bothers *me* the most. The movie has no heart; there's no center to that picture. I wrote the book as a tragedy, and if it *was* a tragedy, it was because all the people loved each other. Here, it seems there's no tragedy because there's nothing to be lost. And yet, the movie as a whole *is* scary. The camera angles and the use of the Steadicam are very upsetting and unnerving to me. So even though the family relationships are all screwed up in terms of storytelling, there's something uneasy about the whole film. And I'm not sure that what the movie achieves it could possibly have achieved if it had gone a more conventional route."

Obviously, King's devotion to the "never-let-up" ethic in horror is not quite absolute. In fact, he insists that there must be natural, humane limits on the sort of horror. "I don't know how much you're supposed to want to hurt people," he explained, "how deep you're supposed to go. I don't think that artistically there's any limit on that kind of thing. I just wonder whether morally there isn't. I worry about the morality of this stuff a lot. George Romero says that *Dawn of the Dead* is an *a*moral movie, and the film seems to bear him out. But there has to be a dividing line between the *a*moral and the *im*moral. And the line may just be whether the writer entices you to the point that you're vitally concerned with these people. *Friday the 13th* is an *im*moral movie from my point of view; it's saying, 'Come in and watch people get killed.' It's like a porno novel, in which the writer of this Beeline Original says, 'Come and read this book and you'll see people fuck and fuck and fuck and fuck and *fuck*!' And they don't even give you a plot; what they give you are these hangers, and they can hang fucks on these hangers. That's what *Friday the 13th* does, except. . . well, basically, it's a snuff movie, isn't it? Simple as that."

Just as they can always spot the fakes and carpetbaggers, the real horror specialists seem able to spot one another immediately. On the evening of the day this interview was conducted, I sat in Stephen King's living room while he screened David Cronenberg's *The Brood* on his large-screen video-beam TV, because he would shortly be writing about the film in the second draft of *Danse Macabre*, his non-fiction "love song to the genre," due next spring. The second of his three children, a diabolical seven-year-old horror *maven* named Joe Hill King, sits watching it in one of the white-on-black "Brood" t-shirts his father had purchased when he caught the film at the late Central Square Cinemas. On the screen, Frank Carveth, the father, is comforting the small daughter, whom he believes has been beaten by her mother. "See that," King tells his wife, "*that's* what Kubrick missed in *The Shining*." Later, he added, "*The Brood* really is very *a propos* of *The Shining*; the passing on of violence to children, and so on. But I think Cronenberg blows Kubrick out of the water."

With Ben Herndon

Q: Now that you have the screenplays for *Creepshow* and *Cat's Eye* under your belt, what have you found to be the pleasures and pitfalls of adapting your own stories for the screen?

KING: I like it because it's fast, I like it because it's visual, and I like it because it's work for idiots in the sense that it's all like skating—it's this totally surface phenomenon. I don't like the fact that everybody in the world wants to put a handprint on what you do. Everybody in the world wants to say to you, "This doesn't work, this isn't enough motivation, this isn't deep enough, or this situation is too static, you need to bring in a new element here." It's the major culprit in the business of failing to bring books and stories to movies.

Q: What is the reason your books have not adapted well to the screen?

KING: I just gave it to you. The movie result is something like the victim of a vampire. That is to say, it *looks* like Lucy Westerna, but it really *isn't* Lucy Westerna anymore, you know what I mean? It's very cold at that point.

Q: Do you feel you'll have better control of the film if you write your own screenplay?

KING: Well, I don't know. At this point, I've had two screenplays produced and actually brought out. One was *Creepshow*, which was a good-sized success, and the second one was *Cat's Eye*, which, financially speaking, was a good-sized failure. There are reasons for that which don't have anything to do with the movie. They have to do with the production end of it. At MGM, the whole top echelon of executives fell, and all the pictures that had been produced under those people became orphans. There were maybe six pictures, and *Cat's Eye* was one of them. There were no trailers, no publicity, and no promotion—that sort of thing. But beyond that, there were a lot of other factors. The point is, both of these movies were anthology movies. It'll be interesting to see what happens with *Silver Bullet*, which is actually a "movie" movie.

Q: Is this the film based on your *Cycle of the Werewolf*? How were you involved with that project?

KING: I wrote a screenplay for *Silver Bullet*, and wrote and am going to direct a film called *Maximum Overdrive* for Dino De Laurentiis.

Q: Is your desire to direct based on the need to protect the integrity of your work?

KING: You're not quite right when you say it's one more step to "protect the integrity of the work." I don't care about the integrity of the work at all...well, I do a little bit. But no more than, say, a father who sends his daughter off to college. You hope that the girl is not going to get gang-banged at a fraternity, and you hope that the girl is not going to turn into a little roundheels but at the same time, if you've got any intelligence, you realize that at a certain point she has to go her own way and her virginity—her propriety or whatever—is no longer your personal concern. And in the same way, if somebody pays a lot of money for the rights to a book that I wrote and they're going to make a film out of it—I hope that it will be treated well. I have a logical right to expect that it will be treated well because I want to protect my own investment, correct? But at the same time, if I'm not involved with the project, it has nothing to do with me. If it's good—fantastic. But I didn't have anything to do with it being good any more than I had to do with *Carrie* being a good movie. If it's bad—as *Firestarter* was bad—I don't have anything to do with that. In the case of *Maximum Overdrive*, what I'm doing is seeing whether or not I can take whatever it is that makes people like the books, and buy the books in big numbers, over into the film and see if people will really like it.

Q: How did Rod Serling's work on *The Twilight Zone* influence your style of writing?

KING: It taught me some bad things, man. It taught me that short stories had to have O. Henry endings, which is something that I later found out isn't necessarily the truth. It isn't always a cheat to the reader to progress in a straight line; endings don't always have to be a funky double-reverse. But I still don't believe critics of the short story who say the O. Henry ending is inherently bad. You remember *The Twilight Zone* where the guy finally had time enough to read and he broke his glasses? There's nothing wrong with that. To me, that's a perfectly acceptable ending. What's a *better* story ending is the one in the TZ show, "The Shelter," where it [the UFO warning that induces a family to lock their neighbors out of its fall-out shelter] turns out to be just a mistake and they have to go up and face each other. That's *real* short story telling. But you know what the show really did for me was bring me into contact with a lot of writers whose names I first saw as credits on *The Twilight Zone*. And then later, when I was sensitized to those names, I began to see their books, pick them up, and read them. Chuck Beaumont in particular...also Richard Matheson.

Q: Of the 156 episodes, I believe Serling wrote 92 of them himself.

KING: I'm on record in *Danse Macabre* as saying that. . . well, Serling himself said that "a third of what I wrote for the series was crap," and I think that's about right. I think a third of what he wrote for the series was crap. I also think a third of what he wrote was inspired, and the rest of it was pretty good. But what he did have was this very clear view of what this series was about—so that it achieved a remarkably high consistency and quite a lot of quality too. I mean Serling was *The Twilight Zone*. It's amazing if you sit down and figure out what he wrote. You wonder how he ever did it. I mean, people think *I'm* prolific! What is especially amazing is how many he did that were really, really good that were just pulled out of thin air. They weren't adaptations of stories. Matheson adapted—people don't know this, but "Third from the Sun," was a short story before it was a teleplay. And I think some of the Beaumont stuff were short stores before they were teleplays. Most of what Serling did were not adaptations. Serling came from a sort of radio and TV drama background and came to fantasy through the back door. He didn't know what had been done, and so he had the courage to just try everything. But I have written this kind of stuff since I was a kid. I have always loved it, whereas Serling—so far as I know—wrote very little fantasy until he started to work on *The Twilight Zone*. And then he was like this guy observing a huge untilled field—because he didn't know that other people had worked in it—saying, "Think of all the things that I can do!" And he just went out and did 'em, and a lot of 'em were great. The first couple of years you're looking at the work of a man who was just entranced with the idea that he didn't have to be totally realistic in every way. The first two years—and they were the best—were the work of a man drunk on fantasy.

Q: You've certainly taken horror/fantasy into a more realistic realm.

KING: No, that's nothing I did. Matheson did it, and *The Twilight Zone* did it too. That was something that maybe I did take from *The Twilight Zone*. How many of those things had backgrounds like you remember, the episode about Shatner finding this little devil in a restaurant? It's the most prosaic setting in the world. If not for that little devil, that would have been a boring story. So I owe some of that to *The Twilight Zone*, certainly.

With Paul R. Gagne

Q: How did your first novel, *Carrie*, develop from the initial story idea to a finished novel?

KING: Originally, it was going to be a short story. I had an idea about a girl who is at the very bottom, the pits, of the high school pecking order with just nowhere to go and everybody just turning on her. I wanted her to get her own revenge on them through some kind of a wild psychic talent. I'd read an article a long time ago in *Life* magazine about a case of telekinesis that involved a young girl. The hypothesis was that a lot of this stuff comes from young people. So I sat down and started to write it, and I saw that it was impossible for it to be a short story because it needed too much developmental material. In order for you to really be delighted when Carrie destroys everything you have to see her really put upon.

Q: You were quoted in *Yankee* magazine as saying that you were "the kid who got picked last for baseball teams" in school. Do Carrie's experiences reflect your own adolescense?

KING: I was quoted out of context. The fact is, I was the last to be picked for baseball teams when I was a kid because I was fat and wore glasses. I just wasn't too cool. But I was never picked on. I never had Carrie's kind of a life when I was in high school. I played football. I wasn't the kind of kid who would get elected to student council, but neither did I lurk around the lockers looking like I was just waiting for somebody to haul off on me.

Q: How do you feel about Brian DePalma's film of *Carrie*?

KING: I think it was very good. First of all, I put this in the context of all the really good fantasy novels I've seen turned into cruddy pictures because the filmmakers don't care. A lot of people in Hollywood only see the buck, and they're perfectly willing to take a fine fantasy novel, something by Fritz Leiber or H. P. Lovecraft, and turn it into a piece of drive-in tripe that's gonna play for two weeks and be gone. They don't care, because they only laid out about four hundred thousand dollars on the picture anyway. They make back the negative cost and another million, and everybody goes home happy. It's enough to make you cry if you really love fantasy.

They only had a small budget on *Carrie*, but the people who were involved had made an agreement that it wouldn't be a cheap drive-in picture. Everybody put out really hard, and I think they made a really good picture out of it.

Q: Was there anything about the film which disappointed you?

KING: Well, I was disappointed that the destruction of the town at the end wasn't in the film. But on the other hand, I understand that it just couldn't be. They only had about a two million dollar budget. It was before the big horror craze, when Frankenheimer could get twelve million for *Prophecy*, and it looked cheaper than *Carrie*! DePalma is a really good low-budget director, which is one of the reasons he was picked for the project. He made *Sisters* for about four hundred thousand dollars, and it looked like two million. He made *Carrie* for two million, and it looked like six. Now, Kubrick is doing *The Shining*, and he spent twenty million dollars. Hopefully, it'll be a twenty million dollar film that won't look like a twenty million dollar film!

Q: Were you involved at all with the production of *Carrie*?

KING: Only in the most basic way. There were actually a number of offers on the film rights to *Carrie*. The fact that it didn't do too well in hardcover didn't seem to make any difference. It was there, and it was filmable; it had a lot of the things I feel moviemakers must look for. One of which is a storyline that's going to interest your basic moviegoing audience, let's say fifteen to thirty-two, or whatever. And of the offers that were presented before us, I suggested that we go with Paul Monash, because I had seen his other work and I though he'd make a decent picture. Beyond that, I wasn't involved. I wasn't invited. I kept my nose out of it, because one of the things movie makers buy when they purchase a book for film is the right to a little autonomy!

Q: What inspired your second novel, *'Salem's Lot*?

KING: I was teaching a course called "Fantasy and Science Fiction," and *Dracula* was one of the books. We got sitting around and rapping at the dinner table about what would happen if Dracula came back today, in modern dress. And my first reaction was that he'd go to New York and get run over by a taxicab! But that question wouldn't go away; it kept coming back when I was bored or just sitting around. And I put him in different settings—I put him in the west, I put him in the city, and finally I put him in my own native New England. And the more I thought about it, the better it began to seem to me. And finally I had to sit down and write it. A lot of other things came into play. The *Dracula* thing was the basis, but then I started thinking about the old E.C.

comics, and I thought I maybe I'd work this in. I also started thinking about Thornton Wilder's play *Our Town,* and *Peyton Place,* both of which tried to get below the surface where everything seems all right to what's real. It was very exciting to write that book and to balance those three things off. And I think they work in the book to varying degrees.

Q: Your trademark of writing about "ordinary" people gives the vampire tale a new slant; it becomes less exotic than the stereotypical characterization, and therefore more accessible and believable.

KING: I try to make ordinary people seem ordinary, but yet I think most people are mainly good. I feel that way about people, even when I see them on the street; that they probably have something inside them that's decent, you know? Maybe that's just a piece of sappy philosophy, but when you take that decency and contrast it with the evil of the vampire or the supernatural, it kind of makes it stand forward.

Q: How did your feel about the television movie based on *'Salem's Lot?*

KING: Basically, I liked it. Most of what television touches within the horror genre turns to absolute drivel. I think Richard Kobritz and Tobe Hooper made it rise well above that. The gore and the violence were toned down, but they still managed to maintain the fright and the intensity of the story. There are a couple of things I disliked about the picture, though. First of all, I wasn't happy with the makeup they used to bring Barlow to the screen. The fact that they wanted to make him truly horrifying rather than charming and sophisticated didn't bother me, but they made him look too much like the vampire in *Nosferatu.* This is the third time that particular makeup concept has been used, and I think they could have been more original.

The other thing that really bothered me a lot was the fact that CBS chose to show the two parts of the film a week apart, rather than on consecutive nights as they originally intended. A lot of the film's continuity and intensity was lost between that and the constant commercial interruption. I saw the film at a special screening shortly before it was shown on TV, and there's quite a difference when you see it straight through.

Q: Do you feel that the considerable plot and character changes that were made from your novel work well in the film?

KING: Yes. In order to get the story down to an acceptable length for filming, Paul Monash had to combine some of the characters and events. I felt that his combinations worked quite well, though certain things could have been built up a little better in the first half of the film. One thing that comes to mind is the priest, Father Callahan. There's a scene where Barlow takes a cross away from him. The audience is given the impression that Barlow is too powerful a vampire to be affected by crosses, and that simply isn't true. Barlow can take the cross away because Callahan's faith is very shaky. This is explained in the book, but not in the film. Overall, though, I think Paul Monash did a fine job. I read his script, and it was quite good. The intensity of the story was even greater in his script than it was in the film.

Q: One of the things in the book that Richard Kobritz felt very strongly against showing in the film was Ben Mears's vision of Hubie Marsten hanging upstairs in the Marsten house.

KING: In a way, I'm glad they didn't show that. The first couple of screenplays all focused very heavily on that. Ben's vision and the Marsten house were both very central to the story in those scripts, and that was wrong. I mean, if I intended the story to be *about* the Marsten house, I would have called the book "The Marsten House"!

Q: Is there anything in the book you would have liked to have seen in the film?

KING: Well, there are two scenes in the book that I really like. One is when the vampire children attack the driver of the school bus in the middle of the night. The other is when Sandy McDougall discovers that her baby is dead and tries to feed him chocolate pudding. Obviously, those scenes were just too gruesome to be done for television.

Q: To what extent do you feel the integrity of the book was sacrificed for the sake of not offending television viewers?

KING: When I first learned the book was being done for television rather than as a theatrical release, I was very disappointed. That initial disappointment did not extend to the finished product. It was done for television, but it was done well for television. Most of the reviewers I've talked to since the thing was shown on TV seem to be expecting me to really come out against it, but I just didn't feel that way. Sure, it probably would have been better if it wasn't done for television, but I'm not gonna run around screaming "They wrecked my fuckin' book!"

Q: I understand that at one point you were working on adapting some of the stories from *Night Shift* as television movies.

KING: I did that, and it was shot down by NBC. Basically, all of the people involved with it on the creative end, myself included, were very happy with what we had. It was presented to NBC, and their Standards and Practices just said "No, too gory, too suspenseful, it's too intense." They axed it for those reasons.

I'm pretty sour on TV. I feel like I've been bitten a number of times. I've been approached by several groups about actually hosting a series of supernatural, horror-type stories on TV. The pitch was "TV needs another Rod Serling; You'd become a fuckin' STAR!" All those incentives; the new Rod Serling, the new Alfred Hitchcock, or something like that. And I'd tell these people, "You are in a position now where you can't show somebody getting punched in the nose more than once in one hour of prime time television, and you want to put horror on TV?" My reaction was that I didn't want to do it simply because I didn't want to be on TV for six weeks and then be axed because everybody tuned out when they found out there was nothing there to watch!

Q: Moving on to *The Shining*, that was inspired when you were on vacation in Colorado and stayed at a hotel similar to The Overlook in the novel?

KING: It was the Hotel Stanley, up country near the Rocky Mountain State Park. Somebody had told us we ought to go stay there—you know, a piece of Americana, part of western history, Johnny Ringo was shot down there, and all this other stuff—and finally my wife and I did go up to the hotel. It was the last day of the season, and they let us stay there because we could pay cash. They'd already shipped out their credit card slips! The hotel was totally empty except for us. We were the only guests, yet all the service help was there. They were there by contract until the last day. The band was there, playing in the deserted dining room with all the chairs turned up on their tables, except for ours. It was very eerie!

Q: How did *The Stand* develop?

KING: That's the hardest one to talk about. I was actually trying to write a book about Patty Hearst! I was convinced that the only way anybody ever could really understand the whole Hearst case was to lie about it. All these things that nobody knows but her, and she's not very interesting anyway. She knows certain facts, but she doesn't really know what happened. How's that for an arrogant statement? So I wanted to write a novel about it, and *The Stand* is what came out instead.

Q: How would you describe your depiction of the concepts of good and evil in *The Stand*?

KING: Well, I tend to see evil as being very powerful, but ultimately stupid. I tend to see good as powerful in a more subtle way, and ultimately the force that has all the variation and all the real excitement. I see evil as having a superficial excitement, but underneath it's dull and monotonous, and that's where the real terror is. As Joseph Conrad said, "the only horror is that there is no horror." That's what I see as the basis of it.

Q: That view is clearly personified in the character of Randall Flagg, the novel's embodiment of evil.

KING: Yeah, it is. A lot of people were disappointed in *The Stand* because Randall Flagg kind of peters away to nothing. But to me, the ultimate thing about evil is that it leads nowhere. I believe that with truly evil people, the evil leaps into them from somewhere outside. Like Charlie Starkweather, or Charlie Whitman, the guy who went up in that Texas tower and shot all those people. At the end of it, they either kill themselves, or if you get hold of them there's just nothing left. Those who support the death penalty want to put these people to death in an electric chair without realizing that the thing they want to kill has gone.

Q: In *The Stand's* final confrontation between the forces of good and evil, there are scenes where Randall Flagg is mocked, berated, openly laughed at by the protagonists. I'm reminded of a similar scene in Ray Bradbury's *Something Wicked This Way Comes*. Did the Bradbury novel influence you at all?

KING: I suspect it did. I taught *Something Wicked This Way Comes* when I was a writer-in-residence. The basic concept, and I've come to believe more and more in the validity of this over the years, is that you can laugh evil out of existence. Evil can only exist when it creates a feeling of awe and overmastering fear. I didn't think that Bradbury handled it very well at the end of *Something Wicked This Way Comes*, because I think he was tired when he finished that book. I was certainly tired when I finished *The Stand*, and I think it shows to some degree. But I think you're right; the influence is really there.

Q: What led to the writing of *The Dead Zone*?

KING: I don't really know how to answer that one, either. Originally, I wanted to write a novel about a person who could tell the future. It was as simple as that. And little by little it refined itself into this psychic talent that's known as "prolepsis." The Peter Hurkos talent. I guess that Uri Geller claims to have it to some degree, too. It's the ability to be sort of a human bloodhound—to touch objects and get visions from them.

Originally, I'd simply visualized a single scene where this guy, the hero of the book, would be teaching a high school class. He would touch a student who handed in an examination, and he'd say to her, "You must go home at once; your house is on fire!" And it would be true, and everybody would sort of shun him as a result of this. Everybody would be afraid of him. I sat down to write it, only I went back a little further and began to ask myself all these other questions about what would happen if you could really see the future. The more I wrote, the more it seemed like just a really fucking horrible thing, you know? People wouldn't like you!

Q: One of the things I liked most about *The Dead Zone*, from a stylistic standpoint, was your careful use of interrelated images and symbols throughout the plot.

KING: To me, everything that's symbolic in *The Dead Zone* points in one direction. It seems as though our lives are governed by these little "chance" events. If most people look back at the way they met their wives, for example, it all seems random. You know, you could have spent five minutes to get your shoes shined or walked in another direction on a particular day and you'd be married to somebody different. Or think about how your grandmother and grandfather met. On that slender thread of coincidence hangs your very existence. The book tries to convey the idea that maybe chance isn't entirely chance. If you look closely at some of the images, symbols and events in the book—the wheel of fortune, the burning tire, the bad hot dog that Sarah gets at the carnival, Johnny Smith shaking hands, or whatever you want—it appears to be coincidence. But if you draw back and take a longer view, maybe there's a pattern to it all. I like to think there is; I'd hate to think that life is all random.

Q: With both *The Dead Zone* and *The Stand*, you've gotten away from the straight horror story and into more philosophical and socially conscious themes. Is this your rebuttal to every critic who's asked you "Yes, but when are you going to do something serious?"

KING: No, I don't really think so! I don't have a game plan or anything like that. You write what comes out, and that's all that you can do. Otherwise, you start to lie, and that's no way to run the game. Fiction is all lies anyway, and if you start to lie about the lies, you're really in terrible shape. I don't think you can deal with it on that level. That's the level that Harold Robbins deals with it on. It's no good.

Q: *The Dead Zone* takes a pretty scathing point of view with regard to religious fanaticism and yellow journalism.

KING: Yes. The view of religion in *The Dead Zone* is pretty specified in terms of what sort of religion it tries to cover. I don't have too many problems with Roman Catholics who want to go to mass and do their thing and all that. I don't personally like it, and I want to disassociate myself from it. We've got millions of churchgoers in this country who, by their attendance, are giving their stamp of approval to the church which recognized the Inquisition and is, whether intentionally or not, the balance wheel of so much misery over the entire world, from Northern Ireland to wherever. But I don't really have anything against religion, because most people see it as the means to another world and have a good handle on it. Vera Smith, Johnny's mother in *The Dead Zone*, has gone one step beyond that. She's not over the line into religious mania the way that Carrie White's mother is, but at the same time she's supplanting the Bible and the power of God with a lot of what I think of as pagan stuff.

And as far as the yellow journalism goes, I just have utter contempt for that. That's taking people's most miserable fears and using them to turn a buck. That's terrible.

Q: With regard to religion, there seems to be an underlying theme in *The Dead Zone* which parallels Johnny Smith's life to Christ's life in the Bible. Like his father being a carpenter, and the very ending of the book.

KING: And don't forget that he's described as being the only child of a sub-standard womb, though that doesn't really describe Mary, the mother of God, because she had other children. I guess I see the entire latter half of the book as being sort of a Gethsemane for Johnny Smith, but that sounds so fucking pretentious that let's just say certain parallels are there and leave it at that!

Q: What can you tell me about the genesis of *Firestarter*?

KING: It came mostly from occasionally reading articles about pyrokinesis, or maybe I should say auto-pyrokinesis, people who just burn up under mysterious circumstances. The fires are supposedly very, very hot, but they don't spread; they're concentrated in one very small area and there's nothing left but ashes afterwards. I got to playing with the idea of what would happen if somebody had that ability and could control it. I had a lot of fun writing the book!

Q: Its premise is similar to *Carrie's*, but I felt it had even more in common with John Farris's 1976 novel *The Fury,* particularly with regard to the idea of a government agency attempting to develop and control psychic power as a weapon.

KING: One of the things that happened with *Firestarter* is that when the book went for movie rights, my agent asked me how much I wanted. I said, "Let's go for a bundle. Let's ask for a million. We'll keep it out there for awhile, and if nobody buys it we can drop the price." We actually did sell the rights for one million before the book was even published, to an Egyptian producer named Dotie Fyet. His production company just finished a picture called *Chariots of Fire,* which is about the 1936 Olympics. But before that, it looked as though 20th Century-Fox wanted it for Zanuck and Brown, the people who made *Jaws* and all that. When I heard at one point that they were in a screening room watching *The Fury,* I knew we could kiss that one off!

When I wrote the first half of *Firestarter,* I don't think *The Fury* had even been published; it was that far back. I never noticed the similarity until somebody pointed it out to me. Whether there was a subconscious plagiarism going on I don't know, but it seems to me that there are more differences than there are similarities. *Firestarter* deals with a father and a very young girl. It's ironic—after Brian DePalma's film of *The Fury* came out, I had people asking me if John Farris had read *Carrie* when he wrote *The Fury*! I don't know if he had or not, but he's an awfully nice guy and those things happen. This field is so goddamned narrow that you're always on somebody's feet. I remember people coming to me and asking "Does it strike you that the framework Peter Straub used in *Ghost Story* is a lot like '*Salem's Lot*?" My answer would be "Sure it does. And it strikes me that the framework of '*Salem's Lot* is a lot like the framework of *Our Town*!"

Q: I recently interviewed David Morrell, and he mentioned feeling very paranoid about that from time to time. You know, he would see something he had just written creep up in another book.

KING: I had a bad moment when I was working on *The Stand.* I'd been involved with the book for about two years. I felt like my blood was really flowing out of my stomach, and if I didn't finish the book and staunch the flow I'd just die. Then I look in a bookstore and there's this book out called *Survivors* by Terry Nation, the guy who writes *Dr. Who.* It was about a virus decimating the world and the survivors that were left, and I thought, "Great, this guy has just written my book."

Usually, writers are working without any conscious knowledge of that. I'm sure we all plagiarize each other subconsciously, but there are still enough differences to make it interesting.

Q: I'm reminded in *Firestarter* of the stories that have surfaced in the post-Vietnam era about the Army experimenting with the effects of drugs on American soldiers, and the whole controversy over Agent Orange.

KING: Yeah, there was this thing that came out about the Army administering LSD to people on the pretense of saying "Here, have a gin and tonic." The next thing, these poor guys are tripping their brains out! The big scandal was that one guy jumped out of a hotel window and killed himself.

There's also the story that figured in my mind of the Army lining up a bunch of guys about a hundred and fifty yards from the first nuclear blast they did at White Sands. They wanted to see what the radiation effects would be like, so they just lined these guys up and gave them sunglasses, which I thought was very big of them.

Q: Besides *Firestarter*, you've recently published a novella entitled "The Mist" in Kirby McCauley's *Dark Forces* anthology. That story has tremendous potential for a movie.

KING: Yeah, "The Mist" is a good story. You're supposed to visualize that entire story in a sort of grainy black and white. It's sort of an homage to Roger Corman and Bert I. Gordon, the heroes of my misspent youth! The film rights were optioned by Kirby McCauley, who is my agent. He's shopping it around, and there is some moderate interest, but no more than that. I think the major reason is that the market is sort of overloaded right now with Stephen King product.

Q: How are you able to put out so much material every year?

KING: Well, I don't even write a lot. I just sort of write every day and keep it rolling along. I think a lot of writers have a tendency to stand back awhile and sort of sniff around a project if it's not going well. That never works for me; I find that once I get out of the driver's seat, I don't want to get back in. The story gets old for me very quickly, and I begin to lose whatever feelings I had for the characters. So when I run into tough sledding, my impulse is to just push straight ahead. If it's bad, I can always rip it out later. That's what I've done, so the material piles up day by day.

Q: What amazes me is your ability to work on so many things at the same time, like a novel, a couple of short stories, a non-fiction book, two screenplays. . . .

KING: Well, sometimes I feel a bit scatterbrained about the whole thing, but I do try to keep it rolling along one project at a time as much as I can. Whenever I'm between larger projects, that's when I do short stories now. And they get harder and harder to do. Of course, every now and then a really good idea will come up, and I can't say no; I have to just put aside whatever I'm doing to write it.

Q: What is your official opinion of Stanley Kubrick's film of *The Shining*?

KING: It cancels out to zero. There are things about it that I like an awful lot, and there are things about it that I don't care for at all. I think the problems are mostly with the scripting, not with the acting, *per se*, or the directing. There are weaknesses in the script, places where Kubrick and Diane Johnson apparently didn't think, or maybe where they thought too much. I think Kubrick quite consciously set out to transcend the genre. It comes off looking like a technicolor *Twilight Zone* more than anything else. You almost expect to see Rod Serling out by the hedge maze: "Jack and Wendy Torrance. . . your next stop is. . . The *Twilight Zone!*"

Another big problem, the more I think about it, is that Jack Nicholson shouldn't have been cast as Jack Torrance. He's too dark right from the outset of the film. The horror in the novel comes from the fact that Jack Torrance is a nice guy, not someone who's just flown out from the cuckoo's nest. People have said to me that Nicholson is crazy from the beginning of the film; there's never any progression. That is not right. The man is sane at the beginning. People impute that craziness to Nicholson because of the other parts that he's played. When he smiles you think he's crazy just because that's the kind of smile he's got. What's ironic is that Kubrick did *Barry Lyndon*, and I think Ryan O'Neal was terribly miscast in that picture. I think that if Jack Nicholson had been cast as *Barry Lyndon* and Ryan O'Neal had been cast in *The Shining* they both would have been better pictures.

Q: But Nicholson is wonderful when Jack Torrance finally goes completely off the wall; it's hard to imagine anyone else playing the role. Perhaps if there had been a more clear-cut transition from loving father to total madman. . . .

KING: Well, I'm concentrating on the negative here, but I got the impression more and more every time I saw the picture that Kubrick really did not know how to show a warm relationship between this father and his son. There's the scene in the bedroom where Jack takes Danny on his lap and tries to reassure the kid—"I'd never hurt you; I'd never hurt your mother." It's very cold and stilted, and you have the feeling that it's there because Kubrick knew that something had to be there at this point purely from a story perspective.

On the other hand, the photography is beautiful, the execution of the film is wonderful, the hedge maze works as a metaphor for the family, and the tracking shots are nice. My feeling is that anyone who paid five bucks to see it got their money's worth, which is maybe the bottom line, ultimately. I mean, compared to something like *Terror Train*! Honest effort should always be applauded.

Q: Ultimately, though, fans of the book have objected to the film because it just isn't scary. Tensions and expectations are built up nicely, but you're eased through the film without any real payoffs.

KING: In a way, this is what I mean about Kubrick trying to transcend the genre. He knew where all those scares should go, where all the payoffs should come, and he simply said "This is too easy; I'm not going to do it that way." So he didn't, and what he wound up with was very little, I think. The genre has never been transcended, so far as I know, unless maybe by William Golding in *Lord of the Flies*, or something on that order.

Q: At one point you had written your own screenplay for *The Shining*. Did that follow the book more closely?

KING: No, only about as much as the screenplay by Kubrick and Johnson. It was pegged a lot more to the history of the hotel, because I was really interested in the idea that an evil place calls evil men, which is a line from *'Salem's Lot*. The place isn't evil because these people come, but these people come because the place is evil. The screenplay that I wrote began with voices talking over a totally black screen. It turns out that they're mafia hit men. There are shotgun flashes and screams, and then this voice says "and get his balls." There's another scream, and then you see the hotel. Nominally, the story follows from there, except I didn't bother with the home life in Boulder or any of the job interview; I simply had the Torrances going up to the hotel.

Q: The most recent film based on one of your books is *Cujo*. It strikes me that while this isn't the best film adaptation of a Stephen King novel, it comes the closest to capturing the overall mood and spirit of the original.

KING: Yeah, in terms of being true to the book, this is probably the first Stephen King novel *per se* that's been put on film. I actually worked on the screenplay before the two writers credited on the film were brought in, but I ended up not getting any credit for it. That was a Writers Guild decision. Taft, the distributor, submitted it with my name only, and I believe Barbara Turner (who used a pen name, Lauren Currier, in the film) objected to the fact that Don Carlos Dunaway wasn't given top billing for the screenplay. The Writers Guild has a process that's very fair and totally objective for adjudicating credits. I was in England at the time, and I just didn't have time to mess with it, so I didn't.

Q: How much did the other writers change from your screenplay?

KING: There are some passages that are totally different from mine, but they're minor. The finished screenplay runs close to the book; mine ran a little closer. I think there was more stuff about the Sharp Cereal Professor in my screenplay than there was in the movie. On the whole, I think they probably did well to deep-six that.

Q: The one really big change made from the book is the ending. Allowing Tad to live significantly alters the whole point of a story that's essentially about fate and tragedy, the idea that life's "monsters" often do get us. Was this change in your script?

KING: Yeah, my script had the kid live also. This goes back to when Taft first bought the film rights. I had seen their film *The Boogens*, and I thought they were really clever. They were doing low budget stuff that was pretty classy. Anyway, we all sat down together in a suite at the U.N. Plaza to talk about *Cujo*, and they said they wanted the kid to live. That didn't really surprise me. The book had gotten the same reaction when it was still in manuscript. Alan Williams, my editor on the book, asked "What would you think of the kid living?" I said "That's non-negotiable; the kid died." But my view of films is that they're not life; they're something else. Films exist on a much more emotional level. It's all happening on a screen right up there in front of you; it's very ephemeral. So when they brought this up, I said "Fine, let's let the kid live and see how that works." I was never really against the idea. In a way, I feel like there are two Stephen Kings. I feel different ways on different days. It's like something Donald Westlake used to say—on sunny days, he wrote about Dortmunder, the comical thief from *The Hot Rock*, and on dark days he wrote about Parker, this thief who kills people. So what I'm saying here is that *'Salem's Lot* is a much sunnier novel than *Cujo* is. *The Shining* is a sunnier novel in a lot of ways. There's hope. I haven't given up on hope; most of my stories do have happy endings. With *Cujo*, you're looking at a very dark story. As it turns out in the film, even the characters are a lot more appetizing than they are in the book. Again, that comes from seeing them up there in front of you, and seeing a lot less of them than you see in the book.

Q: The film did quite well in its opening weekend; didn't it make something like $6 million in three days?

KING: Yeah, it did. Overall I think it's going to do about $20 million, which is about the break-even point according to the formula I've been given. I think that if the same level of quality in the acting, the direction and the writing were brought to any of my other books, you'd be looking at about $60 million. You know, the traditional movie rule of thumb is that it's the man who says "Let's go to the movies," but it's the woman who picks the movie. I think that a lot of women out there said "I don't want to go see this woman stuck in a car with her son having convulsions," and I understand that. I had a pretty good idea of what the playoff was going to be when I screened the picture with some friends in New York City. There's a group of people I've regularly invited to screenings in the past. This time, none of the women showed up. It's like the opposite with *The Dead Zone*—we screened it the other day, and when the lights came up, most of the women were crying. I know that picture's going to make money! From a commercial sense, I thought Taft was crazy to want *Cujo* from the beginning. I think they were sort of hypnotized by the name, by the idea of saying "We have a Stephen King novel," which has become a little bit like saying "We've got Paul Newman!"

Q: You've been in a fairly unique position for a couple of years now as far as that goes. Almost all of your novels have either been filmed or optioned for filming, and they've attracted some of the horror genre's most highly-regarded directors. What's your reaction to all of this?

KING: I'm a little bit amazed by the whole thing, and I don't really understand it. Writers are not stars; they're not supposed to be stars. It's a thing that will play itself out in time. It'll pass.

Q: Do you think it's coming to a saturation point?

KING: I don't know. Probably.

Q: Do you have any involvement with *Firestarter*?

KING: I saw Stanley Mann's screenplay, and I passed some critical comments along on it that I think were pretty well taken, because they were mostly favorable! I had seen the screenplay John Carpenter had done when he was involved with the project, and it was really quite weak compared to this one. It remains true to the book in most places, but not entirely. The guy has done some things that are almost brilliant in terms of the genre. There's a scene in the screenplay where the parents are trying to fire-train the little girl, and they've got her cooking toast! Her father is holding up a piece of bread with tongs, and it's going brown as the little girl looks at it! It's a knockout! You just read it and laugh! Then, if you're me, you say, "Goddamn, I wish I'd thought of that!"

Q: Tell me about *Christine*. The story is set in Pittsburgh; did the idea develop while you were there during the filming of *Creepshow*?

KING: No; the book was first drafted back in '77 or '78. In fact, the time sequence in the book is pretty accurate to the time in which the first draft was written. I'd had an idea for a long time to write a story about a kid who got an old car with an odometer that ran backwards. The kid would be delighted to find that as the odometer ran backwards, the car got newer and newer as it progressed back through time. It was supposed to be funny; the kicker was that when the odometer got all the way back to zeroes across, the car would just fall apart! It started out as a short story, the way *Carrie* did. In fact, if you ignore the prologue, which was added later and gives the sense that this is a novel, and you go back and read just the first chapter, you can see that it was supposed to be a short story. The whole business about the discovery of the car is really accelerated. As I worked on it I became more and more interested in the interaction between Arnie Cunningham and Dennis, and the difference in their lifestyles. I got entranced with Dennis's *Happy Days* sort of lifestyle. In fact, Arnie's name was originally Randy something, and I changed it to Arnie Cunningham because it was a *Happy Days* name!

Q: Yeah, I thought about Richie Cunningham a lot when I read it.

KING: Yes, and the name of the place the characters in *Happy Days* go to hang out is "Arnold's"!

Q: Along the same lines, Douglas Winter pointed out in his book on your work that *Christine* is the dark side of *American Graffiti*, the movie *Happy Days* grew out of.

KING: Yes. One of the things that *American Graffiti* never dealt with was parents. It was like the *Peanuts* comic strip, where adults are never seen. You can talk about peer groups and everything, but sixty percent of a teenager's life is still the struggle to get free from his or her parents! That was the catalyst for the rewrite—the idea of the car as a symbol of escape from imprisonment. A guy from *Locus* magazine who reviewed the book mentioned Henry Gregor Felson, and it really gave me a jolt. It was like finding out a corpse is walking! I was really influenced as a kid by Felson's books—*Hot Rod, Street Rod, Crash Club*, all those things where he dealt with the violence that's implicit in the automobile. That was a part of it too. And I wanted to go back to high school. I wanted to do that teenybop thing one more time and see if I couldn't get it right!

Q: You use a lot of quotes from rock song lyrics in your novels, and in the case of *Christine* the book even seems scored like *American Graffiti*. The music is a constant presence.

KING: It wasn't that way in the first draft, and it came to me that it should be that way, because so many rock n roll songs deal with kids and cars.

Q: John Carpenter's film of *Christine* will be out less than a year from the novel's publication in hardcover. What are the effects of this from a publishing standpoint?

KING: That's a complex question. Nobody really thought it would be made so fast. Nobody believed Polar Film when they said they were going to make it that fast, and nobody believed Paramount when they said they wanted it for Christmas. I felt that a delay of even one week in the shooting schedule would throw the whole thing off, and it never happened. As for what it means in business terms for the hardcover publisher, the book was published in April of this year. It's still something like number 6 on the *Times* best-seller list. By having the movie out in December, Viking will effectively lose four months of the twelve-month run that they usually have on the hardcover edition. Granted, they're the four downside months, but you also have to keep in mind that Christmas is a very busy season for books. I think they're less concerned than they would be under other circumstances, because I have another book coming out in November, *Pet Sematary*, and they all realize that that would take some of the attention off *Christine* anyway.

It made a lot more problems for New American Library, who'll be publishing the paperback. They've got a *Coma* fixation at New American Library. They talk about *Coma* the way World War II hardliners talk about the Battle of the Bulge! *Coma* was perfect as far as book-to-movie goes, because they brought out the paperback a year after the hardcover, and they had a run of about six to seven weeks that was just fantastic. Just when it started to lag a little bit, *bang*, the movie came out, and it shot right back up. So I hear this a lot.

Right now they're chasing their own tails at New American Library. They've re-released *Cujo* to tie in with the movie, they're going to have a *Dead Zone* movie tie-in, and on top of everything else, they've bumped the publication of *Christine* to late November-early December. They're going to run about three weeks with a regular paperback edition, and then they're going to bump that for a movie tie-in. They're worried that all the expenses and all the backing and forthing will cost them money, and they've got a legitimate bitch.

On top of everything else, I think that they're unhappy that we had a disagreement over the cover price. I held them to a lower cover price because, quite frankly, they only paid a dollar for the book! It seemed awful to me for them to say, "Well, we're going to have to price this book at $4.50, because we're in this terrible position." That terrible position is a best-selling novel that's going to be a movie at the same time. There are two really different perspectives here.

Q: Would you mind going into the story of why you sold the book for a dollar one more time?

KING: I'm just tired of people sort of saying "Hmm, best-selling novelist. You take the money and run. The book doesn't matter to you; the money matters." And this business of tying up dough in advances for best-selling writers is ridiculous. When you see that Sidney Sheldon, Judith Krantz or somebody like that has just taken four million dollars as an advance for a book, and then the *New York Times* publishes a story about how that could have been sixty advances for first novels, well, they've got a talking point there. Book audiences are very loyal; you can be quite certain that they'll come back and re-purchase if they were happy with what they got before. So in terms of royalties, that money will come home to the writer within a year or two anyway.

Q: I heard the film rights also went for a dollar; is that true?

KING: No, we sold the film rights for a lot of money! I think it was something like four hundred thousand! With movies, it's a different ball of wax. I'm perfectly willing to be a great guy and everything else, but movie people are sleazy. You give them an inch and they take a mile. If you sell a book for something like $15,000 you don't know whether the movie will actually be made. A lot of these people will just boff around at cocktail partes, have a drink or snort up some cocaine off a mirror, and say "Well, I've got an option on the new Stephen King. . . ." You know, a lot of them are real sleazebags, and they just don't care! But if you tie them down to a lot of money, you've got more assurance that the movie will be made, because somebody wants to get their money back.

Also, it's better to get as much as you can up front, because with movie guys the accounting is so creative that you never know who's down in Mexico running away with your money! Quite frankly, I have never seen that much money in terms of residuals. We've seen a fair amount on *Carrie*, and when I say "fair," that's what I mean—it was a fair payout. Brian DePalma, Lawrence D. Cohen and I all got together and audited the company, and I don't know if that has anything to do with it or if it was just because it was United Artists and they have a tendency to be a little bit straighter.

Q: I understand you've expressed the opinion that the script Bill Phillips wrote for *Christine* is, on paper at least, the best adaptation of one of your books so far.

KING: No, the best on paper is Stanley Mann's screenplay for *Firestarter*, by far. But the screenplay for *Christine* is very, very good. It's very tight. It's not real true to the book, but that doesn't matter—what matters is whether or not it can be filmed. I think it could be a really fine picture. I haven't seen any footage. I've seen some ad copy and promotional material that I'm not really pleased with. I've seen a trailer. Have you seen the trailer for it?

Q: No, I haven't.

KING: That just confirms my feeling that you are a critical human being, because it played with a picture called *Yor, The Hunter from the Future*!

Q: Umm, yeah, I stayed far away from *Yor.* . . .

KING: I really wanted to see that picture, because it looked so dreadful! You must have seen the poster for *Yor*—here's this guy with a Hollywood Rodeo Drive blowdry standing on top of a blimp fighting flying saucers, and I thought, "Jesus Christ, Herschell Gordon Lewis, where are you?" I love that stuff!

Q: On a final note, it's been rumored that Forrest J. Ackerman has a story you sent to him when you were about ten years old.

KING: Yeah, I've talked to him about that. I used to subscribe to *Spacemen, Famous Monsters,* and all those other magazines. Those bastards still owe me two issues of something, because *Spacemen* folded! Actually, Forry did give me some Transylvanian earth, so I have no right to bitch at him at all. . . .

Anyway, he shocked the shit out of me, because he came into the Change of Hobbit bookstore in Los Angeles when I was signing books there, and he showed me this letter I had written in 1961, or something like that. I knew it was from me, because it was written on this old typewriter I had that was missing the "n" plate. I would write letters or stories and I'd have to fill in all the "n"s by hand! The letter mentioned the story I had written, and Forry said he had lost the story, otherwise he would run it. That made me glad he lost it! I don't know what it could have been.

The first story I ever had published appeared in a fanzine published by Marv Wolfman, who now writes for the comics. It was called "In A Half World of Terror," and I have a copy of it somewhere. That goes back to my Sophomore year of high school, which would have been 1964.

With Darrell Ewing and Dennis Myers

Q: What do you feel are some of the scariest moments in your film adaptations?

KING: You mean that scared me in the theater? When that hand comes out of the grave in *Carrie* at the end. Man, I thought I was going to shit in my pants.

Q: You had no idea. . . ?

KING: I knew they were going to do it, and I still almost shit in my pants. The first time I saw *Carrie* with an audience they previewed it about a week and a half before Halloween. They didn't do a screening in Maine, but they did one in Boston, so my wife and I went down to the theater, and I just looked around in total dismay, because the regular picture that they were showing was *Norman, Is That You?* with Redd Foxx. The theater was entirely full of black people. We looked like two little grains of salt in a pepper shaker, and we thought: This audience is just going to rate the hell out of this picture. What are they going to think about a skinny little white girl with her menstrual problems? And that's the way it started, and then, little by little, they got on her side, you know, and when she started doing her shtick, I mean, they're going, "Tear it up!" "Go for it!" and all this other stuff. These two guys were talking behind us, and we were listening to them, and at the end they're putting on their coats and getting ready to leave. Suddenly this hand comes up, and these two big guys scream along with everyone else, and one of them goes, "That's it! That's it! She ain't never gonna be right!" And I knew it was going to be a hit.

Q: What do you think of the movies adapted from your books?

KING: *Firestarter* is one of the worst of the bunch, even though in terms of story it's very close to the original. But it's flavorless; it's like cafeteria mashed potatoes. There are things that happen in terms of special effects in that movie that make no sense to me whatsoever. Why this kid's hair blows every time she starts fires is totally beyond my understanding. I never got a satisfactory answer when I saw the rough cut.

The movie has great actors, with the exception of the lead, David Keith, who I didn't feel was very good—my wife said that he has stupid eyes. The actors were allowed to do pretty much what they wanted to do. Martin Sheen, who is a great actor, with no direction and nobody to tell him—and I mean there must have been literally no direction—with nobody to pull him in and say, "Stop what you're doing," he simply reprised Greg Stillson from *The Dead Zone*. That's all there is; it's the same character exactly. But Greg Stillson should not be in charge of The Shop. He's not the kind of guy who gets that job.

Q: You were disappointed in *The Shining*—if you were directing it now, what would you do with it?

KING: Oh, I would do everything different.

I wanted to like that movie. I was so flattered that Kubrick was going to do something of mine. The first time he called, it was 7:30 in the morning. I was standing in the bathroom in my underwear, shaving, and my wife comes in and her eyes are bugging out. I thought one of the kids must be choking in the kitchen or something. She says, "Stanley Kubrick is on the phone!" I mean, I was just floored. I didn't even take the shaving cream off my face.

Q: It sounds as though he was trying to rewrite the horror genre.

KING: I'm sure that he wanted to bust it open, to do something new with it, but it is very unbustable, which is one of the reasons it has endured as long as it has.

Q: What was it you liked about David Cronenberg's direction of *The Dead Zone?*

KING: If there were no element of horror in my books, they'd be the dullest books ever written. Everything in those stories is totally ordinary —Dairy Queens—except you take one element and you take that out of context. Cronenberg did the ordinary, and nobody else who has used my books really has. I thought that Lewis Teague, who directed *Cujo*, did to a degree, except that Teague always seems to me to get his kind of soap-opera look in his people and his sets.

One of the guys who worked on *Dead Zone*, someone I respect very much, told me that Dino was the first producer David Cronenberg ever had who forced him to direct. Who forced him to approach the job, not as this gorgeous toy that was made for David Cronenberg, but as a job where he had a responsibility to the producer and to the audience. And that's another reason why *Dead Zone* was a good picture.

Q: Where did you get the idea for it?

KING: The story was supposed to be about this guy who eventually would shake hands with the man who is going to blow up the world. I got interested in the idea of whether it would be possible to write a moral novel where an assassin, an American assassin, actually was a good guy, or where the act would be justified. When you write a novel—well, at least for me, because I never think about theme as a starting point—I just think about story. But sometimes, about three-quarters of the way through the first draft, you'll discover that there is a theme, or the potential for a theme. Or you discover what it is that you were actually talking about all along.

In *Dead Zone*, I thought what I was talking about was the way that we sometimes think gifts or special talents are actually the things that cause people to be totally rejected by society. Books like *Carrie* and *Firestarter* are instinctive rebellings against that. I think that *Dead Zone* is the only time that I was able to go back and actually approach the whole rewrite of the book with one unifying idea in mind, which made it into a novel. I mean, it's actually sort of thoughtful.

Pet Sematary to some degree is the same: It's supposed to be a reflection on what happens when people in a materialistic society, people who live only for materialistic reasons, come into contact with questions of faith and death and outside forces.

Q: What do you think of America at present? Is it ordinary?

KING: I think the same thing about it that I always have thought: I think it's fantastic. We're killing ourselves; we're fiddling while Rome burns. I mean, while we've got enough explosives to turn planet Earth into the second asteroid belt, the largest weekly magazine in the country is talking about where celebrities shop, and why people in Hollywood don't want to serve finger foods any more. It all seems really ridiculous to me, but I love it. I love everything about it.

With Jessie Horsting

KING: First of all, let's get one thing up front—I like most of the adaptations pretty well. The only two real exceptions to that are *The Shining* and *Children of the Corn*. The other stuff I can deal with. I don't like it all equally, but I can deal with it.

Q: Why are *The Shining* and *Children of the Corn* such exceptions?

KING: The major thing has to do with why *audiences* turn away from them, or why they have turned away from movies, since *The Shining*, which is the one that really turned off the Stephen King book fans, is because they don't find me in the movie. Whatever writers have isn't so much style as it is soul or something that's between the mind and the prose that they write. It's that interior tension, the stuff that you *don't* say rather than the way that you say the things that you *do* say. A perfect example is you take the novel *Stick* by Elmore Leonard and then you look at the movie *Stick* and even though Elmore Leonard did the screenplay, he's not present—well, he got a co-credit for the screenplay. He's not present in that. And when you look at *Christine* and some of these other things, I'm just not there for those people and so they don't like it.

Q: Isn't that a problem with film all the time, though, is that you have to sacrifice? You don't have the luxury of narrative.

KING: No, I don't think so. I think that Ken Kesey is very much there in *One Flew Over the Cuckoo's Nest*. And I think that James Dickey is there almost completely in *Deliverance*. And I think that the spirit of that book and that movie are exactly the same. The soul has made that transference. It can happen. The same thing is true for *Rosemary's Baby*. I think it's a very faithful adaptation of the book and it keeps the spirit of Levin's novel. For instance, you take *Firestarter*, which is very faithful to the novel and yet I'm not there. I'm just not in that movie.

Q: What is missing? Is there one particular thing or is just your voice or the characterization that you're able to put in the novels?

KING: It's the spirit. It's between the lines of the book. It's whatever it is. It's whatever flavor that readers come to expect and they come to want. It's the sort of thing that they come to crave. It's the only reason they go back to buy more. They don't even exactly, after a while, go back because they say this Stephen King book looks particularly interesting. They go back because they say "it's a Stephen King book and I will get that flavor," the way somebody who likes coffee will say, "I want coffee. I want Maxwell House coffee, and I want whatever that is." And it's the same reason they *don't* go to see the movies. They say, "Ah, it's just another shitty adaptation of a Stephen King."

Q: Does that make you crazy?

KING: No. Why should it? It's just movies.

Q: Have you seen *The Body*?

KING: Yeah.

Q: I think it's wonderful.

KING: I do, too. I think it's a great movie.

Q: I think they really hit right on the nose with this one.

KING: It's fantastic. I loved it. I'm glad to hear that you said you like it.

Q: I was stunned because it's one of my favorite stories. I was a little, ah—what's the word?—hesitant.

KING: Of course. That's what we're talking about.

Q: I was enamored with the whole thing, start to finish. I thought it was so right. And my immediate question was, why didn't they do this eight years ago?

KING: I don't know. You know, you couldn't have got the backing for it. What you can spend is about four million dollars because what they're looking for is a exploitation hit that's going to last two weeks. Nobody's looking to make anything quality out of my stuff. They haven't since *The Shining*.

Q: Can we talk about *Cujo* for a minute?

KING: Yeah.

Q: The director, Lewis Teague, really maintained your interest for two hours about a woman being terrorized by a dog.

KING: That's my favorite adaptation of all of the movies, really, because it does keep some of the spirit and flavor of the work. It has no finesse. It has no pretension. I thought Dee Wallace should have been nominated for an Academy Award.

Q: And that kid, Danny Pintauro, was amazing.

KING: Yeah.

Q: Do you think it should have been a movie?

KING: Uh, yeah. I don't know about *Pet Sematary*, but I thought *Cujo* worked fine and, you know, I suggested selling it to Taft International, although they couldn't pay as much as some of the other people wanted, because I'd seen a low budget picture called *The Boogens* and I thought it was really good. And I suggested Lewis Teague as the director because I'd seen *Alligator* and I thought *Alligator* was great. It's very funny and everything like that, but it showed that he could work with animals 'cause he did work with real alligators there. And so they said, "No, we're gonna use the guy who did *Woodstock*." I think his name is Michael Wadleigh. I'm not sure. And whoever he was he lasted one day and he just walked off and said "I can't do this. I can't deal with this." You know, like a breakdown. So they brought in Teague on the spur of the moment and Teague directed the picture. And then I worked with him on *Cat's Eye*. And *Cat's Eye* was another movie that I like a lot. I think it's a good movie. I think it's witty and stylish. And you talk to people about it and they say, "Was that any good? I never saw it." Well, nobody in America saw it. It went into the toilet.

Q: I saw it and in fact—you don't mind skipping around like this, do you?

KING: No.

Q: I had gotten a copy of the script that had a pretty extensive section in the very beginning of it where—

KING: Oh, it was all shot. It was cut at the behest of Frank Yablans even though we screened it with that in there. There was one audience in America that saw it with the woman with the machine gun and everything. And verbally they responded to it very clearly in the theater and most of them responded to it on the critic cards pretty favorably. There was a percentage and there's always a percentage that said they really didn't like this because they felt it was cruelty to animals or something like that. But the real thing was that the difference between the comment cards without that section in at the beginning and with it, was that the people who saw the prologue said they understood the movie. And there was a huge response without it from people who said, "I don't know what the fuck's going on."

Q: You lost most of the back story there.

KING: It's very funny. Patty Lupone is very funny as that woman chasing the cat around with a machine gun.

Q: That's one of the two original screenplays of yours that have been made, right? Or is it three?

KING: Three. *Silver Bullet* and *Cat's Eye* and *Creepshow*.

Q: Of those, which do you feel is the most successful?

KING: Well, let's see. In terms of money *Creepshow* is the most successful. And *Silver Bullet* made a little bit of money, I think. You know studios think of it as a loss if it doesn't make at least 20 million dollars. I think that *Silver Bullet* earned back about 800,000 dollars first run.

Q: I mean more—

KING: In terms of execution and all that stuff.

Q: Yes.

KING: I would say probably *Cat's Eye*.

Q: *Cat's Eye*. All right. *Creepshow* is one of my personal favorites. I just loved it.

KING: I would have picked that a close second.

Q: Yeah, now Romero has *Pet Sematary* and *The Stand*?

KING: Yeah.

Q: And, which of those are going to get done first?

KING: I really don't know. I think that Laurel has come to an agreement in principle with Orion Pictures on *Pet Sematary* so conceivably that could film this year. But that's still all murky and I've done I think four drafts on *The Stand* and George has also worked on *The Stand* screenplay and we now have a very saleable screenplay and it would be fairly cheap to do.

Q: At what length?

KING: I think the screenplay, it would run about the length of, let's say, *Out of Africa*. It would be about two hours and 45 minutes. And basically when you look at the screenplay it looks like a real long road picture, like *Wild Angels* or something like that, one of the old motorcycle pictures. A lot of people on bikes.

Q: A lot of people on bikes.

KING: Yeah.

Q: Have any of these films ever exceeded your expectations? Any of them?

KING: *Carrie* did.

Q: *Carrie?* That must have been a big thrill being the first one.

KING: It was, but it was also a real stylish thing. In all of the pictures— well, no, that isn't quite true. In most of the pictures you see things and you say, "Shit, I should have done that." You know, *Dead Zone* with the thing with the guy and the scissors and all that stuff and having put Johnny Smith *into* his own visions. I thought that was a wonderful thing. I would say that *Carrie* exceeded my expectations and probably *'Salem's Lot* exceeded my expectations for what they could get away with on TV.

Q: Those were early. Now that you have twelve movies under the belt and years have gone by, do your expectations grow? Do you have a wish list of directors?

KING: Pardon me?

Q: Do you have wish list for directors? Somebody you'd really like to—

KING: Well, I directed my own this time. I went in and did *Maximum Overdrive*. Yeah, mostly to find out if it would work because so many people have said, "I just don't go anymore. It's not you and that's it." And I thought just once let's go in and find out, if you can, if it does carry over. I think it does.

Q: Now that you've directed one, does it make you more forgiving about any of the other ones?

KING: I'm not forgiving or unforgiving. I go to see 'em like a fan. They don't do a thing to the book. I mean a movie is a very ephemeral item. It comes to a theater near you and it's there for like two weeks unless it's a mega-hit, like *E.T.*, and then it might be at that theater near you for ten weeks or twelve weeks.

Q: Yeah, the hit and run phenomena.

KING: So, say a picture like *E.T.* plays for three months and you say, "Holy shit! That picture's been there forever." But, I mean, I just had a book that fell off the best-seller list, *Skeleton Crew*, and it was on the list for 32 weeks.

Q: Does that astonish you?

KING: No, what I mean is, I'm saying books live damn near forever, while movies will have a first run, maybe if it's successful they have a second run, they turn up on cable TV, they turn up on network TV, and they'll be on the shelves at the video store. And you say, "Well, shit, they're at the video store now. You rent 'em and they're there forever. It's like a library." But that isn't true. After a while they just simply disappear.

Q: They lose their popularity.

KING: There's a question of shelf space there, too. After a while somebody's going to take *Eaten Alive* off the shelves because nobody watches it, so the movie is gone, it's gone.

Q: It's gone and sometimes thank God, right?

KING: Yeah.

Q: You've done screenplays for almost every adaptation but you've had a number of them turned down?

KING: Jeez, I've done a bunch. Let's see what I didn't do. I never did an adaptation for *Carrie*, I never did one for *'Salem's Lot*. I did one for *The Shining*, I've done it for *The Stand*. I did it for *The Dead Zone*. I never did one for *Firestarter*.

Q: *Christine* did you do?

KING: No, I didn't. *Cujo* I did. You sound like you got a cold.

Q: Yeah, I do. I think it's Captain Trips. I really do. It's all over the place here. Producers are dying like flies.

KING: Take some Tylenol.

Q: Okay. That'll either cure it or kill it. I was in Chicago when they had that big Tylenol scare.

KING: It happened again today.

Q: Yeah, I heard that some lady got another cyanide-laced—do you think that's a serial killer or do you think something's going wrong in the plant?

KING: This is a case of murder. That woman had like seven or eight cyanide-laced Tylenol tablets in her bottle. No, I think somebody set out to kill her—

Q: —to kill her, just did a copycat murder.

KING: Yeah.

Q: There's an idea, right? Put me out of my misery. I've had this thing for two weeks now. I'm ready to die. Gosh. Stop this. Stop being funny.

KING: My wife thinks she's a good cook. She made a leg of lamb, I couldn't get past the wool. Okay.

Q: Yes, I just flew in from Chicago, take my wife please. Umm, do you hear the new one about where you get your ideas? Now they just say *why* do you get your ideas?

KING: Oh, great.

Q: Are you possessive anymore about your stories?

KING: Possessive? No, not in that sense that—my view has always been that movies are not books and book are not movies. And I don't understand writers who get all wound up in the film adaptations of their novels, as though somehow the novel could be tainted, the novel itself could be tainted by a bad adaptation. I've taken several chances and I've gone in a couple of cases with low budget people, but for the major books, the only thing I've ever insisted on was that somebody pay me a lot of money up front. There's two reasons for that. The first thing is that you start off with the idea in mind that in any collaborative venture, the chances that somebody is really going to fuck up are very high. Look at the space shuttle. Nobody knew it was going to blow up. Most movie adaptations of work are shit and you know that going in and you figure that if you're going to get plastered with shit, somebody oughta pay you to do it and pay you a lot of money. The other possibility is that if somebody pays you $500,000, $700,000, a million dollars, which is what this guy Dotie Fyet paid for *Firestarter*. If they pay that much money, somebody's going to make a reasonable effort to make a good movie so that they can get their money back.

Q: Well, no one sets out to make a bad one, right?

KING: Ah, nobody ever sets out to make a bad movie, but sometimes they're just set out to make money and that's just as bad. That's a recipe for disaster.

Q: Yeah, always the wrong reason. So what's the motivation to keep selling stories?

KING: There's really very little motivation to keep selling stories now. The motivation now is to see who wants to do it and to do it on that basis. But there's also no reason in the world just to hold back. I mean, that would be irrational, particularly because I like most of the adaptations that have been done. There are some that leave me cold, like *Christine*, and there are some that I actively dislike, like *Firestarter* and *Children of the Corn* and *The Shining*. And it doesn't taint the book. That's the major thing. Why not? It doesn't hurt the book. Somebody makes a terrible movie—*Firestarter* with a couple of changes could have been really awful, the *Mommie Dearest* of horror pictures. You know, you've got Martin Sheen saying, "What if this ability to light fires is just the tip of the iceberg."

Q: Very funny.

KING: They're close there in a couple of places.

Q: We were talking a little bit about what your brand of horror is—

KING: Brand X.

Q: Brand X.

KING: The low priced spread.

Q: And you're less a horror writer than I think—well, psychological horror is how I'd describe it rather than a lot of gore like *Reanimator* or *Dawn of the Dead*. Did you see that by the way?

KING: Which one?

Q: *Reanimator.*

KING: Oh yeah.

Q: Is that great?

KING: I loved it. Absolutely loved it. It's the only time in the history of films that a head has ever given head. I couldn't believe it. I couldn't believe what I was seeing. I can't wait for it to come out on videotape.

Q: I know. It was like watching an accident. You don't want to watch anymore, but you can't tear your eyes away.

KING: Did you see *Return of the Living Dead?*

Q: Yes. Was that a stitch.

KING: I thought it was wonderful.

Q: "Send more paramedics."

KING: That's what I was going to say. "Send more paramedics."

Q: Yeah, that's my kind of movie—low.

KING: Yeah, real low.

Q: That was a riot.

KING: It's like the blurb on this paperback. I remember it from about 1954. It was a Beacon novel called *Liz.* It said, "She hit the gutter and then bounced lower."

Q: Oh, my God. That's wonderful. She hit the gutter and bounced. What I want to open the book with is a quote by George Romero I read that says, a reporter asked him about *Dawn of the Dead*, to describe the story, and he says, "Well, you got your good guys and you got your bad guys and you got your dead guys."

KING: Yeah, right.

Q: You seem to deal a lot about the nature of good and evil and that's even reflected, I suppose, in the films, though not as well, and your bad guys are always clearly defined, but sometimes the good guys are a lot more fuzzy around the edges.

KING: Uh-huh.

Q: Is that an important theme to you? Or are the themes of the books a little less ambitious?

KING: Well, I would always like to have the good guys come through stronger and if they do that they do it more by force of personality than by their actions. My own view of good and evil is that a lot of times good people and good intentions are handcuffed in the face of evil, and good responds to evil. So that it becomes—you know, you can present people like say Stu Redmond or Franny Goldsmith or Andy McGee in *Firestarter*, and say "Look, here are good people. They're good *per se* by their actions, even though they're not doing anything that's very important, even though they're not important people in themselves." But people have even remarked on Tolkien's *Rings* trilogy, the scenes of evil are depicted much more forcefully than the scenes of bucolic peace and quiet in the Shire and all that stuff. I don't personally agree with that. I think that he makes good very attractive in those books. And I've always tried to do that as well, but evil, let's face it, has a certain flash that good just doesn't have. Particularly for readers and viewers who are voyeurs by nature and who are generally attracted to things that they know they themselves will never be or couldn't do.

Q: But I suppose that the stories give them hope that, if their backs are against the wall, they'll do the right thing and maybe that's all that good is.

KING: Well, in most of the books, they either do the right thing or they try to do the right thing. I mean Vic Trenton goes home and does not slaughter his wife after he finds out she's been screwing the tennis pro or whoever it was. And in most of the books, things turn out okay. I do think that you pay a price for doing the right thing. You always pay a price for doing the right thing.

Q: So what price does evil pay?

KING: Well, I don't know.

Q: Mostly, they get off scot-free. Let's talk a little bit about *The Shining*.

KING: I seem to remember having described *The Shining* as a great big beautiful car with no engine inside it. It's a film that has all kinds of style. It's gorgeous. I could watch it any day. I think it's marvelous to look at, but Kubrick wanted to make a horror movie. And he made *The Shining* and what I felt was that he made the movie in a total vacuum, with no understanding of the basics of the genre. And I'll just give you one example. I think it's important because it goes to the heart of what we're talking about. And again it goes back to this thing where I said there are things in a lot of the movies that I wish I'd thought of myself. There's a thing in the movie that isn't in the book. In the book Jack Torrance is writing this really terrible play called *The Little School* and in the film he's working on something in the lobby and what we have after a while is this little allegory of Bluebeard's story where Bluebeard brings the last wife home and says you can go anywhere you want to except for this one place; the door's locked; you can't go in there. So that's the one place that she wants to go. By the same token, Wendy Torrance, even though she's been told not to look at it, wants to look at that book. So finally she's drawn to it like Bluebeard's wife is drawn toward the room with the locked door. She looks down through the key plate and then she sees the key and she goes in. While Jack isn't around, Wendy starts to look through the book and on every page is "All work and no play makes Jack a dull boy," written all these different ways and different styles and everything. Kubrick cuts from her face to the pages, from her face to the pages, from her face to the pages; you're getting more and more frightened by what's going on here. And you know what's going to happen. You don't want it to happen, but you know it's going to happen. What the horror movie is, is it's something like a girl jerking you off in a car. You know that sooner or later there's going to be an orgasm. The question is when is it going to come and how intense is it going to be. Okay. So back and forth, back and forth. We know Jack's going to find her. The hand's going to come down on her shoulder and he's going to say "Do you like it?" But we want that to happen, we don't want it to happen, but we do want it to happen. It's the same way that in a lot of senses you want to have the orgasm but at the same time you don't want the orgasm to happen because then it's over. You know what I mean?

Q: Yeah, but the one alternative that's not picked is for no one to come, right?

KING: That's exactly what happens here because Kubrick for some reason—God only knows what it is—elects to cut away and show us Jack Torrance approaching her.

Basically it goes back to pride, to a man who's so sure that he's unable to make a mistake that he's elected to do a picture in a genre that he doesn't understand. And he's made a mistake that fundamental but you can't explain it to somebody why it's wrong. They either know it's wrong or they don't.

Q: Yeah, but you just explained why it was wrong and I think you're right on the money.

KING: I explained why it was wrong except what I can't explain is why it's wrong to cut away and show him approaching. This is something that Hitchcock does all the time. Except I think it's because Kubrick only shows it toward the very end and he only shows us for a second and he doesn't allow any build, so that it's totally empty and totally flat. I tried very hard to get Warner Brothers and Stanley not to cast Jack Nicholson. They talked about Jack Nicholson in the beginning. I think that Jack Nicholson is an excellent actor and I think that he did everything Stanley asked him in the movie and did a tremendous job, but he's a man who comes across crazy.

Q: Yeah, well the moment he turns around and looks in your eyes, you have no story. You don't have the same story *The Shining* was about.

KING: So, everybody said to me, it wasn't any fun because the guy was crazy from the beginning. But Jack didn't think he was crazy from the beginning and Stanley didn't think he was crazy from the beginning. He wasn't supposed to be crazy. He didn't think he was crazy. It was just everybody in America who went to see that movie. You look at those eyes and you see Randall Patrick McMurphy.

Q: Yes, yes indeed.

KING: And you say, "Okay, the guy's as crazy as a shithouse rat. He's going to get his whole family up there and kill 'em." There's no moral struggle at all. I wanted 'em to cast Michael Moriarty or Jon Voight. They wouldn't. Not bankable.

Q: I like either one of those, but what's not bankable here is that when you have no story, do you have a movie? Not really.

KING: The movie made 91 million dollars. It's just not a profit. Kubrick spent a lot. He was playing with his Steadicam.

Q: That sounds filthy.

KING: That's what he was doing.

Q: Can we talk about *Children of the Corn* for a couple of minutes here?

KING: I think it was done by a lot of people who hopefully will go on to do better work. It could have been a better picture. I'm not down on New World Pictures or anything like that. What happened was that there was a Maine-based group of filmmakers; they're still there. They're in Rockport down the coast from me, called Varied Direction. And I was interested in getting the thing produced in Maine and they had sent me some scripts that were terrible and I sent them *Children of the Corn* and I said, "I think this would make a great movie" and they said, "So do we. We don't have any money." So basically I sold it to 'em as a partnership for $500 or something like that, did two drafts on the screenplay. They kept sort of insisting that I add some kind of Vietnam metaphor for this thing. You see this is what I mean when you make a movie you get a lot of people in collaboration, someone really fucks up. I wouldn't do it and so finally the project lapsed. And then about a year after that, this would be about 1980 or something like that, the two partners split and the idea was that each one of them, one of the conditions of the split, was that each one of them would have a year to try to get the project off the ground. And one of them tried and didn't make it and then the second guy, Harry Whealen, tried and United Artists almost produced it. I wished that had happened because I had good experience with them. The one movie that they did was *Carrie*. And they got ready to produce and then for some reason they backed down. So Harry Whealen turned around and sold the property to New World Pictures and what came out was *Children of the Corn*, which is still not as bad as it could be, but it's not very good.

Q: 'Nuff said, 'nuff said. It just is something that got out of your hands a little bit. Are you not going to let that happen again?

KING: No, no, I'm not going to say I won't let it happen again because if you don't take a chance on people that don't have any money or anything—in fact, for all I know it's happening again right now. I sold "Graveyard Shift" from *Night Shift* to this total unknown from Pittsburgh for I think $75 or something like that because he seemed interested in it and he seemed bright and most of all he seemed to have the right sense of humor—and maybe he can bankroll it and we'll have something that will be really outrageous like *Evil Dead* or maybe he can turn around and sell it and make a buck.

Q: And hope that his instincts are good and to do the right thing.

KING: Yeah.

Q: It's always a crapshoot, right?

KING: But the worst thing you can do on something like this is just say okay, Universal, Paramount, *blah, blah, blah*. I mean that takes all the fun out of it. You gotta take a chance once in a while.

Q: Well, that's good for you. I understood that *The Running Man* has been sold. They're going to do that?

KING: Yeah, I mean again it's, we're getting right back to *The Shining* again. They had cast Christopher Reeve, who's right for the part, and they pulled him out, not bankable, and it's going to be Arnold Schwarzenegger. I'm sorry, I just don't believe this guy against society. It's just—

Q: He looks too healthy to me.

KING: Yeah, that's right.

Q: What about *Maximum Overdrive*?

KING: I had a good crew and we worked really hard and we came in under budget, ahead of schedule and I'm happy with the picture.

Q: Good God, that's incredible. That never happens. Are you going to try and get an R?

KING: Yeah, we should get an R. That's where it is. If they proved to be totally intractable, I think that if push came to shove I would try to persuade Dino to go unrated, but I don't think that I could and technically speaking, by contract, he has final cut. And although he promised me he would never exercise that and he would be a man of his word, if we really get down push to shove I will say to him, "You cut this film, I'm walking away and I'm washing my hands of it." I don't think it will come to that.

Q: He's done that on a few occasions, hasn't he? Didn't he go in on *Cat's Eye* and, that's what I understood from Lewis Teague, that he went in on *Cat's Eye* with the ending, with the troll sequence at the ending and had some more be added.

KING: He may have done that. Lewis never told me that he did that and Dino's ideas are not always bad. I think that the troll sequence at the end of the movie is pretty good. And Dino did act very proprietary about that so it wouldn't surprise me. The troll sequence at the end of that movie would have been better if you'd been allowed to see the troll at the beginning because the troll was in the Prologue. They went from the crying woman to the wall and you saw him in the wall, the little red eye. So it actually became book ends. He was very fond of that troll.

Q: He can have it for his very own now. You're a movie lover, you've watched them carefully and speak with great reverence for 'em in *Danse Macabre*. Is a movie lover necessarily a good movie-maker?

KING: No, I don't think so. But on the other hand I don't have any real reverence for movies anyway. I go to see 'em because it's a way to check out my mind.

CHAPTER FIVE

†

SCREAM PARTNERS

†

With Stanley Wiater *(1980)*

Providence, Rhode Island—the birthplace of H.P. Lovecraft—seems the appropriate town in which to hold a gathering of artists, writers and filmmakers specializing in fantasy and the macabre: the Fifth World Fantasy Convention. Stephen King was here as Guest of Honor; George Romero arrived to make an appearance on a panel discussing "The Modern Horror Film." The result—an opportunity for the fans to meet two giants of modern terror.

Considering the popular and critical acclaim both men have received for their work in their respective media, it's not surprising to learn that the two are mutual admirers. Neither men give any outward sign of being overwhelmed by their enormous critical and financial successes in the field.

What did excite the pair were their own plans to work together on *two* major film projects, one an adaptation of King's ambitious novel, *The Stand*, the other a film collection of short horror comics of the Fifties titled *Creepshow*. Little more can be said of the latter—King had left all copies of *Creepshow* at his home in western Maine.

"I am very embarrassed about that, because the screenplay's all done and it's sitting on the dresser! It's just like show biz."

In regards to the filming of *The Stand*, King continues: "I guess I never really had considered *The Stand* as a movie, seriously. Then George and Richard Rubenstein, Romero's producer, came up; they were out in Hollywood after doing *Dawn of the Dead* and talking to people. And they kept saying, 'What about *The Stand?*' And people would say, 'You can't do that. It's huge!' And George and Richard would say, 'But have you read it?' And they'd say, 'No, but it's huge!' This is a ridiculous way to approach a project for a movie. So you have to wonder if the studios are reading at all."

"What the studios balked at essentially is this: *The Dead Zone* is a one-character book. There's a guy named Johnny Smith, and he *is* the book; everything revolves around him. He is the story, and everything thing around him is the setting for that story. But *The Stand* has no essential hero. There's Stu Redman, there's Nick Andros, there's all these other people. And they said, 'You've got all these people—you can't handle it.' But on the other hand Coppola did that with *Godfather*."

Leaning back in his chair, Romero constantly nods in agreement with King's statements. Their collaboration is certainly logical in one sense: King's stories and novels are known for having the most unspeakable terrors taking place among the people next door, in Anyplace, U.S.A. While all of Romero's films, no matter how outré the subject matter— ghouls, biological warfare, vampires—all have taken place in the same mundane and most ordinary of surroundings. The settings for *Night of the Living Dead*, *Dawn of the Dead*, *The Crazies*, *Martin*—small towns and cities on the East Coast—differ little, except by name, from the basically ordinary settings of King's novels.

"That's why I'm attracted to a lot of Steve's stuff," Romero readily admits. "I also find in *The Stand* a lot of social significance, if you will. Although on the surface, we're just out to make a movie." And what sort of horror directly appeals to Romero as a writer/director? "It's hard to pinpoint. It's such a personal thing. I like it to have a certain kind of logic, and a certain kind of craft. And a certain integrity to the form—to the genre. I tend to be a little more outrageous and a little more—I know it sounds cliché—sociopolitical. *The Crazies* is very political, up front. But even with the *Dead* films, there's a sociopolitical underbelly to them. I like things like that, and I like satire. I really haven't tried to make a 'scary' movie since *Night of the Living Dead*—none of the others are really scary movies."

Romero explains that to the viewers who found *Dawn of the Dead* to be no longer frightening after the first 10 minutes, that this was precisely the point when he first planned the film. "*Dawn of the Dead* isn't a scare film. It's a *shock* film. It's a satire, and to me is funny. It's in the genre, but it's not in pure form. Neither is *Martin*. In fact, none of them are, except for

Night of the Living Dead, which, while it has a socio-political-philosophical underside to it, on the surface it's a pure horror film. And even *Dawn* on the surface is still just a movie. It's just not a scary *horror* movie."

Although Romero has made his reputation as a sort of a maverick, producing his films without major studio backing, the success of *Dawn of the Dead* finally has the studios seeking him out. Yet Romero is hesitant as to what sort of creative control might be lost by gaining either a large financial backing or a solid distribution package for *The Stand.* Although he did not mention anyone by name, Romero cited several examples of young, independent directors who were hired by a major Hollywood studio to do films, had one box-office failure and were never heard from again. Overall, he's still optimistic about his own chances.

"I'm very excited about *The Stand.* We're going to try to produce that with or without a studio's involvement. There might be some studio involvement up front, but it's a lot different when you go to a studio and say, 'This movie's going to cost $10 million,' and you already have six. And getting that first six doesn't involve the studios at all."

"*The Creepshow* is an anthology; I think one part was originally a short story, but whether it was previously published or not I don't know because I haven't seen the script! Steve and I just had a couple of very broad conversations, just kind of respecting each other's jobs, in regards to what each of us is going to do. And Steve just said, 'Terrific, and I'll see you again when it's ready.' I really look forward to reading it, even though I know what it's like, what it's intended to be."

Both men have long been in love with horror movies; it's a love that dates back to their childhood days. King laughs. "If you love horror movies, you've got to have a love for pure *shit.* This is not an aspersion on anyone in this company, but you turn into the kind of person who would watch *Attack of the Crab Monsters* four times. You know how shitty it is, but there's something that appeals to you. It doesn't mean you don't want to do better."

Elaborating on his earliest influences, Romero states, "When I was growing up in the 1940s, genre movies were what were around...the double-bills on weekends. But I loved all the genre movies—jungle movies, war movies. And horror movies were *it.* The first one that I think had a real influence on me was Howard Hawk's *The Thing,* which I carried around for a couple years in my psyche. Roman Polanski's work has had an effect on me, too. I'll say the same thing Steve said: I like to watch 'junk.' I *do* like to watch it, and I'll always opt for that. Always. Some people forget that's what movies are: a popular form. And enjoyment is at the heart of the form."

With Paul Gagne

Q: I understand George Romero recently purchased the rights to film *The Stand*. What can you tell me about it?

KING: Basically, he took an option that's kind of open-ended. First we're doing another project, called *Creepshow*. Our idea here is simply to do something original that we can do on a low budget, get it out there and hopefully make a profit. It will show people that we're for real. Then we can go ahead and make a deal with one of the majors for the production money for *The Stand*. The money to do *The Stand* would be there right now, actually; the question is one of how much control over the project we can get, so that George, in particular, can do the kind of film he wants to do. We want to give it every chance; if no one likes the picture, at least it won't be a result of studio interference. On the other side of that, if we make a good picture and people like it, I'd hate to see some vice-president in charge of ass-scratching at one of the majors come out at the end saying how this wonderful idea was all his simply because he controlled the money. So basically, we're doing *Creepshow* as one step up to doing *The Stand*.

Q: What is your role in the project?

KING: I did the screenplay. The film will be a series of short segments. It's an anthology film, like *Dead of Night* or some of the Hammer films, only it's done in a much more violent, throat-gripping kind of way. There will be four or five segments aimed at really scaring the wits out of the audience. George and I both believe that for an anthology film to be effective you have to make each one of the segments scary as hell. That's the only way to keep people interested. In the past, the trouble with this type of film has often been that one of the segments will be great, but the other two or three will be sort of low-key and not very interesting. So we're trying to make each one of these strong and punchy.

Q: Will you also be doing the screenplay for *The Stand*?

KING: I wouldn't trust it to anybody else. In fact, I've been offered option deals on *The Stand* before and I've turned them down. Some of them have been for pretty good money. But this is maybe the one thing I've done where I want as much creative control over the movie as I can get. If it's gonna get bitched up, I want to do the bitching up. I don't want to let somebody else do it.

Q: What aspects of *The Stand* would you like to see emphasized in the film? It's much too long to try to convey all of the plot in two hours' time.

KING: This is something that I've turned over in my mind. Mostly, I've gone at it from the standpoint that we have to break it down to where we can get it on film in about two and a half hours. That in itself is going to be a job. I think that I'd like to see most of the emphasis come down on the "post-apocalypse." That is, what happens to the survivors after the superflu has burned itself out. I'd like to maybe concentrate a little more on the dark man, Randall Flagg, and the whole aspect of evil. I still want it to be a strong adventure story with those mystical overtones. I know that's what attracts George.

Q: It'll be interesting to see how Randall Flagg is personified in the film. The character in the novel almost comes across as some sort of a living shadow, which leaves it wide open to interpretation from a visual standpoint.

KING: I'd make him just a regular guy. When he is described in the book as "the man with no face," in many ways that means he looks like *anybody.* There is nothing about his physical appearance that sets him apart from anyone else. I'd love to see Robert Duvall play the part.

Q: He was a lot like Randall Flagg in *Apocalypse Now!*

KING: You're right! Maybe if he's in *The Stand* he can wear that same hat! But actually, Marlon Brando is really the dark man in *Apocalypse Now.* That's the way the dark man should be. He's in and out of the shadows, and every now and then you see him, but mostly you just see shadows.

With Paul Gagne

Q: In one of our earlier conversations, you briefly explained how your collaboration with George Romero on *Creepshow* evolved as sort of a stepping stone to doing *The Stand.* Can you elaborate on how it all started?

KING: Yes. It was in the summer of 1979, I think. George came up to Maine with Richard Rubinstein to talk about *The Stand*, which they owned by then. I think it was my idea to do a low-budget "tune up" project first, because it would cost so much money to do *The Stand*. I was thinking in terms of something we could do more or less on a shoestring that would go out and make money to prove that we were for real. The thing kind of snowballed from there, because it isn't exactly a low budget picture anymore. I was thinking in terms of, say, $2 million. I think George was thinking $3-4 million. It snowballed to six and then went to eight when they decided on a "name" cast.

Originally, George and I were just tossing around the idea of what could we do as an original piece that would really scare people; you know, a high-wire effect that would go through a whole movie. This was the time that all of the *Halloween* ripoffs started to come out, and none of them seemed particularly scary. The idea was to do a bunch of blackouts—eight or nine different things where you wouldn't really need a lot of buildup or motivation. They'd be situational, like some of the *Out* radio programs were situational. Because they would be situational, they'd almost be the equivalent of comedy skits, only this would be horror. Comedy and horror are very closely intertwined.

The idea to make *Creepshow* a comic book evolved out of the decision to expand these little blackouts into stories. The E.C. horror comics from the Fifties were very close to what we were thinking of—everything was pared down to the bone, and they got it off in a big hurry. We started to talk about some of the anthology films that were based on the E.C. comics, like *Tales from the Crypt* and *The Vault of Horror*, which hadn't really worked, and a couple of things that almost worked, like *The House That Dripped Blood*. *Creepshow* was the result.

Q: Visually, George has taken the approach of literally making *Creepshow* a comic book come to life, using brightly colored lighting and back-lit patterns which appear behind the actors at key dramatic moments.

KING: That was his idea. Originally, George had talked about doing the blackout idea in a number of different styles. One would be in black and white and small screen, another would be wide screen, and one would even be done in 3D. When the blackouts developed into the comic book idea, George started thinking in terms of comic book panels, the color fades and everything. At one point, he had the idea of setting it all in the

Fifties, when the E.C. comics were first published. Not to make a big deal out of it, but to have people in Fifties hairdos, the hemlines would be Fifties-style hemlines, or when Henry took the station wagon out in "The Crate," it would be a "Woody" from the Fifties. I wasn't wild about the idea, and there were problems in terms of the costuming and things like that, so we dropped it. I'm really glad we didn't go that far, because it would have been sort of overboard.

Q: Your script uses the *Creepshow* comic book itself as sort of a framing device for the five stories in the film. A father catches his son reading a horror comic, throws it in the trash, and as the wind whips the pages open we go in and out of each story. . . .

KING: Again, that was George's idea, I think. Most of the anthology films within the horror genre have used the idea of a framing story, which goes back to Chaucer's *The Canterbury Tales*. You know, these people are traveling to Canterbury and they're telling these tales. In a Milton Subotsky film, you'll have people going down in an elevator, and they sit around and tell these stories, and then ho, ho!—they find out they're in hell. Or maybe they're on a train and they're telling these stories, and then—ho, ho!—the train ends up in hell. At least in *Creepshow*, Billy and his father don't end up in hell!

I wasn't wild about the idea of a framing device from the beginning; I thought we could just do the stories and that would be it. I think George had said something about the Old Witch who introduced the stories in the E.C.'s, and how that was kind of a framing device, in a way, and I said "Okay, fine." My feeling is that if you can't collaborate with the director on a creative level, why are you involved at all?

Q: The five stories in *Creepshow* all fall into the category you refer to as "Tales of the Hook" in your nonfiction book, *Danse Macabre*.

KING: They're pretty primitive, aren't they?

Q: They have the barest of all possible plots, each of which serves strictly as a buildup to some big shock or scare, although there is a lot of character development. But these are essentially "Tales of the Hook."

KING: Yes. They're efforts to get at that childish center of horror. In a sense, I always relate humor and horror, and in some ways *Creepshow* is very funny. People sit there and roll at the dailies. My idea is that the audience should be laughing and screaming at the same time, almost. If there's any one scene in *Creepshow* that's indicative of all this, it's the scene in "The Crate" where Hal Holbrook lures Adrienne Barbeau down the stairs to where the monster is hiding, and he's trying not to laugh at her, biting the insides of his cheeks. She's saying "What are you laughing about? Your best friend gets into a scrape and you're laughing?" He says "It's pretty funny; wait until you see!" And it is sort of funny in a horrible way.

I had one of my first experiences with this in college. They had a place called The Coffee House. It's been renamed since then, but in the Sixties it was very beatnik. You know, we'd go down there in our pattern stockings and smoke cigarettes, very hip. At that time, I had sold about three stories to various markets, and they were all horror stories. Everybody in college who wanted to write wanted to be Ezra Pound or Flannery O'Connor when they grew up. Or Anne Sexton. Dead people, in other words. Here was this story I had done about a guy with eyes all over his hands, and they all thought it was pretty amusing! So when they had this Halloween thing at The Coffee House, I was asked to read some stories, and I said, "Okay." People listened, and they were obviously entertained. I don't know if you could say they were engrossed, but they were certainly more engrossed than they ever were by my guitar playing! But they would laugh at various points in the stories. I was really taken aback, and I thought, This must not be working.

It took me a long time to realize that it was working and that people were laughing for a reason. One of the reasons is to relieve tension, but another reason Peter Straub always cites is that any horror story is an entry for the mass mind into the surreal, and it's one of the only entries. Whenever we enter that surreal world, we laugh. People laugh at Dali paintings, too, even while they're engrossed, because those images are so ridiculous. Tabby, my wife, pointed out one Dali painting where this guy is in a corner shitting his pants; you see it squirting right out. At that time, in the 1920s, everybody was into Freud and everything, and sex in these surrealistic paintings was considered okay. You know, "That's Freudian." But shit? People had to stand back and say, "Well, it's Freudian, but is it in good taste?" Along the same lines, Ted Sturgeon had a great story published in the *National Lampoon* about an alien from outer space who was a shape-changer. It came to Earth and took the shape of a toilet. People would sit on it to take a crap, and it would suck out their life force. It's hilarious, but at the same time the very idea is horrible, because you're at your most vulnerable then. I've never had the guts to do a real crap story, though a lot of my critics would say that's all I have done!

Everything funny is horrible, and everything horrible is funny, really.

Q: George Romero's films combine horror and humor with wonderful results. Like *Dawn of the Dead*—I saw it in a packed theater when it first came out, and we were all cringing and shrieking but laughing hysterically at the same time.

KING: Well, George is a guy with a great sense of humor. He laughs a lot. Things strike him funny. But that line is very, very close. He was pointing out to me one time that most comedians have reputations for being real shits. Guys like Buddy Hackett, and I guess Mel Brooks has a reputation as somebody who's apt to just explode if you push his buttons. On the other hand, most horror people are alright. They laugh a lot and they're easy to get along with. When you think about it—and I got into this argument with my wife after seeing *Scanners*, which just turned her off violently—most humor is based on somebody being hurt in some way, and we laugh at it, because thank God it isn't us. In some ways, horror is almost more humane, because when we scream, we're showing sympathy rather than non-sympathy. We express the non-sympathy with this kind of laughter, which is sort of an apelike sound; it's a triumph sound.

Q: I'd like to get into the specific background of each of the stories in *Creepshow*. "Father's Day," for example, is particularly reminiscent of the E.C. comics. . . .

KING: "Father's Day," of all of them, is a deliberate E.C. pastiche. I don't mean that it was plagiarized—it isn't any one particular E.C. story, but to my mind, it's like the archetypal E.C. story, with the dead guy coming back to life and just relentlessly offing his family one after the other. There's nothing more to it than that. I just sat down at the typewriter and said "Okay, somebody's going to come out of the grave." I very rarely work that way, but it worked this time.

Q: You're playing the lead in the second segment, "The Lonesome Death of Jordy Verrill." That was taken from "Weeds," one of your short stories. Did you include that specifically for yourself?

KING: No. I've been telling people that if I had written it for myself, I would have put at least one sex scene in there! Or maybe not a sex scene, but at least a fantasy vision of Jordy sitting there with some painted woman who would look like something out of one of his magazines—a real Fifties-style "whoor"!

That particular story is one of two in the screenplay that have been previously published. It appeared in *Cavalier*, during that period where I was writing stories and selling them to the men's magazines. This was before *Carrie*, back in 1970–71. Originally, "Weeds" was written as the first chapter of a novel. I got to about twenty thousand words when I ran out of inspiration for the thing. Instead of being compressed into a day and a night, it was more like a day and a half. It took place during the Fourth of July, and there were fireworks in the sky throughout it all, which made it nice. Jordy originally had this neighbor who was a lot smarter and a better farmer than he was, and the weeds started to spread to his side. But once the weeds started to grow beyond that closed world and toward the town, I couldn't find any more to say. It seemed to me that that was all I really cared about, and I ran out of caring about it. Not only was there no third act, there wasn't even a second act.

Q: The original story as it appeared in *Cavalier* was a lot more grim and painful than it is in the screenplay. You've taken a more broad, comic approach to the story, particularly in your own performance as Jordy.

KING: I think that would be true no matter who played Jordy. It was George's idea that this piece should have a different mood than the others. I go along with that, because I think it's bad to have an anthology picture where you're playing the same note over and over again. Corpses that come back from the grave are allright once or twice, but by all means let's not stick with those things for two hours. George's idea was that we'd play it real broad, and it was his idea that Jordy should become real broad. It was good for me because it gave me a hook to hang the performance on. Some of the humor in "Jordy" happened almost naturally, like the scenes where he's having these fantasies of striking the big time, getting rich. When we actually see those fantasies played out, they become funny. I think that's the point where it changed, in my own mind, to a piece that's really a comedy.

Q: Yeah, those fantasy scenes are some of the funniest bits in the screenplay.

KING: Well, some of then have turned out even funnier on film. George was shooting all of this with really skewed camera angles, so it looks like what you get sometimes in the old *Twilight Zone* programs, where everything is slanted. He shot all of the fantasies that way. We were looking at some of the dailies of the scene in the doctor's office, and the continuity girl said, "Wouldn't it be funny if things started to roll back and forth because of that slant?" The next day, George had decided it was a great idea, so they had these things like a skeleton in the background rolling back and forth. It has a very uneasy effect, and at the same time it's very funny!

Q: "The Crate" is the other story that's been published before, in *Gallery*. What was the inspiration for that?

KING: I was working on *The Dead Zone* at the time. I had the radio going, and there was a local news item about this crate that was found underneath the stairs at the University of Maine, which was where I went to college. They were closing down the chemistry building and moving it to a new location. They found all this stuff, including a crate that had been there under the stairs for something like a hundred years. Nobody knew it was there. What got to me was to think of a hundred years of students going up and down those stairs with that crate right underneath. There was probably nothing in it but old magazines, but it kind of tripped over in my mind that there could have been something really sinister in there.

Then one day my kids were watching one of those Warner Brothers cartoons about the Tasmanian Devil. You know—all teeth! I thought, "Jesus Christ, that's not funny! That's horrible!" But I got to thinking, suppose it was the Tasmanian Devil in that crate? And it's really like "Pig Pen" in the *Peanuts* comics—you never really know what it looks like, because there's all this whirling dervish kind of effect. I never really wanted to describe the creature, so in the original story it isn't anything like Tom Savini's conception of it for the film, but it isn't anything *not* like Savini's conception, either. Some choices have to be made in a movie; the camera's eye doesn't blink.

It was funny, though—when I finished that story, I sent it to *Playboy*, because they really wanted something from me at that point. You know, I was hot. One of their editors liked it a lot, but she reluctantly turned it down. When my agent called her up to find out why, she said "Well, I think it's really scary, but every time that creature pops up I think of the Tasmanian Devil in the Warner Brothers cartoons!"

I had several other existing stories that could have just as easily been included in the *Creepshow* screenplay. One of these was "The Float," which was originally published in *Adam*. That's the best horror story I've ever written. It's about these four college kids, two guys and two girls, who go down to this lake for a dip. There are some obvious sexual overtones to the thing. It's after the season is over, and they swim out to this float which hasn't been taken in yet. There's this slime thing floating around on the water that gets underneath the float and starts to suck them down one by one, and they're screaming and going down. There's nothing left of one guy but his class ring stuck between two of the boards. Finally, at the end, you're left with one guy trying to stand on the boards and swaying back and forth. That was one of the possibilities that I rejected for *Creepshow*.

Q: "Something to Tide You Over," one of the original pieces in *Creepshow*, certainly fits the E.C. mold.

KING: Again, that came from trying to think of some kind of situation that would be very ominous but at the same time absurd and almost ludicrous. It's like the Jack Davis story in the E.C. comics, where at the end you have guts strewn all over the baseball field, and these guys are running baselines made up of intestines and using a human heart as home plate. I wanted to do something in that vein, and I just flashed on what we used to do at the beach when we were kids, which was to bury ourselves up to our necks in the sand. Then I remembered this movie about Bluebeard where they shot him in the hips and left him below the high tide line, and I thought, "Aha, that's it!"

Q: That one's quite a bit like "The Ledge," one of the short stories in your *Night Shift* collection.

KING: I've never thought of that! As a matter of fact, the original draft of the script had some very "Ledge"-like things in it, like the bird and the crab who come after this guy when just his head is sticking up out of the sand. They were cut out because the bird was just impossible, and the crabs they got were nasty! I mean, Ted Danson was in this hole up to his neck, and the crabs were gonna do a number on his face!

Q: There seems to be a lot of this nervous anticipation on the set over the 25,000 cockroaches that are being brought in for "They're Creeping Up on You." At one point you were thinking about replacing that particular story with something else about a hitchiker in case the bugs became impossible for budgetary or logistical reasons.

KING: All I can say is that everybody liked the bugs. I liked the bugs. Having a backup story was strictly a case of my being super-aware of the budgetary limitations. In the original script, there were all different kinds of bugs, not just cockroaches. It was this mixture of cockroaches, spiders, beetles, and bugs that don't even exist, like the little rubber horrors from novelty shops. After I wrote the script, Tabby read it and said "How are they going to do it with all these different kinds of bugs?"

My standard response is "That's their problem, not mine." My feeling is that if I can do something in a book then I can put it in a screenplay. Let someone else hassle with the special effects. If they can't do it, then we'll work something else out. In this case, they decided to make it strictly cockroaches in order to keep it as simple as possible. It seemed easier to get a whole bunch of one kind of bug than to try to incubate six or seven different kinds.

We've actually got a bug wrangler on the picture, a guy from the American Museum of Natural History. We did some screen tests on the bugs last summer! They built a little mockup of Pratt's room it was like a miniature living room with plexiglass walls, and it had curtains. Our bug expert was giving us all this advice—you know, if you smear vaseline on the tops of the sets they won't crawl over it, they'll always go for the corners, etc. Everything that he said was true, within limits. I mean, some of these cockroaches were really fucking enthusiastic, and they did manage to crawl over the vaseline, and people had to push them back down. Chris Romero, George's wife, was just out of it! She left the room! She couldn't dig it at all! Anyway, that gave me some practical experience when I went back and did the shooting script, and the idea was to go for enclosed areas, to set things in the corners of rooms, and to keep Pratt's apartment really sparse. George's idea was to make this guy not necessarily a Howard Hughes type, but to have him living in this kind of antiseptic environment. Then we also changed the ending when they decided to bring in these really gigantic cockroaches from Trinidad. In the original draft, there's a single bug at the end that comes trundling out of Pratt's nose after he's dead. I talked to Tom Savini about this— your nostrils are only so wide, and these bugs are big. We talked about a number of different options, and we finally came up with something that should be quite striking. It should be a buster, the way some of the stuff in *Alien* was.

Q: Tom took a life cast of E. G. Marshall the other day for some effect where the cockroaches are apparently supposed to burst right through Pratt's chest. Is this what you're trying not to tell me?

KING: Yeah, that's what I'm trying not to tell you. The idea is to come in on Marshall totally clean, and whether these are fantasy bugs that became real or real bugs that were supernaturally inspired to come after this guy, he's simply internalized them all. The image you should get on screen is that all of these bugs are now inside of him. The skin begins to bulge in a number of different places, and then everything bursts through at once!

Q: How do you feel about the way the actors have responded to the parts they're playing, and specifically to your dialogue?

KING: It's great. They've all been really nice to work with. I think that George felt a little dubious at first about using "name" actors, which he had never done before. We didn't know what to expect. My hope was that they would simply be pros who would come in and do the work, and they have. I think we've gotten some really good performances.

Q: How about yourself as an actor? Is "Jordy Verrill" the first thing you've done aside from playing a cameo role in George's last film, *Knightriders*?

KING: It's the first piece of film I've done other than that. I did some stage work off and on in college—my minor in college was speech—and I've done some community theater bits, so I *have* acted before. I've always felt like it was something I could do. George just kind of asked me off the cuff if I'd play Jordy, and I said yes. I was aware that I was going to get into something that was *work*. I think you're okay if you approach it with that in mind. Beyond that, I'm aware of certain other things. You know, whether this performance is good or bad I may be in for a hard time critically, because people don't want you to be able to do two things really well. And I'm sure a lot of people will feel that I got to play this role because of who I am, which is probably completely true. With that in mind, you just go into it and try to please yourself. I guess that's the only thing you *can* do. And, of course, to try and please George. He's been great to work for, because I don't think he's ever played the part cheap or anything like that.

Q: Not many writers get to actually live out one of their characters; has playing Jordy been fun for you?

KING: It isn't that I haven't had fun playing Jordy, but I really just think of it as work. It isn't fun or not fun. I mean, you just try to do it. You know when you're doing a good job and you know when you're doing a bad job. Sometimes I'm too shy to say this, but there have been days, like a couple of times today, where I've said, "Let's do another take; I felt I was just getting that right and I'd like you to have at least two to choose from." Like this scene we did where Jordy puts his fingers in his mouth with the blisters and realizes he's making the weed infection spread. I was just yanking the fingers away. George was trying to put across to me what he wanted, and I finally realized what he was saying—that Jordy's reaction should be like when Wile E. Coyote is chasing the Roadrunner and goes off the edge of a cliff. He thinks he's still on the road, and as soon as he realizes he's walking on air, down he goes! When I knew that, I thought to myself, Gee, I could do this five more times, and maybe a couple of them would be real good!

You know, the first step toward forming any kind of a creative thing that reflects your own individuality is when you can isolate the bad things in other people's work, particularly the first time you look at somebody else and say, "I can do it better than that." One of the reasons I've committed myself to being here so extensively for the production of *Creepshow* is that I'd like to direct something myself some day. I don't want to make it my career or my life, but I'd like to do it once, because I see things in horror films and I say "I could do it better than that."

Q: Did you have any trepidation about the extensive makeup work involved in turning Jordy into a six foot weed?

KING: No, I never thought about that. I don't think you should count the cost on something like that. When I committed myself to this thing, I realized I'd be away from home a lot and I'd miss my kids and my wife. Beyond that, it's a question of whether this is something you want to do or not. It's no good if you get to a point where you're asking yourself, "Do I really want to do this? Do I want to be smelling that awful acetone? Do I want to be in this place at that time?" When you get down to that level, you're a fucking accountant! You might as well forget about whatever you're doing and become something else! It's like the production deal on this picture—if we make money, we make it on the back end. We don't make it up front. My accountant is not wild about that, so I had to give him a couple of shoves—"C'mon, let's go!" Of course he sees things that way, but this is what I do. It's all a crapshoot, really. What else is there?

Q: The fact that you're playing Jordy brings another question to mind. When you're writing, do you put a lot of yourself into your characters? I notice a lot of them are English teachers and writers. . . .

KING: Well, that makes it easier to write about how a character spends their time, or to build the job into the character. I have a book that's been in progress for a couple of years where the main character is a lawyer. It's tough for me, because I'm not a lawyer. How do I write about what this guy does? On television shows and in a lot of books, you get something where the character's work is almost something that's nonexistent. Most of us know that your work is your life, and you can't really separate what you do from who you are. To a certain degree you have to, but most of us think about our work a lot.

Q: Your son Joe is playing Billy, the boy who gets caught with the *Creepshow* comic book in the film's prologue. How old is he?

KING: Nine. That came about when George and Chris were up with us in Maine. We were talking about who could play the kid, and then Joe came in and asked if he could go over to a friend's house. George said something about he how looked like the kid in the *Creepshow* poster Jack Kamen had done for us. Joe read for the part, and George thought he'd be great, so we did it. I was a little bit nervous about it, because I didn't want to get in the position where I was being a stage father, pushing my kid into the limelight and yelling, "Act! Act!" But he tried very, very hard, and it's gonna work.

Q: I understand George and Richard accepted your first draft of the *Creepshow* screenplay without changes.

KING: Yeah, I was really surprised. I thought it was a great screenplay, but my experience with Hollywood has always been that the first thing you hear is something like, "This is the greatest screenplay since *Ben Hur*!" That's followed by "We want to make a few changes," and the "few changes" go on for seven months until they finally drop the project. George and Richard simply steamed straight ahead with the whole thing. Just after the pre-production was set, George went to work on the screenplay and broke it down shot by shot. In other words, my screenplay had around two hundred and twenty scenes, and he ended up with something like twenty-two hundred individual shots.

Q: This is the first screenplay you've written that's actually been produced. Your prior screenwriting experience included a script for *The Shining* that wasn't used.

KING: Yes, but you have to understand that my script was done before anybody had any idea that Kubrick would want to do the picture. I think that they might have gone ahead with my screenplay had it been somebody else.

Q: Then you adapted some of the stories in your *Night Shift* anthology for a project that never got off the ground. I've read that you also did something with Ray Bradbury's *Something Wicked This Way Comes*.

KING: That was just a finger exercise. I had decided that I wanted to try doing a screenplay for *The Shining*, and I had to get some practice, so I adapted that book. There was never any question of selling it.

Q: How do you feel about the relationship between yourself as screenwriter and George as director on *Creepshow*? Given that George has written almost all of his own screenplays in the past, one would think that there might be some ego problems, but word on the set is that George is very respectful of your script and is actually more reluctant than you are to change anything.

KING: Well, George cares about words. There have been times when he's cared almost to excess about words in some of his movies. But he really has a respect for words, and he is a good writer. I just read this book called *Splatter Movies*, and the author kind of dumps on George as a writer. But I've seen some of George's prose, and I've read some of his screenplays, and even in terms of the way his movies work, he's a good writer and he cares about the word. I care about the word; I couldn't give a shit how many books sell to the movies or anything like that. I care about words. There's a chance to do things in this movie with dialogue that nobody's really cared to do, at least in a horror movie, for a long time. It seemed to me that *The Haunting* was a movie that cared about words. I'll never forget Russ Tamblyn at the end, saying "It should be burned to the ground and the ground seeded with salt." They used Shirley Jackson's words, and it worked. There are things in *Creepshow* that are very carefully calculated, like some of Wilma's dialogue in "The Crate." Or in "Father's Day," when Aunt Sylvia says "How can such a beautiful woman be such an utter turd?"—it's a question of words, and the words should sound right. George has shot the words. I don't want it to be all words; I understand that you go to movies to watch something happen. Some of the worst horror movies are the ones where they talk you to death.

Q: Do you think the combination of King and Romero will finally produce the Stephen King film your fans have been waiting for? We've had King/Hooper and King/Kubrick, and both were pretty big letdowns in spite of the directorial talents involved.

KING: Well, none of them have really been King. So in a way, I've been safe through all of this. I've been lucky, in some ways, bacause *Carrie* was a good film, and I didn't play a part in it. *'Salem's Lot* was a good film, considering it was done for television; I think it's better than anything Tobe Hooper's done save *Texas Chainsaw Massacre*, before or since. With *The Shining*, even now people argue about whether it's a good movie or a bad movie. I argue inside my head about all that. But in all those cases, I've been protected, other than in terms of the occasional review where someone will say, "It's a silk purse out of a sow's ear; the guy's just a potboiling popular novelist." But if *Creepshow* is a bad movie and people don't like it, I can't very well duck it, can I? I'm tied to it a hundred ways.

Q: We're sitting in an apartment overlooking the shopping mall where George Romero filmed *Dawn of the Dead.* The other day you mentioned that being here has inspired you to write a novel about cannibalism. . . .

KING: Yes. Being here in Monroeville, and being in a certain state of mind. I've been married for almost twelve years, and this is the first time I've spent any significant amount of time by myself since I was married. That's contributed to the mind-set—you know, the sense of this place as a place that's cut off. It's also a place where everybody's consuming madly. There's a kind of high with consumerism going on here. I've had an idea for a long time of at least a situation that I thought would make a real good story. It's got a lot of what I think of as "macrophotography." People doing things and moving things. A physical world moving around. Under the right circumstances, opening a door can be interesting, if you don't know what's on the other side. Or maybe what I mean is that a door should open but won't. I love that. There's a scene in the book where this guy takes a swing at a glass window with a baseball bat, and it just hits the window and goes "Boonnnnngggg!" He drops the bat like he's hit a stone wall. The main character in the book is a born-again Christian. She's a devout believer in Jesus Christ and being saved and all that. She's very sympathetic, though; sort of the flip side of *Carrie's* mother.

With Tony Crawley

ROMERO: I haven't seen it—finished. Not a full print. We had one screening in Los Angeles of an interlocked version that didn't have all the opticals in. That was the only time I saw an audience we sneaked it for in Harrisburg. Then, we had a screening in New York which was . . . a pretty complete version.

KING: I saw a lot more this time, it seems to me.

Q: But you stayed around, Steve. George split. I saw him hanging about on the stairs as if looking for a fast exit.

ROMERO: I wanted to be able to pace and smoke and all that. After ten minutes. . . I took the train!

Q: You were nervous?

ROMERO: A little bit, yes. I think it's still shell shock from *Knightriders*. Not about the film. It has more to do with the politics and the sales. That's the shit that gets to me.

KING: And that's not a real audience in Cannes. I've seen it twice; completely. I saw it in New York with guys associated with UFD and with Universal. Mostly, you know, hardened film people. They're a soft audience compared to last night's audience. You could take your hot tea and pass it through the chambers of their hearts and come out with ice tea! They're really. . . oh God, they're really a tough audience.

Q: Oh, c'mon Steve, there was a lot of us, your kind of audience, there last night. You must have known that from the applause for individual credits.

KING: Well, we did get some applause and I'm grateful for it. Very nice. But I can't tell how it went down. I can't! I thought they were really with "Father's Day" and "The Crate" stories. Generally speaking, they were with most of it. But again, I didn't get a really strong feeling. Because a lot of them were buyers. Richard Rubinstein and I were saying, if you see a buyer leave after 25 minutes, does that mean he thinks he can't buy this for his territory? Or does that mean, "That's all I have to see, I know I'm going to buy this one and I can go see *Basket Case*"? Or does it mean, he's decided after two or three looks that this is gonna be way outside his league, pricewise, so what's the sense of staying? Or does it mean he just fucking hated the film?

Q: You nearly did *'Salem's Lot* as a team. You're still planning *The Stand* together. Why did you kick off this great teaming with a *portmanteau* movie, a pack of stories?

KING: The reason this actually came about is that George optioned *The Stand* which is a very long novel. I've done a couple of drafts and I've still got a screenplay that's the size of The Bible. And that's cut down. Considerably! So, that's very, very long and it will be expensive and looks like a very long term project. We kinda wanted to establish our *bona-fides*, so to speak. "Wow! They work together really well. This movie said something like, "Wouldn't it be nice to do a horror version of like, Monty Python. A series of blackouts. Very short incidents. Eight or nine. With punchline. Only instead of laughing, you'd vomit or screech or something!" And George said, "Yeah, like the horror comics." And I said, Wow! That was like a real blast. I hadn't thought of them in a long time, those awful, *awful* comics from the Fifties!

ROMERO: Like *Creepshow*!

KING: So that's when we started to talk seriously. Not so much about a multi-part film but the possibility of doing a comic book for cinema.

Q: How did you plan it out between you? Who did what?

ROMERO: Once we decided on the approach, Steve wrote the screenplay. And it was so close, we never had to re-type or publish another version. Steve went in and blue-penciled a few things. But we actually worked all the way through the shoot with that very copy of the script.

KING: George took it in and did a shot-by-shot breakdown of every story. The one thing that was most complete was "The Crate," where every shot, every angle that you see in the film was written down.

Q: Written down—not storyboarded?

KING: No! This is a storyboard that was written out. This is a writing person's storyboard.

ROMERO: A verbal storyboard. A shot list, basically. Without drawings.

KING: In fact, there were things in George's shot-by-shot breakdown that I didn't understand! They weren't in my screenplay. Well, they were in the sense that, for instance, it would say in my original screenplay, "The thing in the crate gets the janitor—the director will know how to shoot this."

ROMERO: Yeah, that's right. I found all these little, personal notes throughout the screenplay.

KING: There comes a point, you know, where it becomes impossible to say anything else. All right, this is where the director becomes the director. I can say, "The thing pops up out of the crate, takes the janitor by the left arm and yanks him in," and it turns out that day that the janitor's got a pulled muscle in his left arm or something. It's up to the director. The director should shoot that. That's the essence of what a director does to create suspense. And so, George had broken this thing down to where the crate falls over. . . and I could never picture it in my mind until I saw it. I never could! I knew that he knew what he wanted and so I was never concerned.

Q: Don't you ever use a storyboard, George—no little scribbles at all?

director. The director should shoot that. That's the essence of what a director does to create suspense. And so, George had broken this thing down to where the crate falls over. . . and I could never picture it in my mind until I saw it. I never could! I knew that he knew what he wanted and so I was never concerned.

Q: Don't you ever use a storyboard, George—no little scribbles at all?

ROMERO: With the designer sometimes and with Tom Savini for sets and effects. Not a shot-by-shot series of sketches, no.

Q: That's strange. Well, maybe it isn't for you. But a director is visually oriented and the only way to really explain visuals is to sketch them so others understand and see what's in your head and not theirs.

ROMERO: I don't resist doing it. I would just write it out. I generally do that work before I've seen all the material. We weren't in a position where we had seven months of pre-production with all the sets designed and a little floor plan in front of me. We had three weeks off between *Knightriders* and *Creepshow*. So, I like to leave things a little more flexible.

KING: George is also very verbally oriented, more so than a lot of directors. It's one of the traits that makes him easy to work with. George *likes* words. When we were making some of the cuts, I found myself in the director's position saying, "We can cut this and this for dialogue." And George would say, "No, I liked that line—that worked."

Q: Does that mean your breakdown itemized the scene of Viveca Lindfors' chattering away to the grave, and all your cuts to and from the gravestone?

ROMERO: Exactly.

Q: With the precise numbers of cuts to and fro?

ROMERO: On her scene, no. [*laugh*].

KING: She was a separate case.

ROMERO: But in the other scenes, yes. For example, where they pulled the grating off the cross-face of "The Crate," and the shots of the flashlights and things like that, those were pretty much as per my shot list.

Q: What happened at the gravestone then?

KING: Viveca happened!

ROMERO: She just. . . she just. . . . She did a jam session with it!

KING: We'd say, "Oh, Viveca, why don't we try it this way? and she'd say, "Yes. But first we do this!"

ROMERO: She just started to jam. So, we just rolled a bunch of film.

Q: Yeah, but then came the editing, and you cut back and forth between her and the gravestone. . . what was it. . . I wasn't counting, of course, I never realized you'd have so many. . . eight, nine cuts backs and forth?

ROMERO: Yeah, a lot of them.

Q: And the jump still works—out came a *Carrie* arm and the people in front of me hit the ceiling. We know it's coming. But not when. That works as well in *Carrie* or in David Lean's classic cut in *Great Expectations*—both graveyard shots, also. I wondered if you'd worked out in advance exactly how many times, how long, you'd tease us like that.

ROMERO: No, I knew there'd be many cuts. The scene runs now about what it was, in terms of length. She basically says what she was supposed to say. But it had been a little more intricate in my breakdown with bits of business with the props, like the bottle. I wound up having to use her and the stone, instead of the details I was going to do. I was a little worried about it—the jump, the conversation and one little thing I did with the bottle is enough to just lull it out further.

Q: It sure worked.

ROMERO: Well, it's also quick movement—loud sound. That works here in Cannes along the Croisette, too, you know!

Q: We'll get to the casting later, but apart from Adrienne Barbeau there are no recognized genre names. So what audience are you aiming at? Because it's tongue-in-cheek horror, isn't it?

ROMERO: I think it will have a large audience in that it will still appeal to the 14–22 audience that is going to the movies. But I hope it will appeal to a wider range. We weren't targeting at any. . . we were targeting at us, I guess. (*laugh*). We were just trying to make the movie. We really didn't have any kind of discussions about audiences while we were shooting it. I mean we had some discussions, peripherally, but nothing to do with the style of what we were doing. We weren't tailoring it to anyone.

Tongue-in-cheek? Yeah. But a New York audience sits and laughs its ass off at it. A Harrisburg audience sits and laughs at the Jordy story. . . and the rest of the time sits there and screams! It seems to play to both. I haven't really seen it yet with an audience. I've only the tape-recording of the audience at the sneak preview in Harrisburg. I wasn't there.

KING: You know the line when Hal Holbrook says, "The last time I saw something like that was in the movies." In Harrisburg, they don't laugh at that line.

Q: Would an under-24-year-old Catholic spinster like this movie. . . ?

KING: Only if she's currently taking a penicillin product.

Q: I'm pressing about your audience because George is said to have said recently, "I don't have a lot of faith in audiences anymore. . ."

ROMERO: I was quoted as having said that. I think it was out of context. I don't mean in the way they respond. What I meant was the audience doesn't go out and try movies anymore.

Q: Movies are expensive these days.

ROMERO: They respond to what's being sold to them.

Q: They're programmed?

ROMERO: They're programmed, right! When you think that *Stripes* and *Raiders* and *Superman* in the States made more than twice the money than all the rest of the product made—it's scary!

Q: If *Stripes* does that, it sure is. Ironically, one of your twin boasts is being of the TV-generation. But isn't TV the reason why today's film-goers are so programmed?

ROMERO: Probably so. TV didn't cause me to lose energy, though. It just made me thirst for more. We were watching television when television was hot, of course.

Q: Was it a hassle convincing the money men of your intuition about *Creepshow*?

ROMERO: There was a lot of interest. Almost everyone bit on the line. Largely because of Stephen.

KING: And you!

ROMERO: Well, much more because of Stephen than me.

KING: No, no! The combination was intriguing.

ROMERO: But everyone came around sort of excitedly. Then we started to hear the standard line about anthology movies haven't been successful since *Dead of Night, blah, blah, blah!* In one case, because someone owned another title, they said, "Well, if you change the title. . . we've got this title sitting in a drawer here. . . ?

Q: Which was, don't tell me. . . ?

KING: *Twilight Zone!*

Q: No kidding!

ROMERO: Yeah! They said, "Take out all this comic book bull, call it *Twilight Zone*—and here's a cheque." We said, "No, let's sit on that." So we left Los Angeles and went back to United Film Distribution, UFD. Richard and I have had a great relationship with them. They picked up *Dawn of the Dead* and released it without a rating in the States, which I was very grateful for. They financed the production of *Knightriders*—writing off the problems with the distribution of that which were not all UFD's problems.[Five days later at Cannes, Steven Spielberg announced that he, John Landis, Joe Dante and Mad Max's George Miller are shooting episodes for a film version of... *Twilight Zone.*]

Q: You've seen the Milton Subotsky anthologies, of course.

KING: That's one of the things that made it hard to get *Creepshow* off the ground. Subotsky had given us—anthology films—a bad name.

Q: Really! They're popular in Britain.

KING: They've never done particularly well in the States. I don't know how they did overseas. But they've been very lukewarm, Stateside. So, there was this idea of ours—to do an anthology film, and...

ROMERO: "Anthology films don't make money!"

KING: I don't think that is proven. I think that with *Creepshow* we have a real shot at showing that anything can work—*if it's done right!* I just don't think Subotsky ever did it right. They were kinda fun, that's all. There was no real fire, no flash to them.

ROMERO: That was my problem with them. They were *just* on the edge. They felt very much like television films.

Q: It's set more in a timeless than twilight zone. The comic book stylization, Jack Kamen's art, Jimmy Novak's lettering, even the music, has Fifties overtures; films seen on TV, the first A *Star is Born* (1937) and W. C. Fields are more Thirties. . . .

KING/ROMERO(ensemble): W. C. Fields was actually in the screenplay!

Q: ...and then we have Bela Lugosi, *Night of the Living Dead*, *Raiders*, *Clash of the Titans* and *Fade to Black* posters in Joe's room; and Leslie Nielsen plays his murder games with a video camera in *Something to Tide You Over.*

ROMERO: Right, there's not really any set period. I talked to Steve for a while about the possibility of setting it flat in the Fifties.

Q: What removes it from that is, to use a quaint euphemism: bad language. In the opening, when the father figure is yelling about Joe's horror comics—they're crap, friggin' crap. Very Fifties. From then on, frig is replaced by the inevitable four letters. You must have discussed this.

ROMERO: Yeah, we did.

KING: George is kinda in favor of removing all the bad language, or at least toning, stepping it way, way down. I kinda stuck with it because I see any concept, like our comic book concept, as something to use but never be handcuffed by. It should be a place to take off from, a launching pad. I'm still not sure if it's the right decision. I know that the comic magazines Stateside now, in the '80s, like *Heavy Metal* you'll find a lot of bad language and bare-breasted women. It's pretty open, now.

Q: Horror, horror!

KING: I know it. Well, that's the real horror. That's what we're all afraid of. A woman who takes off her top! [*laugh*]. Let's put it this way, we've had reactions from people saying blood is perfectly okay. "I don't mind my kid seeing that but I don't want to hear his ears being assaulted with that. . . eff-word!"

ROMERO: The Eff Word!

KING: [*laughing*]: We'd talked to Max von Sydow for Pratt in the bugs story, hadn't we? We'd also talked about him a little bit for "The Crate," too. And the word came back. . . I mean this is the way things go. Yes, the price is. . . er. . . obtainable. But he will not swear in the movie. Well, fine, okay. Author will write out that Eff word all the way through.

Q: Paul Morrissey and I were agreeing the other day that "bad language" works in his films because his cast are unknowns; works fine with the young set, too, De Niro, Pacino, Keitel, even Nicholson but never rings true with the oldies, Kirk Douglas, Burt Lancaster. And yet, your final Pratt, E. G. Marshall, who's 72, was perfectly at home with it. He was such a mean, Scrooge sonuvabitch, it fitted Pratt like an epithetical glove.

KING: He never even hesitated. He was right there!

ROMERO: He wanted to do it. . . after those National Geographic specials on TV.

KING: He has the most difficult lines, you know. Lines, *words*, that'd you'd expect to read in a novel rather than hear out of an actor's mouth.

ROMERO: And he's there by himself with a lotta dialogue.

KING: Thing is, he carries every word of it off.

ROMERO: Yeah, he does.

KING: He's more believable making those words sound right than other people, lesser actors would be in parts that are written more naturalistically. God, I was impressed! To watch him work, too. The way he would just *Krrackk!*—turn it on.

Q: How do you feel sitting there and watching yourself, Steve?

KING: Just real weird.

ROMERO: [*huge laugh*].

KING: I don't know, man.

ROMERO: You shouldn't be at all, Stephen.

KING: Oh, I am. I am! I feel so strange...I can understand why Lee Remick says she's never watched herself.

Q: Many stars say that, and it must be bizarre because you're so hugely larger than life. And it's not the face you see in your shaving mirror, is it?

KING: Absolutely not. I hope not! Man, that's greeeeen!

ROMERO: I think what he did with it, though, was just exactly right. It's exactly what it needed to be.

Q: How much debate went on before you two decided that Steve should play Jordy Verrill?

ROMERO: Not a lot, really. I wanted Steve to do it from the jump and he said, "Well let me think about it." I just wanted to cover him in moss. Make him itch!

KING: I always say that since I played such a total scuzzo in *Knightriders*, George decided there was an endless capacity for vapidity and stupidity there that he asked me to do it. I said Yes because it's very hard to say No to George when he wants to do something.

Q: Your comic strip saturation lighting effects are great. You worked long and hard on those, I hear. Two colors on your face, and all those backgrounds, jagged lines, spirals, lighting stabs, all on...well, not backdrops...animation, I suppose.

ROMERO: Those were backdrops, those effects were on the set, actually.

Q: Really?

ROMERO: Yeah, exactly. It's a stage technique. We could put a wash of light on the front of the scrim and bring colored lights through from behind and get our patterns. We did all those right on the set. Much easier than trying to do them optically. We could see the results straight away. You can see whether or not it works—*you have the film!* You don't have to have a piece of leader in there, taking the place of the unfinished opticals. I had enough pieces of leader as it was. A shot—leader—leader —shot—leader! It was difficult to get a sense if the film was playing because all the opticals we needed were in a lab someplace. And the matte paintings. All of that. You know, I've never shot anything that wasn't there before.

Q: How did the actors cope—their heads were clamped firmly in place like in the Victorian photographic studios?

ROMERO: No, the screens were big. They had to be on marks and they had to stay in place. But it was much easier to do it that way. They all had fun doing that.

KING: It was like posing for stills.

ROMERO: Steve had one of those scrims. There were like about 14 dimmers on your shot, because the light had to change so much on your shot.

KING: That was like the last thing we did—and I was wild to get out and go home! But some of the dimmers weren't working very well . . . . I think everybody did one of those things—and in three or four takes. I don't know about Adrienne. I wasn't there when she did hers.

ROMERO: That's all it was, three or four takes.

KING: It worked pretty well. I thought they looked great.

Q: As per your grand design. You may not have thought, first of all about backdrops, but you wanted this kind of comic-book backgrounds —and the strip animation openers and panels effect. The panels were splendid. Particularly the first with Aunt Bedelia's car arriving in long-shots and close-ups, five shots on the same screen.

ROMERO: The car, yeah—well, I'm glad that works for you. I was concerned about it. But I said, Hey, let's go for it. Steve backed me up on it. . .

KING: Sure.

ROMERO: . . . and we let it fly. I hope it does work.

Q: One positive difference, and maybe a problem, was working with name actors for the first time.

ROMERO: Yeah, I was up-tight about that. Intimidated.

Q: Why? They all worked well.

ROMERO: Well, we talked a lot about the types of people we wanted and discussed each individual as the names came up. And, yes, we're really happy with them.

Q: How did you choose the cast?

KING: We had boundaries. The budget itself dictated certain choices—

not this person and that person, but another. I can't remember anybody specific, but let's say X actor—and I'm not, you know, not trying to say names, I just can't remember. But X Actor would be fifty or a hundred thousands dollars out of our reach in terms of budget. They would have broken the budget so we had that to think about. I think from the jump that both George and I went for guys who have a reputation for working fast and well and honestly. Guys that just are good, workmanlike actors, who maybe don't have the Burt Reynolds reputation, the people that you would nominate for The Strother Martin Award!

Q: Or the L. Q. Jones Trophy?

KING: That's right. Character actors. Then, you also have guys like Fritz Weaver and Hal Holbrook, people who are above that. George was saying the other night that it'd be great to work with Fritz again, be great to work with Adrienne again another time.

ROMERO: Everybody had a good time. As Steve says, we didn't cast it to make a deal from it. We cast it from people—it was a protection factor.

Q: If you were up-tight about the cast, George, were they nervous?

ROMERO: Perhaps, I don't know.

Q: Obviously Adrienne knew who you were, maybe Holbrook too as he's been through Carpenter country, but what about Fritz, E. G. Marshall, Leslie Nielsen and the others?

ROMERO: Well, most of them knew *Night of the Living Dead* and had *heard* the title *Dawn of the Dead,* but had probably not bothered to go see it. I think a few of them came in with reservations, thinking, "My God, I'm going to Pittsburgh—what am I getting into here?"

KING: I'd never worked with stars any more than George had. My experience with stars was, you know, at a supermarket opening. I took my son, Joe, to meet Batman! So at the beginning of the thing, I was depressed. Then, Viveca Lindfors came in. I'd seen a lot of her movies and I said, "I'm Steve King, and it's wonderful to meet you." And she said, "It's very nice to meet you, young man. Is it tunafish or egg today?" She thought I was the caterer!

ROMERO: [*bellows with laughter*].

KING: And that sort of misinformation, misapprehension went on for about three days. So, what I did was, I got her the sandwiches... which added to it. See, she was dubious, too. She didn't know us. She said, "I've never been killed by a monster in a movie before," and this sorta thing. She didn't know. . . . She thought George was all cut and hack and slash, it took her awhile to warm up, but when she did she was terrific.

ROMERO: Most of them had fears about, you know, "I've gotta get out of here and fire my agent next week." Only because they didn't know what we'd be up to. I think had it just been me, it would have been more difficult, but because Stephen's attachment to the project, it made it a lot easier.

Q: Well, sure. Every movie needs a good caterer. . . . I hadn't realized the terror of the graveyard, Viveca Lindfors, has been working so much in America recently, so I had wondered. . . why her?

ROMERO: Most recently she was in *The Hand* and she looked pretty good. And we need an Aunt Bedelia. That was actually the toughest part to cast. Unless you go with Ruth Gordon, there aren't a lot of character women around.

Q: Ruth Gordon would have killed the monster. Talked him to death. But Viveca, of course, used to be married to Don Siegel and goes way back to Joe Losey's *The Damned* (1963).

ROMERO: She goes back to Errol Flynn, *The Adventures of Don Juan*.

Q: Don't know about you, but the grandstand actor for me in the entire movie was Fritz Weaver in "The Crate."

KING: Oh, right. He was wonderful. Wow!

Q: When he comes out of the cellar having seen the Thing, bumps into the kid in the corridor and goes completely inarticulate, he was. . .

ROMERO: Extraordinary!

Q: I don't know how much of what he's trying to say, is as per script or improvised.

KING: The lines are exactly verbatim. But the way he did it! I'd read somewhere he'd said, "I don't want to see the creature until he pops out. I want a reaction that's 100% genuine." So that's what he did.

ROMERO: He's an incredible craftsman. Amazing. Watching him, sitting near him and watching him work is incredible.

KING: And what a gentleman!

ROMERO: Even when I'm doing handshots of him with the little chess pieces, he's in such control of his body and his voice. I was knocked out. *Knocked out!* The other real big revelation for me was putting someone who was doing such a big, theatrically technical performance like Fritz next to someone like Holbrook—whose performance I never saw until I got him twenty feet high. Because even sitting across the table from Hal, you don't see him working. And yet it works. Yeah, but those two styles together: I thought we were in trouble until I started to cut it together.

Q: So as well as all the jumps we have Tom Savini to thank for Fritz Weaver's astonishing performance. Tom made the creature, of course.

ROMERO: Of course! Well, Tom is a very close friend of mine and we work very well together. I just love Tom's work in *Creepshow*. Tom has a chance to do more than just *body-wounds*! He gets to show his stuff a little bit.

Q: How did it work—hydraulics, puppetry or both?

ROMERO: The costume was built and worn by an actor and controlled by several technicians. So, the top of it, the arms, are the principal actor. His head is in the face mask, his eyes are seen through it. And the rest of the snout comes out. The cheek and lip movements and everything else are controlled by hydraulics, outside the costume... and its feet were worked by other people as puppets. We were actually able to make him scurry across the floor at one point. We dug a hole in the floor of the gymnasium and we had these collapsible sliding floor panels, so that when he walked, the creature's feet, above the actor's waist, were being operated like puppets and the actor is halfway under the floor. We decided to just 86 that. There's quick shot of it, but you can't really see it well.

Q: Tom gave up his directing debut *Night of the Burning Moon*, to do *Creepshow*. Is that right, hype or was his movie postponed?

ROMERO: I don't think it was entirely postponed. I shouldn't be presumptuous enough to talk about it, except that I think it was a sort of frivolous offer on the part of William Friedkin. I gather Tom went back to him and said, "Look I really wanna do *Creepshow*; can't we arrange things?" And there was no deal. There wasn't even a script! All Tom was asking for was four months and it came down to one of those awful scenes—"If you do this, you'll never be working on this waterfront again."

Q: No wonder you guys stay in Pittsburgh and Maine. . . . The bugs episode must have presented the most problems in shooting.

ROMERO: Actually, no. It was the most unpleasant! But not the most difficult. It was a small set, easier to light—and one actor. "The Crate" was the most difficult, the most involved; we had to keep moving the walls all the time. "Father's Day" was tough because it was all location. And "The Tide" was not easy.

Q: What's all this about needing your own method of making waves on the beach. Didn't you just use a New Jersey beach, and shoot down low?

KING: We weren't allowed to drown actors. Too bad. There's a lot that deserve it.

ROMERO: No, it's something that I'm sure none of us thought about until Cletus said, "You know you can't really bury someone in the sand below the high tide line and wait for the tide to cover them." And we said, "Oh my god, yeah...!" So we worked up the beach a little and lots of people came up with these wave-making machines. They were like *The Guns of Navarone*! The size of a flight of stairs. They had three huge water-chambers in each one. They'd give you a single shot, a double—all the way to six shots, or waves, which would completely cover the actors. And boy, those actors were game.

KING: The woman and Ted Danson? Oh yeah!

Q: The woman is Gaylen Ross—Fran in *Dawn of the Dead*. She's up another end of the beach, also buried up to her chin and awaiting drowning like her love—some reward for surviving *Dawn*! Yet we see her only in black and white on Leslie Nielsen's video monitors. Did you shoot her on film or some form of video-transfer?

ROMERO: We shot all film. Then we went to videotape and back from videotape to film, just to denigrate, break up the image a little...and out the video lines on. Then, we matted it into the TV sets. We couldn't use real video—we were outdoors, again—and we needed all six monitors for the interior set. So there was really no way to do it all with video.

Q: You two love scaring people, right? So come clean now—what was the first movie to really scare the pants off you?

KING: *The Creature from the Black Lagoon*. That was terrible!

ROMERO: The original *Frankenstein*, which I saw as a kid on a re-issue with, I guess, *Bride of Frankenstein*. The scene with the tramp, that shook me up. But the first to knock me out was *The Thing*.

KING: See, I'm exactly two years younger!

Q: As your producer, Richard Rubinstein, told us, it was Warner Brothers that brought you two together. It's still difficult to credit such common sense—even though they also let you get away!

ROMERO: I don't think they were think in those terms right way. They were looking for somebody to make *'Salem's Lot*. Christ, how many screenplays were written for *that*?

KING: Five or six.

ROMERO: They got in way over their heads on story costs. Somebody from Warners had seen *Martin* at a festival and in inimitable studio fashion saw the connections—vampires in a small town! What they saw in Richard and I was an ability. So, basically they said, "Can you take this, here are all six scripts"—and I'm going *'Salem's Lot*!—"Go talk to Steve. Make the movie and come back in six months." And I'm going, "Yeah, Yeah, YEAH! You mean I don't have to work here? I don't have to use Studio C? Great!" They just wanted somebody to make it—fast. Because they had this incredible investment in story costs.

And they were worried about all these vampire movies coming out. They wanted instant-movie. And it was going to be a negative pick-up deal or whatever. So I called Stephen and Steve said. . .

KING: I dropped my pants. . . ! I mean, I couldn't *believe* it, man! I just walked in and said, "Do you know who called me on the phone today? George fucking Romero. . . called me on the telephone. You hear me." And Tabby said, "Who's that?" And I said, "*Night of the Living Dead* . . . the movie you walked out of because you were so scared."

ROMERO: Well, you're kind to say that stuff. Actually, I was doing that on the other end. I said, *Stephen King*!!

KING: I was so excited man! That was really somethin'. People would come to laugh at *Night of the Living Dead*. This was in the old days before it became a "cult." And they'd be stunned to silence. About halfway through the film, all the joking would stop and they would be *stunned* to silence. These college kids who were supposed to be smart asses, they'd be sitting there. . . . I mean, there were girls who were literally being helped out by their boyfriends with their faces deadly white.

Q: And the girls didn't look too hot, either!

KING: It wasn't just from sickness. It was from terror. It's a terrifying situation in that film. That house was so relentless. What an awful place. There were so many ways to get in!

ROMERO: Well. . . I read a couple of those screenplays of *'Salem's Lot*. One of them was ludicrous. The one with the snakes and all of that. I don't know who did that one?

Q: Who did do them?

KING: Stirling Silliphant. . . .

ROMERO: Larry Cohen, Paul Monash.

Q: He produced *Carrie*.

KING: Yeah, Monash did the one that was produced finally. But even that was hybrid.

Q: Did you watch it on the tube?

KING: Oh yeah. Now listen: This is an interesting case and George would agree with this. The man who produced *'Salem's Lot* for TV is someone that is very like a genius. He may be the last one left in American TV. I would imagine that Blake Edwards was much like him when he was in TV. His name is Richard Kobritz and among other things, he got a director named John Carpenter, that no one had heard of because it was pre-*Halloween*, to do a picture with Lauren Hutton called *Someone Is Watching Me!* One of the best suspense films ever made for American TV with the exception maybe of Spielberg's *Duel*.

So when he didn't get George when he succeeded to this property for TV, he got Tobe Hooper. And the movie was mistaken. It's wrong in a lot of ways. But I like it much better than *The Shining*. It's got this sick, feverish energy that is running through it. And there's things in there that are the way I think you would have shot them, George. Like when the woman wakes up, you know, in the morgue. . . I don't even know if you saw it.

ROMERO: I saw it. I liked it a lot. I thought it was the best translation of your stuff.

KING: Yeah! And she sits up and he slashes her hand. Have you seen it by any chance?

Q: Only the movie release version.

KING: It works pretty well. I like the movie version better. It seems tighter.

Q: No lead-in commercials, no continual climaxes like that.

ROMERO: I agree with you. The biggest problem I had with it was that the vampire wasn't the lord. The vampire was an attack dog for James Mason.

KING: I know. . . and it looked like *Nosferatu*. It was just a dreadful steal on the makeup. That *was* bad.

Q: Right—now to the big question. What's the situation report on *The Stand*?

KING: We had some talk about doing two, like *Superman I* and *II*.

Shoot them together and then release them a little bit apart. But actually shooting them as one complete movie and just splitting them because of length.

ROMERO: It's a tough problem. It really needs to be a long film—and that's expensive. And this is the wrong time to be pitching a long, expensive movie!

Q: So, as usual, money is the villain: fifteen million dollars, I gather.

KING: No, the major roadblock is screenplay, I think. We're not talking or thinking about budget at this point.

ROMERO: Well, the screenplay isn't a roadblock in that sense at all. We haven't tried to pitch the project yet. We have, on that level, been waiting to see what happens with *Creepshow*. . . . and waiting to see what happens with the business. I mean, my God—*what* do you do? Do you go for length and go for cable television? Do you just make half of it as an individual picture? So many problems. And the biggest is the delivery mechanism, that's really tough. Yeah, if somebody could say, "Hey guys, we'll let you make a three hour film, here's the check" then we would seriously sit down and try to go that way.

Q: So it's not money holding things up—but a backer. But that's money, isn't it?

KING: Ironically, after two drafts of the screenplay, it doesn't look like the expensive movie that everybody seems to think it would be. The biggest problem that I saw, as I told George, is trying to make Las Vegas look deserted—that's a 24-hour town! You can shoot New York at dawn, at 5 a.m. like they did in *The World, The Flesh and The Devil* and make the entire city look totally deserted.

Q: But Vegas is on the go 24 hours around the clock!

KING: Right. But then, Richard, George's partner, found out that Francis Ford Coppola has a scale model of Las Vegas left over from *One from the Heart* and he's going to rent it out from. . .what is it?. . . Zoetrope Studios? So there's a possibility there. And the rest of the film looks a lot like a biker movie from the Sixties. A lotta guys riding around on motorcycles.

Q: Wouldn't Coppola's model be part of his studio sale, though?

ROMERO: Well, that's the problem now. . .!

Q: You may have to buy the whole damn studio just to get the model!

ROMERO: The full twenty million dollars.

KING: Oh, we can afford *that*!

ROMERO: I don't want to get in a deal where they say, "Hey guys, it's gotta be two hours. . . 2:15 tops. You gotta have a cast that justifies these bucks. You gotta do this, you gotta do that." You spend most of your time trying to build as many walls as you can against those kinda things. Then, you have to decide when you're gonna let one crack through.

Q: The first compromise—is rarely the last. . . .

ROMERO: You spend your first ten years in the business trying to figure out how to cover your ass in a contract. Then, you get a little bit hot and you spend the next ten years finding out all the ways they can get you to *relinquish* those clauses. You know the companies they come at you. "I know that you signed this contract and I know that you have this clause BUT. . . look here. . . this is all for the general good, isn't it?" And you're being the sonuvabitch, after all.

KING: But people don't brood over things like that. Like what they did to the book, what they did to the short story or whatever. Man, life's too short to worry about that.

ROMERO: It's too short to brood over, but it's. . .

KING: . . . not too short to get even, of course!

ROMERO: Right!

KING: I believe in that!

ROMERO: Or certainly to campaign against it. It's madness. It's madness! Like the five or six screenplays written on *'Salem's Lot*.

Q: I'm beginning to wonder if *The Stand* will ever be made. . . .

KING: The ideal scenario would be that *Creepshow* goes through the roof and then we've proved ourselves. They'd give us the money to make *The Stand*. And then we could break it in two and do a movie that would be called *The Stand/The Plague*. It would be a little bit like Bakshi's *Lord of the Rings*. . . .

ROMERO: Yeah, well except the first one of his wasn't successful so the second half was never made. But we'd make the first half for a reasonable budget, release it—it would be a tremendous hit and we could do the second half.

KING: And we wouldn't have to worry about Las Vegas until. . .

ROMERO: . . . the tunnel scene!

KING: No, you've got friends in Pittsburgh. We do it in the Squirrel Hill Tunnel. Hell, that's closed half the time, George.

ROMERO: That's true.

Q: But there's your next headache. If *Creepshow* is very successful, won't everyone, your backers included, want a *Creepshow II*?

ROMERO: Yeah, but I don't have a problem with that. Because I'd *love* to do it, if it happens. I'd love to just go that extra bit.

KING: What's this—*Creepshow II*? Yeah, oh man, I'd love to write it.

Q: If you did that, it would take the place of *The Stand* and push that even further into limbo.

ROMERO: It would depend.

Q: The longer you wait, the more expensive *The Stand* is bound to become, Coppola's models or no models.

ROMERO: That also depends. . . . Maybe we should wait until it actually happens and get a lot of footage from ABC News.

KING: Right. We'll wait until Las Vegas is deserted! The black marble ashtray. Is there any significance in a black marble ashtray?

KING: How did you know about that? Did somebody tell you?

Q: I saw it in the first one that she used, it was a murder weapon, and in the second one it was in his nightstand and then I stopped looking for it.

KING: It's there in all of 'em. They just thought that it would be funny. I didn't realize it myself. Then they started talking about the killer ashtray. And I said, "What's that?" And George said, "Well, the grips are putting it in every one." It's somewhere in the Jordy story.

Q: I was looking for it for about two minutes and then after you said "meteor shit" I didn't see it.

KING: Meteor shit. That gives you a big womp.

Q: I want to ask a formal question. Have you been gun shy about making any movies since Kubrick's ill-fated version of *The Shining*?

KING: No, I mean it's just making anything, having anything to do with stuff that's made from a book, has started to really turn me off. There's so much crap involved. They are so many different personalities. And particularly if it's something that goes for a lot of money, up front or if there's a big pre-production thing. When I say up front, I don't mean just what I get. I mean whatever I got, Kubrick got more, Nicholson got more, and pretty soon you got twelve people saying, "Well, we can't let somebody unimportant like the writer fuck this up. We got to go with—"

Q: They got to let the guy who's getting a lot of money screw it.

KING: Yeah, that's right.

Q: Is that why you prefer to go with someone like George Romero who's become a friend of yours now, too?

KING: Yeah, George is a great guy.

Q: You have a lot in common.

KING: Yeah.

Q: Who is more concerned with bringing across on the screen exactly what you wanted to be there—

KING: Well, I don't even want that. I don't—he does. He has a big respect for that. We got into a situation on *Creepshow* that's the exact flip-flop of any writer/director relationship I've ever heard of. In the cutting process, the first cut, *Creepshow* came in at like two hours and twenty minutes. And then it came in at 2:10 and we were both happy about 2:10. But UFD, United Film, who had the thing for Warner Brothers, they weren't happy about 2:10. They wanted two hours, because they still feel like they got their fingers burned on *Knightriders*, which came in longer. So I go into Pittsburgh, right. We're trying to get that last ten minutes out. And here we are arguing this way. I'm saying, "This can go. It's just a bunch of guys sitting around talking." And George is saying, "No! That can't go. That's really important. You gotta keep that in." So instead of him saying "We can get rid of this," I was saying it.

Q: So he had director's cut and you had writer's cut?

KING: Yeah, except we finally just got it together and we did it the way that George wanted to pretty much, which is to just chafe it. You can almost not tell the difference between 2:10 and whatever it is now. I think it's like 1:58 or something.

Q: Is that a problem with *The Stand* now? You guys are working on that?

KING: Length is a problem. Again, it's a problem because like the last time George and I talked about it, I said, "Okay, this is what we've got. It's been through two drafts now and now it's down to a length of what would probably be in shooting time about four hours." In other words, 40 minutes longer than *Godfather II*. So I say, "Okay, we're at this point where we gotta lighten this boat, George. We gotta throw some people overboard. Who's expendable?" And he says, "Well, let me think about it." So he thought about it and I thought about it and I came back to him. And there's this little kid in the book who's kind of a deaf mute kid and pals around with one of the characters. And I said, "Well—

Q: The guy in the jail, the kid in the jail?

KING: No, there's this, he's not a deaf mute, that's Nick. This kid is like autistic. His name's Joe.

Q: Oh, yeah.

KING: I said, "Well, Joe can go." And George kind of says, "Well, I like him." We tried to get rid of a couple of people and they didn't want to stay down. So that's where we are and we're trying to decide what to do next. We've got some places to go now with it.

Q: Is it hard for you to let go of those guys?

KING: Yeah, sometimes, sometimes it is. And mostly it's because as the writer of the book, it's hard to see alternate ways to get across some plot things that you wanted that these guys were advancing. So we're getting it together on that. But the thing about *Creepshow* is that it was original to start with. There was no book. There was nobody trying to say, "Well, you gotta do this, that, and the other thing," and all the rest of it.

Q: Nobody to lose.

KING: *Cujo* we're shooting now and I did a screenplay for *Cujo*. And it was Taft International, they did *The Boogens*. And I said, "How do you want it? Do you want to shoot it quick?" And they said, "Yeah, we want to shoot it quick." I said, "Do you want to shoot it cheap?" And they said, "Yeah, we wanna shoot it cheap." Okay. So I went out and I did a screenplay and I had *Creepshow* for experience, and I brought 'em in a nice, cheap thing. In the meantime, they'd made a production deal with UA or Twentieth or something like that and I'm not bitching because they got the screenplay rewritten. It's a lot better than mine 'cause it's the book.

Q: So someone rewrote it and put more back into it?

KING: Yeah. They just went back to the book. And I was tapped in. They called me up and said, "Do you want to do this job?" And I said, "Not particularly. I've got other commitments now. I did it once."

Q: Well, it seems ironic to me that some of the smaller companies would want to take your work and assume, first of all, that it's going to be a low budget, short screenplay and immediately it's picked up by a larger studio. It seems obvious to me—there already is an audience out there.

KING: Yeah, but that doesn't matter.

Q: But I think they're starting to recognize that now, too.

KING: I hope so. I liked to see *Creepshow* go through the roof, mostly because then George and I could do *The Stand*. That was the major idea to begin with, that we do this thing and this thing would be low budget and this thing kind of started to swell. We got a cast, they're great. On the other hand, I'm not sure that people are drawn out of their houses to the movies because there's a picture down there starring Fritz Weaver and Carrie Nye, people like that. I don't think that happens. So we could have gone with unknowns, but that isn't what he wanted. As a result, the budget went up to eight million. The effects are better than in any of George's other pictures. They're not the same sort of effects that Savini's done before. And they're not certainly the kind of things that this—does he say it Bo-teen, Rob Bottin?

Q: Rob Bottin, yeah.

KING: —has done. It's different stuff.

Q: Was it disappointing for you? The effects?

KING: Not particularly. There are some things that didn't work, but the thing like with the bugs in "They're Creeping Up on You," just incredible.

Q: Yes.

KING: There are things with the monster in the crate that —people ran out in Providence when they tested it. They ran out and threw up. I loved it.

Q: Are they gruesome enough for you? Is the corpse in "Father's Day" gruesome enough? Are the corpses that—

KING: Yeah. The thing with the corpse, we had John Aplus, who was in *Dead Naked* and he was in *Martin*. And he was doing it and everything was fine and George says it's time for the takes with the maggots. And John said, "Uh-uh. I'm not doing the maggots. You get somebody else. You want maggots, not me." So there was a little girl, production assistant, slimmer than you are, and she was, not an entomologist, but she'd had things to do with bugs before. And so she said, "Sure, pour 'em all over me." So they did. They just squirmed and they were great.

Q: And she was lying there with the head mask on her. That was her underneath that?

KING: Yeah. But we've got, this is not with E. G. and the cockroaches. This is "Father's Day" with all the maggots. But, you know, as far as gruesome goes, we've gotten into things now with the ratings. It used to be that horror movies were scary because you didn't know how far this fucker was going to go. You might go all the way. But now, people who go to horror movies regularly know exactly what R means. They know, well, okay, like *Dawn of the Dead* where the zombie, the top of his head comes off in the helicopter and it's just one thing after another. There's people chopping other people up and the rest of it. And in an R–rated picture you can't go that far. And I think that audiences are starting to know that, so that—

Q: There's a certain flavor to *Creepshow* that's different than any other horror movie I've seen, possibly with the exception of the old classic *Little Shop of Horrors*. There's a certain humor that goes along with having fun with the movie that sets you up.

KING: I think it's pretty funny. It wasn't funny on purpose. I think that we both just got comic book motif, the E.C.s and stuff, a lot of those stories were funny. I mean, they had puns for titles and—

Q: Heh-heh-heh.

KING: Heh-heh-heh, yeah. "Irony is Good for Your Blood"—

Q: *It Came for a Drink.*

KING: *We Came for a Drink,* right. So we tried to get some of that in there, but we didn't really try; it was just there. That Jordy Verrill story's outrageous. It was outrageous to begin with, but George kept making it more and more outrageous and he was telling me what he wanted in terms of real, I mean this guy's not there upstairs; nothing ticking but his watch. And I still wasn't getting it. And he said, "Well, you know how the coyote looks just before he falls. When he runs out, he's—" And I said, "Yeah." He said, "That's the way this guy is all the time."

Q: It was very broad. Whose idea was it for you to play that part? Did you write that for yourself?

KING: It was George's idea.

Q: You didn't write that for yourself?

KING: No.

Q: Did you try to do it seriously the first couple of times through?

KING: No, I never tried that at all. I mean, you couldn't when you saw some of the stuff that got cut from it, when he's looking for a bucket to dump the water on the meteor and they had, this was the first night, and thay had a bucket that had a hole in it and Jordy's looking at the sky and there's water going right through the bucket. That was a riot. There was never any question about that. The only thing that George wanted that was probably dangerous about it was to try and little by little bring in a feeling that this guy really is trapped and he's really going to die and then all at once maybe it's not so funny anymore.

Q: That worked pretty well. By the time he went to take his bath you really got that.

KING: He's the only one that really isn't E.C. in the sense that the morality is bad. Everybody else that gets killed, it's like—

Q: You can't say anything funny, and then it's over.

KING: Yeah.

Q: The humor is pathetic. The pathos is a type of humor which can be turned very quickly into very serious sadness.

KING: Yeah. Although I would argue that what we feel is not serious sadness and it's not tragedy. It's more in the line of tear-jerking than that kind of melodrama. But that's okay, too.

Q: Nervous reaction to our fears.

KING: But that was so dreadful to see for the first time, when it blows his head off. And they'd coated the suit he wore. I wasn't inside. It was this guy, Tom's assistant, Darryl, and when he popped the shotgun the first time, the suit caught on fire and Darryl was inside.

Q: I loved the movie because I'm an old E.C. fan.

KING: God love ya. God love ya.

Q: —and those were the days when you kept them hidden in the drawer or put another magazine over the top, or hid them even worse than that so your folks wouldn't see 'em.

KING: I can remember some that were worse than the E.C.s. Cleavers through people's heads, and the brains falling out and everything.

Q: All very graphic.

KING: My mom didn't say too much and then when the nightmares started, she said, "That's it," and they'd all disappear like they'd all walked away. So I went out and got more.

Q: I hear ya. In each of the *Creepshow* episodes, one of the main characters, at least one, makes an error, a fatal error in judgment that eventually leads to their undoing. Is this kind of device a crucial element to a good horror plot?

KING: I don't know. I never even thought of it. I suppose that any kind of plot almost always hinges on some kind of error.

Q: Like the old E.C. comics, the episodes of *Creepshow* seem to be vignette morality plays—

KING: Yep.

Q: —with dire consequences for deserving characters. Well, you could just talk about that, but do you have any favorite human weaknesses that you like to dig at, things that bother you?

KING: Greed, avarice, self involvement. You want my E.C. rap?

Q: Yeah, you bet.

KING: I'll give you my E.C. rap. My E.C. rap is that all the stories used to be this way; the guilty are punished. And this is heavier than E.C. comics deserves, but in a way it isn't, you know, I can excuse it that way. Guilt was always punished. That was the American, that was our view of morality. Even in the novels and the books and things that we thought of as being great literature and stuff, it tended to be that way. And then in World War I and World War II we started the idea that although supposedly the cause of good won in both cases, like there were people who got their guts blown out, there were people who died of inhaling gases, the murder of the Jews, you know, five million Jews, and you have to keep in mind that the people who are doing this up until the time of the Holocaust, people like Williams Gaines and Al Faustein, these guys are Jewish. And to me, I don't know what they say, I never asked them about it, but it's significant to me that it stopped being Biblical comics and started being horror comics after the Holocaust and after the news came out. And to me, I always saw 'em like the last gasp of this romantic idea that evil is punished by forces of good and they couldn't even justify all this old bullshit anymore about how it really happens, because what you have in a lot of E.C. comics is the wife really does kill her husband and really does run off with her lover. They bash the poor guy in the head and drop him into a lake with bricks wired to his feet. They'd get away with it. It's just that you have to at that point go into the supernatural to get the scales put back in balance.

Q: Sure, but just say, like in the movie, that poor janitor who wouldn't hurt a fly, who's the most harmless character in the whole film, is brutally mutilated, massacred.

KING: I explain it two ways. Or I justify it in two ways.

Q: You don't have to, it's not—

KING: I know, I know. I understand, but it's a good point that you raise. The first thing is that when I did it, I wasn't going one-to-one to the comic books. In fact, I was a little bit afraid to try too much for an E.C. flavor for fear that we might get sued. They're great guys and I don't think they'd do that particularly because it's a kind of thing where one idea calls up another. We didn't rip off, I don't believe, any of their story ideas *per se*. So that was it. And that time I thought we were still going for a kind of real vignette feel, almost like horror blackouts. And the second thing is that since the E.C.s, twenty years have gone by and I no longer even cling to the idea that only the guilty get punished. The good get punished right along with the bad. I mean, all those kids they dug up out of John Wayne Gacy's basement, what did they ever do? And they didn't even come back from the dead to get him.

Q: That's the only thing that bothers me all along about horror films.

KING: The good get—

Q: I have a pretty strong stomach. I loved *The Exorcist*, I loved *Jaws*, and not because they had happy endings, but they really dealt with, particularly *The Exorcist*, with real problems. What is it about this trend in the horror films that there's a, no reason—

KING: I know what you're saying.

Q: Gore for gore's sake.

KING: Yeah, I think there's less of that in *Creepshow* than there is—nobody turns on the chain saw in this picture and there isn't a knife. There's not a stabbing in the picture.

Q: They're morally motivated like the old E.C. comics.

KING: To a degree.

Q: Most of the hacker slasher movies that have been out it becomes some girl who's loose morally gets it and she should deserve it because she's a loose woman.

KING: Well, I think that some of the people who go and see the hacker movies are also people who would like to go out and do that exact thing and don't have the guts to do it. That is to say, they would like to get a woman alone and probably—you know, some of them are pretty tabloidish films. They're pretty graphic and they're blunt. There don't seem to be any real twists. The worse one I ever saw was *The Toolbox Murders*. But there's a part of me that, well. . . there's a guy who gets a girl at one point with a nailer, one of these gadgets, right in the forehead. But there's a part of me that reacts to that and says, "Oh, my God, that's awful. Let's do it again."

But you know the E.C.s, too, are like fairy tales. That's the real root of them. Graham Ingles that used to draw for them could have illustrated a book of Grimm's Fairy Tales or something. So they have that feeling of, I mean Leslie Nielsen is a real bad guy. Nobody's sorry to see what happens to him.

Q: When it starts off you don't realize what a maniac he is.

KING: Yeah.

Q: And it's wonderful because he's raving at the end. There's finally no one around but himself and he lets it loose.

KING: Let me suggest to you, too, that nobody in *Creepshow* who is good is killed on purpose. It's sort of undirected forces.

Q: But they do make poor decisions.

KING: Yeah.

Q: I wouldn't touch the meteor shit, not in a million years.

KING: But he's real stupid, I mean, that's the way that I justify it.

Q: You were quoted as saying, and I can't remember where, so what the hell good does that do to say that, but I remember this from someplace. You were talking about *Creepshow* before it was out, that the power of the movie would be in the dialogue, that the dialogue would be the most important part of it. Since I've seen the movie I know what you mean now. Did you write the screenplay with humor intended, in mind, or what was the angle that you had when you decided—

KING: Not intended, not exactly intended. I knew it would be funny, that some of the stuff would be funny. I think there are two kinds of laughs. One is the kind of laugh like Mel Brooks gets, because he says something funny. It's like when Gene Wilder stabs himself in the leg with the scalpel in *Young Frankenstein*, he says, "This is doo-doo!" You laugh because he said doo-doo. That's real funny. But the other kind is, the audience laughs in recognition because this is what they would say in that circumstance. And that kind of laugh very rarely comes up in a horror movie because they're saying things like "I'm going to get you, you little dinglebutt," or whatever it is, which is funny but funny the wrong way. So that, it seems to me, that when we saw the film in Providence with an audience, the audience laughed very hard when Hal Holbrook starts to laugh down in the cellar.

Q: Yeah, when he's trying not to laugh.

KING: Which is not, he's just cleaned up all this blood and the laughter is a hysterical laughter and that whole scene in the story was patterned after Poe's "The Cask of Amontillado" where the guy's—

Q: Laughing madly as he laying the bricks. It was very unexpected.

KING: But there's a lot of visual stuff in there, too. If I said—it sounds too conceited, it sounds more conceited than I want to sound, as though the script were more important than the direction or other parts of the film that are just as important or more important in most cases. And if I said it, I said it before the thing was visualized because I think the staging is even better than the special effects. Cletus Anderson's set design and all that. But I guess I was just trying to say in perspective, well, look, writing in most horror films, you know, *Blood Beach* and all of this stuff is generally speaking written by people who are lawyers. The guy who wrote *Friday the 13th* is a lawyer, Victor Miller or whatever his name is. They're not writers.

Q: It makes you wonder what's bottled inside.

KING: Well, there just has to be something else to say besides "I'll think I'll go out and take a look around."

*   *   *

ROMERO: So what's going on here?

KING: Talking about philosophy, E.C., horror stories.

Q: How much tougher is it to write exclusively for the screen?

KING: I did it and then George took it and did the equivalent of 'boarding it, not with pictures and stuff, but actually breaking it down. And I was there a lot and because it was nothing that was set in print to begin with, I didn't feel any problems if somebody called me up and said, "We got a problem with this," that was fine. I was there, even the stuff like the TV takes. At least where we had to use something else, we used *my* something else. So that he doesn't say "meteor shit" for TV, he says meteor crud or something like that.

ROMERO: You know that they're on our—you know that we're going to have to make some more changes evidently.

KING: For TV you mean?

ROMERO: You know they're not going to allow the word "God." Tell me about it.

KING: It's gawd dang.

ROMERO: You can say "oh my God" in a gangster movie, I think.

Q: Or a soap opera.

KING: You know what happened—this will appeal to you. We asked if we could have a benefit showing in Bangor and Warner Brothers said

"Yeah." So, then it was like who do you wanna do the benefit for because there are a lot of worthy causes. And I finally said, "I don't know," and Stephanie said, "What about St. Josephs," which is the poor relation hospital in Bangor, the Catholic hospital. They never have enough money. I said, "Fine." Then we get the call. "How bad is the language in this? How much blood is there in this?" I said "Stephanie, start looking for another charity quick." They did pass on us.

ROMERO: They don't want *that* kind of money, Steve.

KING: Right, that's *dirty* money.

Q: In *Different Seasons* there's a short story called "The Body" about a boy who seems to be possessed by a desire to write. Is that autobiographical in any way?

KING: It's autobiographical, but there's a piece by John Irving in the *Times Book Review* a couple of weeks ago saying nobody lies as much in their autobiography as a writer. You have to take that into consideration, too. And it isn't conscious lying. It isn't lying like saying I'll pretty this up. It isn't cosmetic lying. What it is, is he'd say, "This is a good story. This is something that happened to me when I was ten." And you're no longer looking at it as something that happened to you when you were ten. You're saying this is a good story. The only thing is, it doesn't have a good enough climax, but if I say this happened, which is what should have happened, and if I say this 'cause it's what I should have said, it'll be a better story.

I've had a chance to say some things about myself and most of 'em are lies.

Q: It seems like the film career of your written work is picking up more and more, all at once it sounds like they're a lot of screenplays going on at one time. You're writing some, other people are rewriting some. You're just writing them from scratch.

KING: I'll tell you, I did two last winter. I called them my double feature. It's true, I did the screenplay for *Cujo* in about a week. And then I did the screenplay for *Dead Zone* in about two weeks. And I thought the screenplay for *Dead Zone* was the best that I've ever done in terms of adaptation. And they started talking first to Michael Cimino, who wanted Johnny Smith to come from Texas and show his sensitivity by talking to horses and I said no, I didn't think so. So it was Dino De Laurentiis and back and forth. This is what I'm talking about, the adaptation, what makes it difficult. You can't just turn in a script and be done with it or go to work on it. It's gotta be something else. So I did screenplays for both and the Taft people, when they got the extra bucks from United Artists, whoever it is, went ahead and commissioned another screenplay. And the irony is that the screenplay they commissioned is much closer than the book to my original one. And I think that David Cronenberg is going to direct *Dead Zone* and he'll do his own screenplay. The guy who's doing *Cujo* is a good director. He's the guy who did *The Changeling* and—

Q: Oh, that's a great movie—

KING: Peter Maydock, I've forgotten his name—

Q: British.

KING: He's good. He's fine. And Cronenberg is good and he's very, very smart. But I just as soon not do it anymore. I'm adapting *The Stand* because I love it and I'm not tired of it.

Q: Is that the one you most like out of all of them? Make the best, a good movie?

KING: It's the biggest challenge, isn't it? Really.

Q: I assume you have expectations about how it's going to look.

KING: I'm not involved in that sense. You can break your heart if you worry about that. The book is there. Like some interviewer was talking to James Cain, who did *The Postman Always Rings Twice* and all that stuff and this interviewer was moaning about how the movies had ruined Cain's work and Cain looks around at the books on the shelf behind him and says, "No, they look just the same to me." It doesn't hurt the book if they do a terrible movie. John Updike said the perfect situation is where they pay you a lot up front and they never make the movie. There's something to be said about that. I'd rather sit down and do my own original screenplay. I'd like to direct at least once to see whether or not I could do it. I see so many movies that are really terrible and you say, it's like, to me, one of the big things that happened to me when I was learning to write, like there comes a moment, I've seen it with all my kids. Your kids are rug rats, they crawl around. They just crawl around. And you have a pet like a cat or a dog or something like that and it's like they're on the same level; they're in the same eye space and the kid is always looking sort of humbly at the cat or the dog, like "I know I'm not as good as you. We're both on four legs and you can run a fuck of a lot faster than I can and you get to eat off the floor and all your food gets in your mouth and I spill all mine and I burp up shit and everything and I know you're better." And then one day the kid gets up and this look comes into his face. It's like "I'm better than him. I'm on two legs." And that look is gone. And when you write or you do anything that's creative, there comes a moment where you see stuff that somebody got paid for and you say, "I do better work than that. I don't care if I'm getting paid for it or not. I know I do." So, that's like the first big step in becoming a creative person who's paid for what he does. And with the movies, I never directed a picture, but I go and see some stuff and I say, "I know I could do it better. I *know* I can." You know what I mean. It's back and forth. It's those head shots—*boom boom*, like playing table tennis—and the scares, they don't work for some reason, because they've been done before or nobody cared or something. You know, the little red ball on the boom mike is floating around the top of the frame.

Q: You think there's any limitations inherent in the film medium that kind of crimp the power of the written word and it's better to write the first screenplay directly?

KING: I don't, particularly not in this field.

Q: Just depends who's doing it.

KING: I think you can scare people a lot badder in a movie than you can in a book just because they're seeing it.

Q: They're seeing somebody else's fears and somebody else's ideas of fears unless their basic gut fear is of mutilation or something.

Q: I think the biggest fears are what you've got up here.

KING: Yeah, I think that, too.

Q: In a book you can just go right in.

KING: Yeah, the worst times in movies are when movies get—it's like when Bill Nolan says, the character's going up the stairs and everybody in the audience is saying, "Don't go up those stairs. I know there's a giant bug up in the attic. Don't go up those stairs." He's going up. "See that god damn fool. I would never go up those stairs. Madge, would you go up those stairs?" "No, I'd never go up those stairs." But he keeps going anyway and when he gets to the top you hear this scratching at the door and you say, "Oh shit"—

Q: Don't open the door.

KING: Don't open the door and he does anyway. There's a 300 foot bug behind that door. "I know, oh, shit, if I see this man, I'd go crazy." So the guy opens the door and there's a 300 foot high roach there behind that door. And what he's saying at that point is "Aw, man, I'm really glad. I can handle 300 feet. I was afraid it'd be 3,000 feet." No matter, and if it's 3,000 you say something else.

What also scares people: violence scares people, when something happens that's really overtly violent. There's a place for that in the movies. It should be there.

Q: They're not releasing it until November something now?

ROMERO: November 10th.

Q: They backed it up again.

ROMERO: They backed it off Halloween because I think, frankly, they thought that it didn't really need Halloween. And that they felt that they might do better over Thanksgiving and in some cities if it hung on they might make it through the Holidays.

Q: I heard various things like the political conventions would be buying all the commercial time up on TV.

ROMERO: Well, they were a little worried about that, too. They thought that the film didn't really have to be attached to Halloween even though it was by its personality, that it didn't need Halloween time to make money. So I'm actually glad they moved it because I was afraid that if it opened at Halloween and it had to go that extra two weeks it might automatically get bumped.

Q: There's not a lot of precedence for this kind of thing.

ROMERO: The thing is, if it had been opened for the extra two weeks, then it would probably be waning by the time the Holidays came along, and I think maybe they're hoping it will hang through the Holidays.

Q: You're one of the few horror movie genre directors I've felt that ever had a sense of humor. And you really got to do it with *Creepshow.* It's just in there. In fact, when I think back on *Creepshow,* I don't think of it as a horror comedy. I think of it as a comedy.

ROMERO: That's the first thing I remember as this enjoyable experience of catharsis coming out in a fun way. Even though it's got those scares in it, it's really like a spook house. I'm glad that you dig it that way, because that's what we were trying to do. We had fun, man.

Q: It shows.

ROMERO: And it bothers the hell out of me. I think sometimes when people think that it's Steve and me getting together, they're just going to have their brains blown out or something. I think it takes the first 45 minutes for them to start looking at it for what it is and say "Oh."

Q: It had a good pace to it. I wonder had you ever considered those stories in any other sequence other than the way they finally appeared?

KING: Every sequence you can think of except—

Q: You kept switching 'em around because they seem to flow really nice in the final one.

ROMERO: They're actually in the order that Steve originally wrote. We played with, after we had them shot, we kicked around with editing and we slid 'em around; we even screened 'em once in a different order, but we kept coming back.

Q: Why did you decide to play Jordy Verrill?

KING: It was George's idea. You didn't have to twist my arm very far, did you. I thought, everybody wants to be in movies and I did a thing for George in *Knightriders* where I played a drunken cowhand and I must have given such good idiot in that one. . . .

Q: I thought you were wonderful and I'm not saying it because I'm sitting here. I loved it. You know why? Because there's a certain fine line in that kind of overacting and you didn't seem to cross it and I don't know if that's you or that's the editing or George's directing.

KING: It's mostly—

ROMERO: Nah, it's mostly yours. It's mostly Steve. I feel guilty sometimes because I know that people are gonna give you shit for doing it.

KING: I get a lot of shit, but I don't care.

ROMERO: I wouldn't either. I think it's great.

KING: It was interesting to do and it was fun. George is good to work for. He doesn't start walking around running his hands through his hair and saying, "Why did I ever cast him? You asshole, you cost me $40,000 today. Let's do it again."

ROMERO: I never had any reason.

Q: Did he make you shave your beard off for it?

KING: No. I never have a beard in the summer anyway and that green stuff, it would have been rank. When I came in to get my face-cast—my rationale is that when the baseball season ends, I grow the beard back. And at the time that I came in to get my face-cast, the baseball season was over because they were on strike. And I had a beard that was a little bit shorter than this one 'cause it was just starting out. And Tom said "If you don't shave that beard, when I take this face cast off your face, your beard is going to come off because this will act as a depilatory and it will hurt." He said, "You wanna shave." And I said, "Yes."

Q: Do you have *The Stand* cast yet?

ROMERO: We've sent several letters back and forth to each other. We've got a cast in our head, but no deals made.

KING: It's really too early, I guess.

Q: Is it going to hurt to ask who you'd like to see do it? How about if I don't write it down?

KING: Gable for Stu Redmond.

Q: Who's going to play Randall Flagg? Anybody? Is he going to have a face?

KING: Oh, sure.

Q: He doesn't, well he does, he's sort of a "Rawhide" face.

KING: Willie Nelson would be okay. I'd like to see Robert Duvall do it.

Q: Another thing that impressed me about the movie was the choice of the character actors you got for it. They just carried that movie beautifully.

ROMERO: I'm glad you feel that way because I thought that everybody was really right and everyone put out a hundred and fifty percent.

KING: They sure did. They worked very, very hard. Even John Warner came in in his white pioneer suit and he plays Nate and all he does is come in and get killed, but he put out; he did all that little bit, "I want my cake, I want my cake."

Q: In the comic adaptation they changed a couple of lines. Did you mind that?

KING: I did it, you know. Because the thing is, it's an R-rated movie. We have things even in the movie that can't be in the comic book because the rationale is a lot of book jobbers don't want to handle it because a comic book is a kid-oriented item on the stands; that's the way you see it. Whereas the ratings serve as a built-in protection against, let's say, a ten year old just walking into the movie and plopping down. In this case my kids have seen it. My youngest kid is six, he's a boy who's six. I took him to the screening, I took my older son. My daughter didn't want to go and this isn't the kind of thing where I twist her arm because she doesn't like that stuff. But the boys did it, they handled it fine, no nightmares, there was no disturbing residue because it's a fairly innocent kind of—it's like a roller coaster.

So the irony is I think it's okay for kids. You know, if you're a parent and you say, "I think my kid can handle some language here," then we're not going to worry about the other stuff. As a parent I judged on whether or not they could see the movie the same way I would for any other movie. But, on the other hand, I understand their feeling that a comic book can't be R-rated. A clerk's job in a bookstore is not to say, "Hey, kid, don't you know that's an R-rated book; put that back." It's a comic book.

With Paul Gagne

Q: When you first sold the film rights to *Pet Sematary* to George Romero and Richard Rubinstein back in 1984, one of the conditions of the deal was that the film had to be shot in Maine. You've cited your concern over Maine's economy as one of the principal reasons for this. *Pet Sematary* is still on hold at this date, but Richard decided to shoot part of *Creepshow 2* in the Bangor area anyway in recognition of that commitment. Would you care to elaborate?

KING: Well, first of all, I didn't have anything to do with Richard's decision to shoot *Creepshow 2* here; it was entirely his own. They filmed about 50% of it here and 50% in Arizona. I think they went away happy with what they got. My concern with the area is dollars. A film production brings broad dollars into a state or region. We've got areas in Maine like Washington County, which doesn't generate in three years the kind of money that's spent in a typical A-type Hollywood production, as far as the working men and women of that county go. I'm talking about the dollars that just flow into a community. There is a lot of inertia now in terms of bringing more film production into Maine. There was no real film commission here until quite recently. I mean, we lost *Golden Pond* by inches in Oxford County, where people eat potatoes because they can't afford meat. And film people pay cash, you know. They come in and they want carpenters, they want people who know how to put a plug into a socket. This is a non-union state. It's dough, and it's good, non-polluting work. Most of the people here who need to put a meal on the table just love it. My brother-in-law is just scrambling right now. He used to be a crane operator. He worked on the *Creepshow 2* production, and he thinks Richard Rubinstein is God come down to Earth. And for coming up here, I do too. I think it was a hell of a thing for him to do. They made a lot of friends up here.

Q: It's ironic and a bit unfortunate that while almost all of your stories are set in Maine, none of the films made from your work have been shot there.

KING: Oddly enough, the one that looks the most natural is *Dead Zone*, which was filmed in Canada right over the border from New York. That's close to New England, so it looked good. But it's funny how if you look at *Cujo*, that's supposed to be in Maine but the ocean's on the wrong side of the screen! You see this guy drinking a brand of beer that's not sold anyplace east of the Mississippi River! It's just wrong. So they came up here for *Creepshow 2*, and the story they shot in Maine is the best story in the picture, I think.

Q: "The Hitchhiker." Is that the story you originally wrote for the first *Creepshow?*

KING: Yes, as a possible replacement for "They're Creeping Up on You."

Q: George Romero has written the screenplay for *Creepshow 2* based on your story ideas. How did you work together on this particular project?

KING: I sat down and did sort of a notebook. I don't know how other people's film treatments look, but I knew what we were after, particularly after the first film. I pretty much scripted the wraparound story, where this kid is chased by a bunch of juvenile delinquents, except they changed it from live action to animation. It follows what I did pretty closely, though. In terms of the stories, I wanted to start off with a Jack Davis kind of story. It was about a dead bowling team.

Q: It sounds close to "Foul Play," the Davis story about the baseball team....

KING: Yeah, you bet it was! Anyway, I put down about seven or eight ideas. Then I did sort of the same thing I did with George when he and I first got together—I just asked him to pick whatever he liked. The notes I sent him were were pretty detailed, and they even had some dialogue, but George really carried it off. He scripted four, including the bowling story, the hitchhiker story, "The Raft," which is based on one of the short stories in *Skeleton Crew*, and "Chief Woodenhead," an original story about a wooden Indian that comes to life. I had actually started that one as a short story, but it fit the film perfectly so we used it there. Anyway, George sent me the script, and I suggested some cuts and some changes, and some of them were made and some were not. He's a darn good writer. The bowling story was later cut before the film went into production.

Q: The first *Creepshow* was considered moderately successful at the box office by industry standards. How do you think this picture will do?

KING: I think the initial turnout is going to be very big, because the original, whether you liked it or hated it or whatever, has pretty much stayed around. It still rents in video outlets, and it still shows on cable. It's had longer legs, particularly on the pay cable movie stations, than a lot of other movies have. That's one movie where I get a check regularly every six months. It's only like eight or nine hundred dollars, but it's something!

I'm somewhat of a closet sociologist, and the closet sociologist in me has been extremely interested in the effect that the cable and video rental invasion has had on the movie marketplace. One of the things that seems to be developing is that with grade B action, horror or comedy pictures that have sequels, the video generates a rebound effect at the box office. It hits and bounces back harder. If you have a picture that just does okay at the box office, and then it does really well on video and on cable, then people are more interested in seeing the sequel when it comes out than they were in the original.

Q: What was the extent of your personal involvment with the production of *Creepshow 2*?

KING: Not a hell of a lot. I played a part—a truck driver. My usual nerd; you'll know me when you see me. The guy who looks like he doesn't quite know what gravity is.

My philosophy about all this stuff is to keep out of people's way and let them do their jobs. That's pretty much what I do, and what I expect people to do for me.

CHAPTER SIX

✝

HIGHWAY TO HORROR

✝

With Stephen Schaefer (1986)

Stephen King is in fine spirits. King is not only Alfred Hitchcock's successor as our most popular scaremonger but a writer now in the position of directing his first film. Based on one of his short stories, *Maximum Overdrive* is a $10 million thriller where machines, energized by the Earth's having passed through a comet's tail, become viciously independent of their operators.

If a lawn mower or electric knife on the attack sounds patently absurd, King won't argue. "It's true of all my stories," he explains, "people laugh at them when I first describe them. They may sound funny but this—"and he gleefully gestures to the commotion surrounding him—"is going to be terrifying."

For *Overdrive's* first night of filming, possessed trucks are circling the fort. Actually, since this isn't a western, the trucks are encircling the Dixie Boy Truckstop, an elaborate fake constructed on Highway 76 just outside Wilmington, N.C., where producer Dino De Laurentiis has built his film studio next to the local airport. The half-dozen "driverless" trucks, all big semis, are quiet for the moment. Led by leading man Emilio (*Repo Man*) Estevez, the cast has just escaped from being flattened in the Dixie Boy via an underground sewage pipe which deposits them in the ditch.

Across the highway, King is in a ditch with his crew and eleven actors. Sipping from his refilled red plastic tumbler, casual in his Bruce Springsteen white satin tour jacket and jeans (Springsteen was an early but unavailable choice for the lead), King is positively jovial. To no one in particular he announces in the voice of a latenight horror show TV host, "It's all part of the *madness of Overdrive*."

The only possible madness, however, is King's hiring Armando Nannuzzi as director of photography. Though a respected veteran cinematographer whose credits include both *La Cage* comedies and the previous King feature, *Silver Bullet*, Nannuzzi speaks no English. It's difficult for a novice director to communicate through ten weeks of filming with his d.p. via interpreter, but "The language doesn't bother me," King says.

In the past, King has voiced his frustrations with film adaptations of his work. *Overdrive*, adapted and expanded by King from his "Trucks" short story, was a chance to direct one right.

To prepare for his attempt at getting quintessential King onscreen, he enlisted the assistance of his *Creepshow* collaborator, George Romero, who visited a month before filming began. "It's amazing what I don't know," he concedes, "but I have a vision of what I want. That's the only way I know how to do this."

Down in the ditch, the actors are stuck in the muck, despite boards laid on the wet grass. An assistant calls to King: "Are we going to rehearse this?"

"Yes," King replies, "but we're going to shoot the rehearsal."

As actors scrunch into the sewage pipe, a halt is called because a real truck has pulled into the Dixie Boy. "That happens a lot," the publicist explains. "There isn't a real truckstop around here for miles."

As the intruding truck exits out of camera range, the cooperative local police (notified by walkie-talkie) stop traffic on both sides of Highway 76. "It's awful down there!" King shouts to his crew, referring to the ditch's wetness, not to mention red ants. "Let's go." A boom microphone is lowered. "Brad," King says, calling to an actor by his character's name, "remember to check back and see Emilio. Then throw your line."

With an ominous roar and a swirl of Carolina dust, the semis begin their circling, like a pachyderm chorus out of an ominous *Dumbo*.

"Brad, remember to keep checking back now. What is your line?"

"Holy shit!"

"Ok!" says King. "Let's *hear*, 'Holy Shit!'"

The two cameras whir, King looks pleased, and with only another take it's a wrap, and the crew positions the camera for the reverse shot. King spreads out on Highway 76, flat on his belly, his jeans hanging low enough like a teenager's to expose the crack in his butt. When the lights are adjusted, the cast is positioned for the group shot. King regroups them closer, squeezing everyone into the frame. "I'm being sodomized!" one yelps.

"C'mon," says the director, "we get this and it's almost Miller Time."

With Stanley Wiater

Q: We must tell you right off this won't be the usual Q&A interview, but a "you-are-there" piece, with me on the set of *Overdrive* talking in person to Steve King, director. As if I was actually there the first day of shooting in Wilmington, North Carolina.

KING: Gotcha! Well, you weren't there the first day of shooting—and I'm going back in my time machine now—you came down when we started principal photography, which was July 4th or 5th, or something like that. When we started shooting I had no second unit, and that was partially my decision because I got down there in May, and I had a full two months to prepare to shoot because I never had shot a picture before. I had time to block, time to work with the actors—Dino was very gracious about all that stuff. So the first day we actually shot, I worked my way into it with these eight guys in the second unit: we were shooting pedals that ran by themselves, with an effects guy that was pulling the device. . . . . But the first thing we *really* shot was a sequence with this dump truck, where the clutch goes in by itself and then you see the shift go into gear, and then you see the clutch pedal go out and the gas pedal go down. We got the clutch pedal, and we got the gas pedal, but we couldn't get the shift because we were on the backlot, and it was Cinemascope lens. And we kept picking up reflections, and kept picking up pieces of the studio roof, and all this other stuff.

So I said, "Let's go around to the other side." And there was this *total* silence in my little crew. This is why it's a good thing to do this sort of thing when there's nobody else around! They all kinda look at you like when you're at a party and you cut a real loud fart. [*pauses*] No. . . it's more like when you're at a party and you have a real big booger hanging out of your nose, and nobody knows how to tell you.

So, finally, it was like they drew straws, and finally the camera operator comes up to me and says, "You can't do that." And I said, "Why not?" And he said, "Because you're crossing the axis." And I said, "What's that?" You know? [*chuckles*] Those weeks of second unit and preproduction that I got was like having a semester in Berkeley film school. And the camera operator didn't have much English, and my cinematographer Armando Nannuzzi had none! If you stay through all the end credits on *Maximum Overdrive* you'll see credits for translators. I had one main translator, and another lady who came out once in awhile to help get it together.

But Armando came with me into my office, where I had these little lead figures like Dungeons & Dragons and a little model set, and explained to me that if you're shooting the same sequence and you switch over to the other side, you confuse the audience. And I didn't fully understand it until I saw some footage cut together later on in the picture where I'd done it, and then I *did* understand.

But the first day *you* were there, was the first day we were on the drawbridge. And it was very, very hot, and we were shooting a model. We had closed off the real drawbridge for the day (it was a Sunday) and we were on a pier that was out on the Cape Fear River. And the trick was to raise the real bridge and the model bridge in tandem so that it would look like the little model cars that were on the bridge were actually stuck there going up there with the real bridge. It's a *dynamite* effect, and you can't believe it until you look at it. Because the action on either side of the drawbridge is *live*; you see people moving about, you see a motorboat going by—so that was a good day. We shot for three consecutive Sundays on the bridge—Wilmington closed that particular drawbridge down for us—and God favored us with good weather on each of the three Sundays except for the last, and we got away with that one, too.

Q: In terms of days and hours, what was the work load?

KING: We worked six days a week, and as far as shooting went, all I can tell you is that for the major part of the shoot we were at the "Dixie Boy Diner." I mean, it *was* a diner that was built in front of a pipe manufacturing company. The result was that it looked like a truck stop, with showers in back, and stalls for the trucks and everything like that. I would leave in the morning, and I would see the sun just coming up in the left rear view mirror of my motorcycle, bright red. And when I left the set, after my first assistant director said that was a wrap, I would see it going *down* red in the right-hand mirror of my motorcycle. Then I would just fall into bed when I got back home. We were playing with temperatures usually anywhere from 90 to 110 degrees. No shade. I wouldn't go directly home, of course; first you'd go back and view rushes, and then talk about the next day's work—yeah, they were 18 hour days. Actually, they were 24 hour days—because I would fall asleep and I would *dream* the day's work.

Q: Just how extensive are the new Dino De Laurentiis facilities?

KING: You go down there to the North Carolina Film Corporation and you get a sense of deja vu for a time. What it's like, it's like being at Warner Bros. Studio in 1946 to, say, about 1963. Dino's got a film *city* down there, and he's built it all in about four years. So when we were down there shooting, we'd be on Sound Stage One if we were inside, and there'd be David Lynch with *Blue Velvet* somewhere, and they'd be working on Manhunter somewhere else. It's a factory. He got a lot of cooperation from the town of Wilmington, which is part of the secret, and another part of the secret I think was non-union labor. But most of it was just the tremendous amounts of cooperation and interest in the projects. And to do him credit, Dino shot a lot of features from that studio that are very interesting; none of them have been, you know, blast-off successes, and yet he's done an amazing range of pictures. Some of them show a lot of courage—films like *Marie*. . . and he's going to be doing *Crimes of the Heart* this year. So he's in there, he's slugging away.

Q: We know you have a good personal relationship with De Laurentiis, but since you were working *for* him as a director at his studio, did the relationship change? Was he looking over your shoulder all the time?

KING: No, he didn't do that. [*chuckles*] We had a meeting about three weeks before principal photography started, when I was still doing my second unit, where we sat there for about four days—all day—and went over every aspect of the script. And he had planned, instead of three or four days, to spend about two weeks doing that because I had never directed a picture before and because he was trying to cover *my* ass. You know? And he'd say, "How're you going to shoot this?" and so on and so forth, and I was prepared by then. What I had done was prepare this huge notebook, because the only way I knew how to approach the project was that I had read that Alfred Hitchcock never looked through the view finder: he already knew what every shot was.

And so what I did, I called Dino up on the phone when I was still in *my* preparation, before I came down there, and I said, "This is an action picture, basically, stripped to its essentials. How many shots are there in an action picture?" He was confused at first by what I was saying, and he said, "Do you mean how many scenes?" And I said, "No—how many *shots*—that is to say, how many shots should be coming out?" He thought about it a little while, and then he understood, and he said, "Anywhere from eight hundred to a thousand." So when I prepared to shoot, I ended up with 1,175 shots. In the final picture, there'll be something like 879. So it worked out pretty close.

Q: Yet we heard you didn't use the traditional storyboard?

KING: No. Dino wanted me to have a storyboard guide down, and there was a guide named Tom Cranham. And in a couple of crucial places he came in and saved us; sometimes with ideas and sometimes by showing me how I could get a fluidity of action that I didn't understand how to get otherwise. But for the most part, I could see exactly where I wanted everybody to be, and I knew where I wanted the cameras to be. And in a lot of cases, I would get a lot more than I thought, because I was thinking in terms of *Creepshow*, where we had one man running the camera, and that was *it*. And I was in a situation where sometimes I had three, and even four, cameras. When we blew the Dixie Boy, we had *six*.

Q: Rather than a one-dimensional storyboard, you had a detailed mock-up of the Dixie Boy in your studio office, complete with various toy trucks and cars.

KING: Yeah, right. I had a model of the Dixie Boy which is now in my home office. I sent my assistant, Stephanie Fowler, out and said, "Get me a whole bunch of toy trucks." And she came back with all these Hasbro and Tonka trucks. I bought the trucks, basically. [*laughs*] And I had a blueprint made of the inside of the Dixie Boy, and had some lead figures that I bought.

Q: What kind of input did your cast have? We're thinking specifically of Emilio Estevez, who recently wrote the screenplay for one of his own films.

KING: I went in there with the view of the actors expecting to beef up their parts. I deliberately worked on a script where I had pared down the dialogue as much as I could, because I think that's been a weakness in some of the pictures... Emilio totally stunned me by saying "I think this can go, this can go. . . ." And he was deliberately cutting the part to the bone himself.

Then Christopher Murney, who played a salesman, said he thought he should go into this whole rap about selling these Bibles that he has. It wasn't in the script, but I said, "Let's shoot it and see what happens." And it was fantastic! He just did this whole thing of going to the waitress and to one of the truckers there, and says [in Southern accent] "This American Truth Way Bible is only $7.95 and you get Genesis, you get Leviticus..." And then a truck would go by and smash his car and he'd say "COCKSUCKER!!" It was great! He's a great improvisational performer.

Q: What about with Pat Hingle?

KING: I did a shot with Laura Harrington—who's the female lead—and Emilio Estevez, where we had this very, very long track built. She simply walks up behind him and scares him while he's looking underneath the truck that's almost run down the guy she's come into the diner with. And she kept fluffing up her lines—it was her first day on the set, she hadn't made many pictures before, and she was understandably nervous. We got to Take 18, 19, and 20, and by then we finally got it. But by then we'd also just about blown the day. So later on we're doing an office scene with Emilio and Pat, and Pat blew a line, and he said, "That's okay—let's just do a pick up." And I said, "What's that?" And he said, "We can pick it up from where I fluffed the line, from the line before." And I said, "You can do that?" I said, "Man, I don't know anything!" [laughs] He said, "You're a good man, you'll do all right." So what I'm saying is, if I'd known what he told me after he came on the set with Laura and Emilio, I probably could have saved five hours that day.

There were also a couple of times where in a scene I wanted him to play it "light," and he said, "This isn't right. These people are in a place I've kept secret for a long time, and they have no right to be there, and I should be very angry." Immediately I saw that he was right and I was wrong—he knew who the character was. But he never fucked with the lines; he read the lines, he knew the character, and he played him beautifully.

Q: It's our understanding that you chose to adapt your story "Trucks" because a good deal of the work you would have as director would be with machines, not human beings. The idea being that you might have a relatively easier time your first time out directing machines rather than people.

KING: My feeling was I'm never going to have a truck that says "I can't do this scene today, I'm having my period." Or, "I'm sorry I shouted at you, I'm having my period." I'm never going to have an actor that's going to walk off and have a tantrum or something if the actor happens to be a Mack truck. But the way it turned out, the trucks and the machinery were the real prima donnas! They fucked up without fail! While my actors and actresses always gave me more than I expected.

We did a scene in an overturned car, with John Short and Yardley Smith, who play this young couple who crash their way into the Dixie Boy a lot like Davy Crockett and his friend into the Alamo. One of the trucks hits them, and their car overturns. And this scene went on for about three hours, and the car's upside-down, and Yardley's in there among all this broken glass, and she's supposed to be all tangled up in the seat belt and everything. It was hot like an attic in there, and I said "How're you doing in there, Yardley?" And she said, [*imitating voice*] "Stephen, I'm as happy as a clam at high tide!" No problem whatsoever.

We had one lady, Ellen McElduff, who had to take a lot of bullet hits and she was three months pregnant, and she was just concerned that the squibs go off above where the baby was. But she went off and did it, and it was no problem. It was a sweet shoot.

Q: We're curious as to how close the film version came to what you originally envisioned in the script, in terms of what the budget allowed —or didn't allow—you to shoot?

KING: I never asked what the budget was, and Dino never told me. I knew what I wanted, and he said "I'll support you." I said, "Do you give me your word?" And he said, "I give you my word." And I went out and I shot the picture. I got everything I wanted. I think we spent maybe four million bucks; it wasn't a big budget at all. We finished under schedule; we finished under budget.

Q: Working with those huge "props," the Mack trucks and huge rigs— did any of the stunts ever become too dangerous?

KING: We *did* have a case where actor John Short wanted to do a scene himself where this truck runs at him and he dives aside. Finally we decided to use a stunt guy and it was a good thing we did because the truck went haywire, and instead of going in a gap between the pump and the gas station, the stunt driver lost control and the truck hit the gas station instead. The stunt man caught like a 90 pound stanchion in one hand—he was a really muscular guy—but if it had been John Short, I think he would have been squashed.

The other thing was that my cinematographer, Armando Nannuzzi, lost an eye on the shoot. But it didn't have anything to do with the trucks—it had to do with this power lawnmower that's supposed to run by itself after this kid. We had the camera set down low, and we had it on chocks, and we asked Armando several times do you want plexiglass in front of the camera? And he said no, because of the shadows and everything. But after 16 takes, the lawnmower was a wimp, it wouldn't do anything. It was on remote control. But on the 17th take, it just came like a bat out of hell, and there were a couple of effects guys and grips standing to either side of the camera to stop the mower, but the power was in the rear wheels, not in the front. So when they put their feet on the front wheels, the thing simply reared up like a bull and chewed the shit out of the little wedges that were underneath the camera.

Armando bent down, and one of those wedges went right into his eye. I also bent down, but nothing happened to me except that one of them hit my arm and I got a tiny spot of blood, but that was it. It appears now he may have lost the eye. He went right to the eye center at Duke, which is located there in North Carolina, and he was gone for about four days. We were shut down for five days, but he came back and, Jesus, he shot the rest of the picture with an eye patch, and he lit it like a champ. He worked with a lot of pain—I mean, this is a guy 65 years old, no English, and never been in a hospital in his life. So we weren't just fucking around, you know?

There was a scene with Emilio one day, where this truck—after all the pumps run out of fuel—he says to it, "I'm sorry guys, it was fun while it lasted, but we're all out." And this fuel truck comes rolling up to him. We had a guy who was behind this black gauze sheet so the cab looks empty, but Emilio was nervous about it. I don't blame him! [*laughs*] The truck was supposed to roll up to him and bump him, and he's supposed to say, "What do you want?" And the truck's supposed to bump him toward the gas pump. . . like a collie herding sheep. Pushing him, and bumping him. But he was real nervous about doing it. And I said, "Look. Now watch, it's going to be all right." And *I* did it.

Now, I'm six foot three, and Emilio is maybe five foot ten—and I was scared shitless. But I figure if I do it, and he sees me do it, and if everybody else sees me do it, *he'll* do it. Not that the guy's gutless or anything like that, but he was worried about it because it was a goddamned BIG truck. And *I* was scared of the truck bumping me. I said to the driver later, "Did you have any problems," and being a good ol' North Carolina boy, he said, "No problems a'tall, boss." So the driver did it with Emilio. And we got the take, and it looks great in the movie. Then, when it's all over, he says to me, "Was that all right?" I said, "Yes, it was fantastic," And he says, "That's good. Because you're tall, and I could see you—but I couldn't see that little guy a'tall." So if his foot had slipped off the clutch or something like that. . . !

Because we didn't use any special effects in the sense of *Star Wars* or anything like that, because I think everybody's hip to it. There's a part of a fake truck in one section of the film, and I defy you to tell me where it's used. You may know, and you may not. But everything else is for real. No fakin'. No messing around. There were no blue screens used, all the opticals that are in the picture have to do with the sky, as the plot has to do with the Earth entering the tail of a comet, which supposedly makes all these machines go crazy. So at night you see an intermittent green glow in the sky. And there's a section in a video game emporium where all these machines go crazy, and there's some optical stuff there. But you pick up on it immediately. But for the most part we lucked out—"fools rush in where angels fear to tread."

Q: We can see how the set-ups might have worked beautifully on paper, but were there any instances where you couldn't shoot a scene as you had envisioned it?

KING: With a couple of exceptions, I got everything I wanted. The *spirit* of everything is there. The only things I would have done over again if I could, is that I wish I had stood up for myself in the beginning and suggested that this picture ended sooner than it does. Because there's a feeling of tapering away. . . but they're fiddling around with that now to bring it back in. But the people who have seen it in the advance screenings say the picture seems like it's only ten minutes long, because of the suicidal pacing. And that's what I wanted, that's what comes across. People don't seem to leave for popcorn. [*chuckles*] I think the final print will be 92 minutes long. There's only three scenes in the picture where you say, "I want a cigarette now," but they have to be there because they're information scenes. But we've kept those to a minimum, too.

Q: Are there going to be any classic "King gross-outs" in *Maximum Overdrive*?

KING: In the three sneaks that we ran with the answer print, they're there. There's one of them that George Romero saw in the work print, and he turned his head away at one point. This is where this steamroller runs over this kid's head, and the kid's head explodes. Dino looked at it in the Movieola and said, "Hey Steeeven, this ess X." We took it to the ratings board and they had 30 objections to the "R" rating. We ended up cutting a number of things back a little bit. . . but the gross-out factor? I don't know. . .I don't think I would ever go in again, if I were ever to direct another motion picture, I would not promise in advance to deliver a picture with a certain rating. Which is what I did with this. Because the "R" in terms of violence continues to shrink. I didn't think it would happen. I thought after P-13, there would be a little more liberality, but . . . .But I was able to go in and talk to them, and in most cases we were able to get what we wanted.

Q: With all the other film adaptations of your work, some of course came off better than others. But this time there's going to be nobody else to blame—or praise—with the adaptation, since *you* are in complete creative control.

KING: That's why I did it. *That's why I did it*, you know? You stop blaming somebody else, and you go in there and *do* it. Because I'm as curious as anybody else. People say, "Nobody seems to be able to translate your stuff to the screen." And this is a blatant falsehood, because David Cronenberg did a hell of a job with *The Dead Zone*, and Lewis Teague did a great job with *Cujo*.

Q: And what are your feelings when your own screenplays have been used, as in, say, *Cat's Eye*?

KING: Shit, *Cat's Eye* is a GREAT movie! It was truncated by MGM, who made a bad mistake by taking the prologue off, which was hilarious, and clarifies the picture a lot. But that was Frank Yablans. I mean, the picture is there, it's literate, it's funny, it's sort of sophisticated in a different kind of way. It just happened to be a picture nobody wanted. I tell people, "I really liked *Cat's Eye*," and they say, "Oh, I haven't seen it." Because nobody went to see it—it went down the toilet. It was Dino's concept—he'd never seen *Creepshow* or anything like that—and I went ahead and did it because it sort of appealed to me. Maybe I'll go out there and make a good picture, and maybe I'll go out there and make an ass out of myself.

Q: We take it that De Laurentiis was the first producer to ever let you put your money where your mouth is, in terms of directing. We know you've been expressing an interest to direct for some time now.

KING: Oh, shit, they've been coming after me for years! But my kids were too young, and my wife has wanted me at home, and I don't blame her—that's where I wanted to be. But finally she says to me, "I know this is something you want to do, so go ahead and go for it." And it was hard on the family and everything else. I can't imagine doing it again until the kids grow up more. Spielberg asked me to direct an *Amazing Stories*—I wrote a teleplay for next season and I said, "No, I can't come out and play." What I thought about saying was, "Don't you think you should see *Maximum Overdrive* before you make those kind of offers?" [*laughs*] But I think I might do it again sometime because I learned enough to say I *could* do it a lot better.

Q: But isn't the real reason for your deciding to direct was to see if you could transport the "pure essence of Stephen King" from the printed page onto the silver screen?

KING: Well, I wanted to go out and see if there was any "Stephen King" if *I* did it! There was no reason to believe in advance—and I never did believe—that I could do it better than anybody else. There was a lot to suggest that I could do it worse because I was a rank amateur. You know? I didn't get this job because, like Steven Spielberg, I did wonderful work on *Night Gallery* on a budget; I didn't get this job because I labored in the vineyards, or been a cinematographer on this picture or that picture. I got it because I'd *written books*—it didn't have anything to do with motion pictures at all!

Q: Did you ever call up your old buddy George Romero for any advice?

KING: On this business about the axis I called, and asked him to explain it to me. I asked him if it could ever be violated, and he said the guy who did *Battleship Potemkin* used to do it all the time! [*laughs*] Then I said, "Do you ever do it?" And he said, "Not if I can help it! It confuses the audience." But, yeah, I called him a couple of times for advice, sure.

Q: Any other directors who influenced you?

KING: Hitchcock. Hitchcock was the guy who said, "Show 'em what's going to happen. Don't all of a sudden just jump people." There's a couple of places in *Maximum Overdrive* where that happens, where all of a sudden you get a nasty jump when something just happens. But Hitchcock said, "You do that and it's over in four seconds. The audience screams, and that's it. But if you show them in advance what's going to happen, *then* they get scared." So Hitchcock. Always Hitchcock. But never to try to be imitative or do the same shots, but to *remember* him. And the only other thing I can say is, whatever worked for me in the books, oughta work in the movies. The one concept that I did bring to this movie—and it was over some strenuous objections from Dino and from some other people—was the idea to interweave a number of stories, the way that *'Salem's Lot* interweaved different stories. And I think it works pretty well.

Q: Author Whitley Strieber told us that he didn't think a novel was really complete until a successful film version of it was done as well. That the work had one life as a novel, and another as a motion picture. What do you say to that theory?

KING: It never crosses my mind. Never even think of it. I don't give much of a shit about the movies, to tell you the truth. Other than as a fan. I go and see 'em, and I either like them or not. And as far as film versions of my own work goes, the only thing I've tried to insist on with the major works is to try and get as much money as possible. Because if they're going to make them—my idea of the trade-off is, "Go ahead, make the picture, give me a lot of money and I'll stay out of your face." Because the books exist in their own life.

Q: Finally, just as an aside, what do you think of the numerous critical studies that have come out on you recently?

KING: Well, there are people who have worked on those books that I know, and people who have worked on those books that I don't know . . . and I can't answer the question. [*pauses*] It's a little bit like Huck Finn and Tom Sawyer going to their own funeral. I'm aware of them. I've read them. For example, Michael Collings's book, *The Many Facets of Stephen King*, which is the latest volume in this parade, has a marvelous and insightful essay on *The Eyes of the Dragon*, which is a children's book that I wrote. That's a good piece. But beyond that, what can I say? They're there, and some of them are good, and some of them are bad, but I'm not going to pick them apart. It's not my place.

Q: But does it ever make you stop and say, "My God, look how seriously these people are taking me?"

KING: No. . . no, I don't think about that at all. That's their business, not mine. I just write stories.

With Stephen Schaefer

Q: What's your reaction to the finished film of *Maximum Overdrive*?
KING: I think it's pretty good! I don't think that it's—I'm not rehearsing my Academy Award speech. It does what I want it to do; I mean, it's a dumb summer picture, so what?
Q: Do you think it's terrifying?
KING: Hmmm. How do I answer that question? There're places where it's real scary. The overall feeling that I get out of it is more one of sort of *kickass, good humored, kickass, things blow up*. In fact it seems to me more like *Cobra* than anything else, except I don't think you'd come out of this one feeling lightly coated with Wesson oil, which is sort of how I came out of *Cobra* feeling. I mean I went to see that at the first showing because I'd heard these things about it. About how it was so violent, all this other stuff. And we had gotten Xed on three counts on *Overdrive*—
Q: Ok, I was going to ask about that.
KING: I mean it wasn't any kind of a big deal. We ended up I think dropping like 18 frames from the movie and we got our R. So I went to see *Cobra* to see what it was. And I went to the first showing and it was pretty crowded for up here for a matinee on a Friday. And my God, man! I came out with these people that looked like possibly they could read the funny papers. It was spooky. They were all guys and they looked real stupid. I sort of hope we'll get a hipper audience than that, although this, believe me, you don't need to have much more than Beetle Bailey to understand what's going on in this picture.
Q: After you finished shooting the film, were you involved with the editing?
KING: Oh yeah. All the way down. From beginning to end, I've been right with this. This is my picture. If you or anybody else is going to tie a can to anybody's tail, it's gonna be mine.
Q: Ok.
KING: Because I wasn't just there from 10 o'clock until I felt like I needed to go home and take my beauty rest. I've been there, you know,

from the first day that we opened pre-production offices to the time when they closed down in New York and sent all the culls back to wherever they put them out there in storage someplace in California.

Q: Now you say you got Xed on three different counts on *Overdrive*.

KING: Yeah.

Q: Did that mean you went back three different times to the ratings boards or they just did that to you?

KING: Well, we went to the ratings board twice. The first time it was sort of, I was overridden by Dino. Dino said, "Stephen, we go, we get an opinion from the ratings board." I said, "Dino, if we go and ask them for an opinion, they're going to think, you know, we're real scared." I mean, it's the same thing, it's this attitude that they've got where they're saying to me, "Stephen, we really think that this is not a critic's movie and that critics will actually like it better with an audience." Which is their way of saying, "We smell turkey all over it and if the critics don't get their hands on it until after it's released, at least we can have a fat first weekend." And that seems to be the attitude that they're expressing. And I talked to Dino about it and Dino agreed and so what they're doing is that they are having critic's screenings, sometimes at two in the morning, sometimes at six in the morning, things like that.

But the critics who have seen it, by and large seem to like it. If we were running for president, we wouldn't win by a landslide, but I'd say, out of every ten maybe seven like it, six, seven, something like that. Anyway, what I was going to say is, it's the same attitude. You go to the ratings board for an opinion. So we went to them for an opinion, not because I wanted to, but because he wanted to. They said, "X. There are twenty different things that may be X." And I got mad and called them up and said, "What is this? We're talking R here. Not PG or PG13." "Well, we're worried about the effect this movie may have on children." "Children? The children are not supposed to be in the theater in an R-rated picture, unless they're with a parent or a guardian. Those are the rules and if they're there, and if you don't like it and you see them there, you ought to complain to the management. And if the management won't do anything, you ought to complain to the exhibitor, because, you know, the self-enforcement is in their interest."

Q: Right.

KING: An unaccompanied fifteen year old who looks like a big kid and is going to pay an adult admission, they're going to let him in. It's just the way things work. But I'm talking about a nine year old who's tottling up there and being let it. That's not in the picture, it doesn't happen, man. It doesn't. It doesn't happen at the Sach theaters, it doesn't happen anywhere.

Finally when we went back, they had to get serious. They said, "Well, we're going to give you an X for these three things here, unless you want to change them." I mean, not like *Herbert West Reanimator*, where those guys when in and the ratings board said you can have your R but you're going to have to cut 40 percent of your picture.

Q: Right.

KING: So we cut. There's a steamroller scene from which we cut the final eight frames and there was a scene that we dropped entirely, just one shot, basically. There's a kid who crawls up to a guy who's supposedly dead in a ditch and waves a hand in his face and says, "Mister, are you all right?" And the guy—the guy's eyes are open and his face is sort of splattered with mud. And the kid decides he's dead and starts to crawl away. And what you see in the picture now is, you see from behind, you see the guy sit up very suddenly. You know, it's a *boo* on the audience. And the kid turns around and you see the guy's hand pulling his ankle. And he says something like, "Help me." And you go back to the kid, and the kid says, "I can't, you're too heavy." And you go back to that same shot of the hand on the ankle because the alternate shot, for which the ratings board didn't care, was you go to the guy's face and about half his face flies off. And that was a no-no. And then there was a machine gun scene where a couple of people get shot, and they wanted that edited down. It's a lot less violent than, let's say, the final scene of *Bonnie and Clyde*, which was PG, but times change. The ratings board is not rating for sex anymore.

Q: Yeah, they're for violence now.

KING: Yeah. It used to be that the sight of you know, some guy fondling a bare breast was going to send the sixteen year olds of America out into the streets to rape the first thing that they saw in skirts, but the ratings board no longer believes that. They believe that if you see a driver on a steamroller run over a guy, then the sixteen year olds of America are all going to go out and find steamrollers and run over their little brothers.

The basic problem is that there's an assumption now both concerning sex—that's the Meese Commission, which is sort of reflected there—and violence, which is, in the standards, the ratings board of movies, that people can't distinguish between fact and fantasy. And that's the belief of people who have no imagination. Unfortunately, they're also the people who are running this country, currently. If you don't have an imagination, of course you believe that everybody's going to think all this is true.

Q: Now what do you think of the changing look, or content, then, of horror movies?

KING: Well, I don't know. I think that what's scary has always been scary and continues to be scary. It's the same kind of stroke that always was. The idea is that you know it's going to come, you just don't know when or how or how bad it's going to be. Those are the givens, that the audience always understands what's going to happen next. If it works, it works because you're scared, you're having a kind of nightmare about things that you're really scared about. You know the funniest thing about horror movies?

Q: What?

KING: Is how people will sit in the theater and scream, "Don't go up those stairs, you stupid bitch." That kills me. I mean, it just kills me every time I hear it. Here you're watching this movie, and this woman comes in the house alone, right? She hears a creak upstairs. She goes to the foot of the stairs and she says, "Is somebody up there?" Nothing. And so she takes a step up the stairs and she says, "Is anybody up there?" And you hear the creak again, and the audience starts, "Don't go up there, don't go up there." So she says something like, "I gotta gun." And she starts to go up the stairs and the audience is all screaming, "Don't go up the stairs, you stupid bitch, don't go up those stairs. I'd never go up those stairs." You know, you hear guys saying this, "I'd *never* go up those stairs." And those guys who would never go up those stairs, get out of the movie theater, they light up a Marlboro. They hop into their cars and they drive back home on the Mass. pike doing 70 with their seat belts unbuckled. *But they wouldn't go up those stairs!*

Q: Yeah.

KING: But they understand. They keep coming back because they understand on an subconscious level that we go up the stairs all the time every day. So it's always the same things. It works, if it's done well, and the ratings board doesn't have anything to do with it, because splatter really doesn't have anything to do with it. Whether it's loose or whether it's tight, they're always waiting for that.

Q: Now, have you seen *Aliens* yet? Did you go this weekend?

KING: I'm going to see it this afternoon.

Q: Okay.

KING: At 12:30.

Q: Okay.

KING: I understand *Aliens* is a scary picture.

Q: Yeah, it's incredibly scary. You know, it's really—the amazing thing, I think, is that it's sustained for over two hours.

KING: Yeah, I know it, and I don't know—

Q: And it's incredibly violent. It's like a war movie.

KING: Bangor is a pretty good movie town, in the sense that what's going to be a hit nationwide is usually a hit here. And what's going to stiff out nationwide usually stiffs out here, and they told me last night, I went to see *Back to School*, that it wasn't doing very well.

Q: What wasn't? *Aliens*?

KING: *Aliens*. Maybe this is just a hinterlands town or something, but man, I loved *Back to School*.

Q: Yeah, wasn't that great.

KING: You know, they're all scratching their heads out there, in California saying "Why is this a hit? Why is this a hit?" You can't tell 'em. Because it's about somebody who's got a lot of *joie de vivre*, who's a human being. You sense that he probably smells sweaty. That he's a real guy. I believed him. It's ridiculous, but I believed him.

Q: Also, it's amazing for movies directed primarily at teenage audiences, they're basically saying this older guy, this old guy knows more than they do.

KING: Yeah.

Q: And that's sort of interesting—

KING: It's also interesting that his son wasn't embarrassed by him.

Q: Yeah.

KING: 'Cause his son kinda loved him. Although—I kept yelling at the screen, "Arnie, go get your Plymouth and run these people down that are giving you a hard time." It's like he's playing Arnie Cunningham again.

Q: Yeah, exactly.

KING: I don't know, the eyes.

Q: You're right. It was funny to see Keith Gordon not play psychoman. Now you've got another movie coming out.

KING: Yeah, *Stand By Me*.

Q: Right, adapted from your story, "The Body."

KING: It's a brilliant picture.

Q: It is, huh?

KING: It is. You're going to like it. Everybody's going to like it. And I think it's going to be nominated for an Academy Award for best picture of the year.

Q: Oh, you do, really?

KING: Yes, I do.

Q: Okay. Now when I heard the story on this, I wondered if this was, first of all, inspired by that incident out on the coast. Where the teenagers had the body there?

KING: No. As a matter of fact the story came from something a college roommate of mine told me back in, I think, 1968 or 1969 one night when we were all drunk, about how he grew up in New Paltz, New York and it was this college town and sort of squeaky clean. The only thing he and his friends had ever seen that was dead was like a squashed chipmunk in the road or something like that. And then one day they were just goofing around and this kid comes along and says, "You guys want to see a dead dog? There's a dead dog on the train tracks." George goes, "Yeah, I want to." They all wanted to, they all wanted to see it. The guy says, "It's all gushy and cut up, with maggots and everything." So they said that they had to be back by suppertime, because that was a big deal. And the guy says, "It's ok, it's only two miles down the track." Well, it turned out to be sixteen miles down the track. What struck me about the story that I could never forget was they couldn't turn around after a while. It was like one of these guys at the Vegas tables, you know. They had to see that dog, and they knew that they were going to get in trouble, but they kept on going till they saw it. So I said to George, "Was it worth it?" And he says, "Yeah!"

So it popped up and down in my mind for about, Jesus, I don't know, four or five years and I finally wrote this novella which was *A Different Season*, and called it "The Body," except I turned it into a human body. Because a dog just don't get it. And Reiner, of course, finally changed the title to *Stand By Me*, which I like, because "The Body" has this horror movie connotation and I'm sort of known for that. Shit, I'm doing this publicity tour and I'm down at the *Atlanta Journal Constitution* and I do the interview and they want a photograph and I go into this studio, and they got a coffin in there. The guy says, "You want to get in that coffin?" I says, "No, I'm not going to get in that coffin. Just take a picture." He says, "Why don't you want to get in the coffin? You write horror stories, don't you?" I said, "That's right, I write horror stories. If you had Louis Gossett, Jr., here, would you want to give him a piece of watermelon?" And the guy says, "It's not the same thing." I said, "Goddamn it, it is to me." You know, I'm done with that part. That was when the kids needed shoes.

Q: Well, you've seen this movie, then, but you really weren't involved with it. It was all Rob Reiner.

KING: I would like to say I was. The extent of my involvement was reading the first draft of the script and telling Rob I thought it was wonderful and thinking privately to myself, "They'll never make this, it's too much like the story." But they did.

Q: I understand also that one of the themes of the novella and the movie is the development of a young writer. People wonder if this is semi-auto-biographical on your part.

KING: It is. I didn't hang with anybody that was anybody when I was a kid. I mean, I grew up in lower-middle class circumstances and my mother worked for a living because my father just shuffled out when I was two. I don't remember him at all. I don't know. For a while my brother raised me, and my mother raised me. And then my mother was working all the time and I sort of raised myself. I sort of hung around with all these kids. Most of them were real, I mean, they just weren't there. But they were my friends and I dug them. And they're all dead.

Q: They are?

KING: Oh yeah, all of them dead. I'm the only one of those, there's something like four or five of us that hung out together. And they're all gone.

Q: Did they die in Vietnam?

KING: No. [*laughs*] One of them burned up in a house fire, the rest of them were car crashes.

Q: Boy.

KING: Two of them together. You know, it's autobiographical in that sense, but writers all lie. You know, you make up the good parts.

Q: Now, when I saw you in Wilmington, you were working, you said, on a book. On a word processor down there. Do you have another book coming out this fall, then?

KING: Yeah, it's called *IT*.

Q: Oh God. I think of *Them* and *The Thing*, and now *IT*.

KING: You're supposed to think of all that. "It" came from outer space. "It" the terror from—I didn't get the jacket I wanted. What I really wanted was just a blank jacket with these great big drooly green letters like on those hokey old movie posters. 'Cause every movie monster that ever lived is in this book. This is it, this is the final exam. Kids and monsters, monsters and kids, one more time, that's it.

Q: When you say, "that's it," that means you want to change after this?

KING: It's just a function of, I think that I wrote about the relationship between kids and adults, kids and parents for a long time because I was trying to understand my own childhood and also because I had small children. The years when most of those books were written that people remember so very clearly, like *The Shining*, *'Salem's Lot* and all that stuff, *Firestarter*, *The Dead Zone*, I had kids, you know, in rubber pants and diapers in all those years. And now, my youngest kid is nine, and I don't seem to have so much to say. I've written a story that's going to come out in January, called *The Eyes of the Dragon*. Basically I wrote it for my daughter because she never read any of my stuff. She doesn't like horror, so it's sort of a, it's sort of a, oh shit, it's a kiss of death but it's the truth. It's not a fairy story exactly, but like it's got dragons in it and things. You know what I mean?

Q: Okay.

KING: It's like a fantasy kinda thing. I don't know how to describe it. Once upon a time, long ago. That kind of thing.

Q: Which daughter is this?

KING: Naomi, she's the only daughter I got.

Q: And how old is Naomi now?

KING: Sixteen. But when she read it, when the thing was done, she was about thirteen, or something like that. She liked it. That was very satisfying to me.

Q: Now will this be published in book form?

KING: Yeah.

Q: I mean, you're describing it as a story, but it's like a short novel, then?

KING: It's actually about 350 pages long. But it's a story. It's like something by the Brothers Grimm, or something like that.

Q: So it's set long ago, in a distant time. And, one thing I read in the production notes on *Maximum Overdrive*, is that five of your works are now under option by the movie companies. Do you think something like *Eyes of the Dragon* would be suitable for a movie?

KING: Yeah, but I don't think I'll sell it.

Q: Why not?

KING: I just don't think that I'm ready to sell anything else. I mean, *IT* is going to be a mini-series for ABC TV. That's something that I worked for very deliberately because I thought that maybe what's needed is just that expanded time frame. Maybe the keyhole's too small.

Q: Okay.

KING: 'Cause I know that what's happened in a lot of cases here, is that these things have been bought because they seem to have a very strong visual sense. I know that's why Dino asked me to direct the picture.

Q: Okay.

KING: Besides a certain freak show value, I imagine he thought people would come for the same reason as Samuel Johnson said that people would come to see women preachers and dancing dogs. You don't expect to see it done well, you pay to see it done at all. So I think a lot of people will come just to see, you know, how bad I fucked up.

Q: Now in the posters, at least the ones I've seen in New York, which I guess are the same ones all across the country, you're sort of coming through—

KING: *It was Dino's idea*—

Q: Coming through a curtain looking like a magician, or a little bit like Orson Welles with a beard, a gray beard. Do you have a beard now?

KING: No.

Q: Did you have one then?

KING: Yes, I did.

Q: How did the beard come into this?

KING: Oh, I shave it off on opening day. When the Red Sox open, my beard comes off. When the Red Sox close, I put my razor away. That's the saddest day of the year. 'Cause when baseball's over, you can't kid yourself anymore, or something. I mean, I grow it in the winter. I live in Maine. It's sort of a protective measure.

Q: Okay.

KING: And you can't keep it in the summertime, because the black flies get in it. Yuck.

Q: Oh, okay.

KING: So at that time, they must not have been playing baseball in fact I know they weren't 'cause that was February.

Q: Right. For the shot. For the art.

KING: It was actually a piece of aluminum that was supposed to look like the side of a truck and I had my head stuck through it and if one of those boxes had slipped, I don't think you'd be talking to me now.

Q: It was in a real truck that they ripped open the side?

KING: It was just this great big piece of heavy gage aluminum that looked like a piece of truck.

Q: Now, have you had other offers since you finished *Maximum Overdrive* to go back and direct again?

KING: From Dino, I have. Dino would be happy to have me go back. I don't want to direct a picture.

Q: You don't?

KING: No.

Q: Once was enough?

KING: Well, for the time being, at least for the next six years. I'd like to do it again, I think, maybe sometime. I'm not in any hurry. It's a primitive way to create. I think one of the reasons people do it is that it seems impossible to do it at all. Women preachers and dancing dogs.

You know, eighty people standing around, drinking Gatorade, while you wait for the sun to come out from behind a cloud. It don't make it. We spent one whole afternoon—there's this guy who gets hit by a Cocoa-Cola can in the head, well, anyway, Coke can, because there is no product in America, I found out, that wants *their* name on a product in a movie if that product kills people.

Q: Oh, okay.

KING: So we made up all these bogus soft drink names. But this guy gets hit in the head with a can. The makeup guy did a thing, you know, he spent half a day putting a prosthetic device on one side of this poor actor's forehead. It was a thing where there was a little tiny bit of blood inside, you know, fake blood. And there was a pneumatic thing so that the idea was when we rolled the camera, it would swell and bloat, and you would see all this blood come through, and then the guy would just sort of pitch forward and set up for the next shot where the thing was all swollen, you know, like a bruise.

Q: Right, okay.

KING: The thing blew open [*laughs*]. Half a day. *Boom!* It's like a flat tire. You couldn't do anything but laugh. I mean, laugh or kill yourself.

Q: So you really realize the frustrations that a director goes through trying to make something, translate something visually.

KING: Yeah, but there's an upside, too, because the—I didn't know if I could work with actors, and I thought, you know, I had this stereotyped picture of actors as conceited monsters. My guys were great. Emilio was great. Laura Harrington was great. They worked very very hard. Pat Hingle taught me a lot of stuff that I probably should have known. I mean, the first three weeks was like a crash course at Berkeley Film School. The first day was like three weeks at Berkeley Film School.

Q: Now, you had mentioned George Romero had come there before, you know, when you were doing pre-production to help you go through. Did he come down to the set at all or work with you on editing or anything afterwards?

KING: No. He saw the rough cut and there were a couple of the shots. . . I could tell from the way he reacted that he really got a kick out of a couple of the shots and he did wince away from the steamroller scene, which was still uncut at that point. That was great. George just goes *sssss!* and covers his eyes. Man, I freaked. That was wonderful.

Q: Okay, now the two of you have been talking about doing, is it *The Stand*?

KING: *The Stand* and *Pet Sematary*. Laurel's got both of them for George, and we're waiting for money. And right now it's tough to get. I mean people will make movies out of my stuff, but—what I started to say before is I'm stopping as far as selling the stuff goes. Because there's a certain droning repetitiveness that's started to crop up, where people will say, "All right, we'll spend four million bucks because we can do 12, 14 million domestic and that's really the ceiling on Stephen King pictures" and, you know, that gives the picture a certain look, one step above New World pictures. In fact, one of them *was* a New World picture. *Children of the Corn.* "Alexander, we have you a woman—"

Q: Those movies, people will do them if they can do them cheap, but they won't commit 12 or 15 million to do one.

KING: Well, George—they budgeted *Pet Sematary*. And they thought that the bottom line, scrimping madly in everything, was a production budget of about 5.7. And the most that anybody would come up with is

Viacom, they come up with 5. Richard was trying to persuade George to do it, George asked me and I said, "Can you do it for 5?" and he said, "Frankly, not very well." And he'd just been stuck on *Day of the Dead*, with a budget, really, creamed a chance to make a picture that really would have looked a lot better. It was a thinkin' picture but it wasn't a lookin' picture. So he said, "I could do it, but it won't look very good." And I said, "Well, shit, let's not do it." So I went back to Richard and I said, "George says no, so I say no." He says, "The problem with George is that George *never* thinks he has enough money." And I said, "You don't understand, the problem is that George never has had enough money."

So one of the reasons that I'm floggin' *Maximum Overdrive*, other than the fact that I've spent a year and a half of my life doing it—

Q: Which is a lot longer than with a book?

KING: Well, not necessarily but it's a different kind of thing. I mean all these people in your face all the time. You don't have that with a book.

If this were a hit, and if *Stand By Me* were a hit, both, then all of a sudden, the purse strings would open wide and someone would be perfectly willing to put 20 million bucks in our hands without turning a hair, because that's the way it is, feast or famine.

Nutty business.

Q: Did you see *Vamp* yet?

KING: No, I'm not busting my ass to go see that; Grace Jones, I know how many teeth she's got. I've seen 'em. I saw *Conan, Part II* or whatever that was.

Q: Do you have a favorite scene in *Maximum Overdrive*, for the last question.

KING: [*laughs*] Yes. The critics won't like it, but I like the scene where Emelio corners this helper, this sort of cowardly, fat dog's body of a guy. It was shot in the bathroom. The guy's in a stall with a men's magazine taking a crap while Billy questions him. And we got a wonderful fart track for that. The first two or three just won't cut it, but we finally found one. I think it's very funny, but I have a low sense of humor.

With Robert Strauss

Stephen King sprawls on a sofa in his Beverly Hills Hotel suite, clad in new blue jeans and a black t-shirt with red lettering that reads "Dirty

Deeds Done Dirt Cheap." He's finishing up an exhausting publicity tour for *Maximum Overdrive,* the latest movie based on one of his stories and the first film he's directed. Beer in hand, his eyes constantly dart toward the national All-Star baseball game unfolding silently on the television.

Q: There is also a theme in "Trucks" about man becoming a slave to his machines.

KING: The thing is, I think about this now, I'm never going to forget every time somebody puts a tape recorder down on a table because it happened today at lunch. Vernon Scott, UPI, did this interview for print, but he also has some kind of radio thing that he does. We were tight for time. He asked me four questions and then I had to go because I had this other guy from one of the rival wire services. *Nothing had recorded.* So I did one more question for him.

But the thing is, if you want to talk about paranoia, about the revolt of the machines, the effect machines have on people, there's a guy who interviewed me from the *Providence Journal.* He was wearing a Batman t-shirt and a baggy tweed coat. This guy was like Wyatt Earp. From each pocket he takes one of these things and sets them both up. And he tells this story of how when Ronald Reagan was first elected—keep in mind this is Providence; so this probably seems like small shit on the West Coast. He got the first interview with Tip O'Neill after Reagan had been elected, which made it a fairly important interview as far as having a nationwide beat because with Carter unelected, Tip O'Neill immediately became the Number 1 Democrat in the country. And it was particularly important for the New England audience. So what he got was 5 minutes of conversation and then *baaaaaaaaaaaaa* for 30 minutes. And this thing had scarred this guy *for life.* So my feeling is that this year he's got two of them. Next year, he'll have four. And the year after he'll have six. He'll be showing people three and hiding the other three because he'll know he's crazy by then.

Q: It sounds like a great idea, carry two of them. . . .

KING: Like if it were me, right now, I'd be turning that thing off and listening to see if I were getting this conversation.

Q: I was just about getting ready to do that. . . .

KING: Right! I've heard that before.

Nothing works right. I know that they're all looking at me. Everyone one of them is out to get me. What happened today during the second interview. I was scared. The alarm went off in this place, the whole hotel. It wasn't just the smoke alarm, it was *the* hotel alarm. There are these people across the hall and the woman's saying, "Should we leave?" And the guy says, "No, I think everything's all right." Famous last words. You're supposed to leave! When it goes off you're supposed to leave, that's what the goddamn thing is for. What's this, "Should we leave?"

Q: Did you find out what it was?

KING: It was a false alarm. It usually is. They get to the bottom of the Chernobyl thing, and what it will turn out to be is one guy turned the wrong switch and someone will have had a dead gauge. So that's what *Maximum Overdrive* is about on that level. What it's about is having a good time, and nothing more. But any fantasy—from the lightest popcorn to the heaviest Sturm und Drang like *Seventh Seal*—is about reality, and it says something about the reality you don't want to talk to.

They don't want to talk about the freight elevator that stops between floors. They don't want to talk about fog, or airplanes falling out of the sky.

Q: You mentioned that even fantasy needs an internal logic. The one thing that stood out as perhaps a flaw in *Maximum Overdrive* is that some of the machines seemed to work for people, and some didn't.

KING: The cars were friendlies. I was hoping you were going to say something else. We knew it when we were making the picture, but the alternative was to rewrite the entire script. I never had the problem in the story. The story starts in there, so you never know how the people got there, except you do know, goddamn it, that the young couple in the story instead of going out to save the kid, the two characters go out—and the guy gets greased instead of coming back alive—they go out to get water. And we know that they crashed in much the same fashion, so apparently that's the truth in our story too.

In the end, I did not even answer that question in my mind, I just justified it. I said: the cars are friendlies. Except that even that doesn't hold water because there's a shot of a guy who's been killed in a pizza VW that's like turned on its own.

Q: And also when they're driving by, there are shots of junked cars blinking their lights.

KING: They've been junked. They've been turned out to pasture. I could justify that, but you're right. That's a flaw; I was hoping you were going to say one or two other things, because then I could have said it was somebody else's fault, but that's nobody's fault but mine.

Q: What are some of the other things?

KING: Why does it have to be a comet? I can tell you why. Because this was an MGM picture, and they said there had to be comet. It's the same reason for "Why does there have to a scene in the fuel office where the girl puts her arms around Emilio and says 'I'm scared'?" Because MGM said there had to be a certain amount of "Oh John," "Oh Martha. Thank God I'm alive. . . . "

They know it doesn't work. Not since *The Towering Inferno, Earthquake, Shake and Bake.* It doesn't work any more. Certainly in The Birds there's no need for that cause. You're right. In any given fantasy you're given that one aberration, and one only, and everything else has to conform to logic.

And we did some stuff, spur of the moment stuff that was not in the screenplay, on that assumption. The exploding jukebox is one thing that I thought to myself, "Well okay, the guy could play that song, but the jukebox should not work any longer because it's in the control of the machines."

Q: The same thing with all the weapons in the basement. How come they work?

KING: They're not electrical. Everything that malfunctions is electrical. We talked about that one too.

Q: I'm told you don't consider movies a real "art" form. . . .

KING: I think that the idea of a serious film is. . . name what you feel is an intellectual film.

Q: *Night of the Shooting Stars.*

KING: You've got to give me a dubbed version, that's number one. You bring in an illiterate off the street, a guy who can't even read a match book cover, he can sit there and might really dig on that movie. He might come off saying "Well, I don't know. It was really messed up. I don't know why all those people were doing them things."

But if you say to the guy, "you didn't understand why all those guys were doing them things, but what happened?" He'll tell you what happened. He's a witness. And I'm the guy that's been called the master of *post*-literate prose. But I can write a sentence and I understand the essential difference between picture and word. And I understand the difference between the exploding now and the ability to. . . r-a-t-i-o-c-i-n-a-t-e. To look backward, to pause in what you're doing and look backward with thought, or to take a look and thumb back three pages and say, "Now wait—what does that mean?" And to go over it again and to parse it out and to think about it.

If you watch *Shoot the Piano Player* or *The 400 Blows* there are great scenes, carefully planned out. But they explode. They're there, and then they're gone. Now we're accepting videotape, which may actually be the biggest influence on the genre ever. It's certainly going to make it a lot easier for people to understand a picture like *Dune* which was a great picture that people I don't think went to see because of that explosive— Here It Is—comin' at you effect.

In a way, watching a movie is a steadicam effect, only you are stationary and the movie flows past your eyes and brain. You can't stop it. That's why it's so hard to do a really good history movie. You can do suspense, you can do chase, but boy is it tough to do a history movie.

Q: Can you compare the creative process between writing and making movies?

KING: You have to listen because everybody on the set has made more movies than you have. And that holds true for Steven Spielberg, who's probably got grips, techs, lighting guys who have made like 250 pictures, who have forgotten things that he'll never learn.

So you listen to people, but everybody's got a movie they want to make. There's a special effects movie, a stunt man's movie, a cinematographer's movie, a set designer's movie, a costumer's movie—they all want to make their movie. Stunt people are the absolute worst, and they're the most insistent because they're the most technical. They know where to hit you, because if you fuck up, somebody dies, so they're the hardest to control in that sense.

That's the difference, when you have people coming and talking to you all the time. The similarities between the two creative processes— and for me, this was a great relief because I didn't know—Dino took me on mostly because the books are cinematic. They've all been bought.

I figured, all right, it's time to find out if I could do this. And I never had a moment's doubt about where the camera should be, or what I wanted to look at, or what I should see. Armando would say, "Why do you want to shoot this?" For instance, there's a scene where the salesman gets *smacked* with his truck, and I said I want to start with the guy's shoes and pan up to see the truck going away. And he says, "Why do you want to shoot this?" through an interpreter.

The thing is, I read somewhere that if you get hit hard enough, it knocks you out of your shoes. And I know if you get run over, a lot of time you get undressed, literally. They find if you're hit by a truck, they find you naked because whatever runs you over, if it's big enough, rips your clothes off and turns them inside out. And I thought those shoes made a statement. Not a big deal statement, but they were just there. Shit, that's all that was left.

Believe me, if I had to do to all over again, there's a lot of things that I could have done a lot better. But that's it. You just go and you do it.

So that was the best part. Nobody had to tell me, and nobody ever got scared that this guy doesn't know what he was doing, he's driving around in circles. I knew what I wanted, and we did get some good stuff, some nice visual imagery of empty roads and empty highways, suburban streets. It's creepy, it's weird. It's surreal.

Q: I really liked the opening scenes . . . .

KING: We had the rail drawbridge for three Sundays. We had a model drawbridge that they had built at great expense on the back lot. Everything was in the wrong scale. We could have put vehicles on there, but do you know what kind of vehicles? Do you want to know? Mercedes, Bughattis, Rolls Royces, Camaros. Can you see Dino De Laurentiis springing for the full-size equivalents that we had to wreck! We could use his Mercedes and two or three Bughattis. The other choice was that just coincidentally, on this day, this whole drawbridge is filled with nothing but Ford Bronco trucks, Jesus Christ! The rolling iron on that drawbridge—what you see that gets wrecked. The total cost of all that stuff was about $1,700. The motorcycles didn't run, they walked. The Trans-Am could barely run at all.

Q: Because there were so many trucks, did they donate?

KING: That was the funniest thing. They didn't give a shit who got run over: men, women, or children. The products were another thing. Coca-Cola—they didn't want their names on these Coca-Cola cans that squirt out of that machine, kill the coach and the little kids. Pepsi-Cola, same thing. You couldn't get Dr. Pepper or anything else. Miller Lite. There's a beer truck that gets blown. You want to see fuckin' strong men cry, it was like a week of 95 degrees, and we blew up a beer truck full of beer inside it. Two or three of those guys were actually lapping up rivulets of the stuff. The only way I could get them to go with the logo was to promise to do a Miller Lite ad and to promise them, solemnly, that their truck with the Miller Lite logo would not kill anybody. We got a few other permissions. We got Bic. And then we got a couple of dope-asso-ciated products: rolling papers and incense, and they didn't give a shit who we ran over, either. They just wanted people to see their logo.

But the truck people—Kenworth, Mack, any of those people—they didn't care who you ran over. An I know I get accused of being a brand name writer, but there ought to be something that people could con-neect with.

Happy Toyz, I wanted to be Toys 'R Us. There was one call from them and the guy says, "Are you kidding?"

Q: Where did idea of Green Goblin come from?

KING: Dino. Except he wanted Darth Vader. I didn't want anything. The Green Goblin seemed like a compromise. I don't like the face on the back, either. You work with a bunch of people, and you make certain compromises. . . . But the Goblin, I thought that was sort of fun.

Q: You've said you wanted to make a film that captured the feel of your books better than the other movies. How do you think you've done?

KING: I think I did pretty good. I think the people who don't like my written stuff, who find it vulgar and tasteless, will find this vulgar and tasteless, gross and grizzly, unpleasant and possibly boring, awkward, stereotypical and all the rest. And people who do like my stuff, are gonna find it vulgar, tasteless, but they're going to see the spirit behind it, which is a combination of Monty Python and Jack the Ripper. Believe it or not, they're the vestiges of an intellect working around up here.

The steamroller that runs over the kid, that's hilarious, but then I'm warped!

Q: I hear there was a before and after shot.

KING: The shot where the steamroller runs over him runs 14 frames farther, and they were just marvelous. I just at the last minute said to Dean Gates, who was our makeup guy, give me a bag of blood. He says, you want a baggie or a freeze-loc bag? I said give me a freeze-loc bag. He says how full? I said about half. He brought it to me and I sealed it up—you know how you can squeeze it so there's air trapped like a balloon, and that's what I wanted, and I tucked it down the dummy's shirts. I thought the steamroller will run over him, the roller will burst the baggie, and if we're lucky, the blood will get all over the roller in one place and we can pan with the camera and get this print, print, print, print, of the blood across the outfield, because the grass was green.

Instead the combination of the live kid with the dolly-arm can, and the switch to the other shot, was that the kid's head explodes.

Q: Did De Laurentiis have any suggestions to make?

KING: He told me, "Stephen, tonight I talk to you about one thing." That night, when we were alone, he says, "Your extras. You forget them in your mind. You think about special effects, about stunt work, but you forget that there are people who must move, who don't understand what is doing on. The way you have them, they are stiff."

I thought, this is great. For 15 days I'm shooting while this guy never comes around. It's 98 degrees out here, my jockey's are stuck to the crack of my ass and there's sweat up to my ankles inside my sneakers. He finally comes out in his air-conditioned Mercedes, looks around for 15 minutes, and says to me that my extras are too goddamned stiff!

So I go back to editing, and I say, "Jerk out every take on the bridge that you've got. I want to see everything that's on the bridge, close." He says, "Everything? You'll be here until 11 o'clock." I said, "I don't give a fuck if I'm here until three in the morning, get it all." So I got it all and looked at it on the movieola. He was right. They were just standing around. I ended up reshooting a bunch of that stuff. So I felt pretty stupid.

Q: Was it Dino's idea for you to direct?

KING: Yes, and no. I thought for a long time that I'd do it eventually. I knew as far back as *Creepshow*. I just got curious. The major thing is that you want to carve out the boundaries. . . you thought all along that writing novels is just a stepping stone to what you really want, directing pictures. . . . But I just got curious. So I watched George Romero, watched how he was directing, and learned as much as I could. That was my first film school. The rest of my film school was the first five days that I shot. I'm not kidding ya, this was earn while you learn— To find out what you could do, to explore new frontiers where no man has gone before, these are the voyages of the U.S.S. Stephen King. You only have one life to live, so you might as well live it as a blond. . . .

Jesus Christ, there are guys who have to go to the same job every day whether they want to or not. It isn't a question of whether they love that job or hate that job—it's called survival, it's called feeding the kids. I did that.

So if you get a chance to try something else, what are you going to do:

be chickenshit? So I did it. So maybe the critics will shoot me up. So maybe the film will be a hit. Maybe the film will stagger two steps, chuckle weakly and die in the street. Either way I can say I went out and at least I took a shot at it. You wouldn't believe how many people have asked me, "Are you going to direct again?" Which immediately makes the supposition that somebody is actually going to trust me to direct again after this comes out. You lose your sense of perspective. I could have made the *Brain of Planet Arous* and I wouldn't know. Not after a year and a half. You have no perspective.

Q: What did you learn?

KING: One thing I learned was that actors were not egomaniacal sons of bitches, total jerks who spend half their time eyes and face pushed into a mirror and the other half calling their agents on the West Coast because their hairdresser didn't come.

It shocked the shit out of me. Emilio came down ready to be a short order cook. He had practiced. There is a scene in the screenplay that was this guy cracking two eggs in one hand because I've seen short order cooks do it. Not that I thought an actor could do it. Actors can't do that sort of thing. Except he practiced, and he could do it. You got used to him after about a week and a half saying, "Who wants a Ruben?" Some guy'd say, "It's too hot Julio, I don't want a ruben."

"C'mon somebody, who wants a Ruben? The krauts going over."

So somebody says, "I'll take it, but only if you have some vienna left. I don't like the rye anymore."

He says, "I got the Vienna. Do you want the slaw up, or do you want the potato salad?"

This guy comes in and he's driving an 18-wheeler, some kind of long-distance hauler. He'd want burgers, beers. You'd tell him it was a movie set, but it wasn't in the sense it wasn't a false front. But *this* guy. . . . We had blown up this toilet paper truck. It was ripped in half, there was burned toilet paper all over everything, there's garbage spread from one end to the other, there's a Cadillac with garbage spread all over its body, there's a blown-up beer truck, there's a blown-up garbage truck. This guy pulls in and he gets out, takes a look around, goes [*belches*] "You really serve beer here? Can I get a hamburger?" He starts to walk inside. In the beginning, we were turning them away.

So Emilio's cooking, and these guys came in—a trucker, and his helper, and someone they picked up hitchhiking. And they come up to the counter and Emilio says " Whatcha havin' today, guys?" And one of them says, "You got any corned beef?"

Emilio says, "Well I think it went over, but I'll tell you what. You got some ham, you fry some up, that ain't too bad."

Guy says, "I'll have that, you think I can get a milkshake?"

Ellen comes out, who plays Wanda June, and says, "I'll get you a milkshake, mister." And the guys in the background are talking.

And they got their food, and they walked out, and they didn't know nothing. The trucks are going back and forth, they're bringing out camera equipment and light standards. And Emilio Estevez cooked for them, *and they're never going to know.* They had one of the pickled pig's feet.

We had a sound guy, Eddie White, who used to talk about pickled pig's feet. And I'd say, "You know what Ed, suppose I gave you $250 to eat one of those pickled pig's feet. Would you take that money?" He says, "No." I couldn't get anyone to eat one. I wouldn't eat one either.

Q: You said you didn't go back and read "Trucks" before you wrote the screenplay. Any kind of operating philosophy you had? . .

KING: I remember what the whole story was, and I took the nut of the story and put a bunch of people around it. I wanted to make some people come to the truck stop, so that I could cut away and cut back, cut away and cut back. Because it's a truck stop, it's not the Death Star, it's not the most fascinating place in the world to look at. But the best part is I was able to get out of Wilmington.

The first shot of this movie is the historic skyline of downtown Wilmington, which is not a skyline that's going to go down in the history of architecture. And I was able to get out of that. In some of Dino's other pictures in the Wilmington area that use the downtown area, it's a generic look. But once you get out of that you're able to show people things that no people have ever seen unless they live in the South.

Q: No other consideration?

KING: Only that it seemed to me that Wilmington should play Wilmington. Because in *Firestarter* it was Washington, D.C., and in *Cat's Eye* it was New York, and Atlantic City. Finally, it got to be Wilmington, to be itself. We were able to get out of downtown, away from those antebellum mansions. It was starting to look like that famous flat rock in the old Hollywood westerns.

Q: What were the toughest things about directing?

KING: The machines. They kept going wrong. That was it, the supreme irony of the experience that I had was that I decided to direct it because I thought a machine will never say to me, "I can't work today because I've got my period."

Part of it was budgetary, because they knew we were going to wreck these trucks and we had to keep them going and they had to nurse them through. But part of it was that they were so goddamned contrary. People would forget to air-up the air-driven trucks; the old ones. The best truck on the shoot was the Mack that chases the kids up the turnpike. It was a great truck, it would do what you want. The worst one was that tow truck, which shows up first, sort of the junk-yard-dog truck. And it shows up again—it was too mean to die. It crashes into the Dixie Boy, the game room. It's the first truck that crashes in, and it still wouldn't stop. I hated that bastard. It would never run when you wanted it to.

Q: What was the most satisfying thing?

KING: I came out alive. Whether I get out of this tour alive remains to be seen.

I guess the greatest satisfaction was finding out how much actors and actresses could do for me, how much more they could do than I thought they could do. You know that thing I told about Emilio coming down as short order cook? Even like the guys who had the parts—you know how they say in acting school, there are no small parts, only small actors? Well, it seems like it's the truth. They all tried their asses off. Even the girl who's in the tennis outfit, in the car at the beginning when the watermelons pile over. She sat in so much shit, and by the third Sunday that wasn't just a truck of watermelons, that was a maggot farm. And she would go right back in there, and get back in there, and she was wearing a skirt that was so short that it made the one Laura was wearing look Victorian in comparison, because it was a tennis dress. And by then, the skylight had broken, and she got glass cuts on her.

They don't complain. They really want to work, and to please you. And goddamn it—they're good! I used to think it was almost like an artificial thing, that there was no talent involved in it, that there was just people who were better mimics than other people. But boy, some of those people can really be actors and actresses.

The most satisfying thing about it, actually, was that I made friends all the way down the line. They were good people, they worked hard, and I respect that. I don't know if I'm a good person or not, but I'm willing to work my ass off. If somebody gives me a job, I'm going to do it.

Dino said when I agreed to do it, "Oh Stephen, I-a wait for-a this-a day."

And I said, "Well, good, you've got the day, you don't have to wait any longer. Just do me a favor. You're a guy who stands by his word. Make me one promise. You'll look at the dailies. And if you look a week, two weeks, and if you decide I can't do this job, cut me loose."

He said, "Stephen, I'd never. . . ."

And I said, "Never mind that. Just give me your word that you'll do that."

And he never came, and I made a lot of friends and they got me out of a lot of jams and saved my ass a lot of times. So I guess that's it.

Q: Now you've directed, do you feel more charitable towards some of the other films you've been disappointed with?

KING: No, not at all. Right's right, and wrong's wrong. That doesn't ever change. Rob Reiner's adaptation of "The Body," *Stand By Me*, is a brilliant piece of work. By far, it's technically superior to my work. It's more thoughtful and has much more range than *Maximum Overdrive*. I'm glad that they're not being released so close together that comparison could be glaringly obvious between somebody who can get the job done and. . . .

Did you see *White Nights*? The difference between the movie Reiner made and the movie I made is like the difference between Baryshnikof and Gregory Hines. I can tap dance.

Q: Where does the public image of the Master of Terror end?

KING: More than anything I'm afraid that after a day like today, talking with reporters from dawn to dusk, I might go to a deli to pick up a sandwich, and some guy will look at me and say, "Aren't you Stephen King?" And I'll say "No. I just look like him." If that day ever comes, that's when I pack it in. I'm done.

King's attention shifts back to the television, where Most Valuable Player Roger Clemens is tipping his hat to the crowd after pitching three perfect innings. "God love ya, Roger," King squeals. "He's just a few miles from his hometown, his whole family's there and everything; that's wonderful. He's like the Robert Redford character in *The Natural*. Too cool." King doesn't seem able to prevent himself from adding, "I can't help thinking someone's going to shoot him."

With Paul Gagne

Q: Part of the reason you were involved so extensively with the first *Creepshow* was that you wanted to direct something yourself some day. After the critical lambasting you took for *Maximum Overdrive*, are you anxious to direct again?

KING: Not soon. I'd like to do it, though. I'd like to remake *Plan Nine from Outer Space*! Hey, Paul, I think there's real possibility there! I'd like to do *Misery*. There's a Fredric Brown novel called *The Mind Thing*, which is a little bit like Finney's *The Body Snatchers*. Sure, I'd like to direct again. I know what I did wrong with *Maximum Overdrive*. I went against every creative impulse that's ever moved me, which has always been intuitive. I've never worked from an outline in my life, so what I did with *Maximum Overdrive* was to work from the most complex outline I could possibly work up. It was wrong, that's all.

Q: One thing I felt the film had going for it was that it didn't take itself seriously at all.

KING: Of course not. It's a stupid movie in a way—it's a chicken circuit movie. I thought it was hilarious when the guy was farting in the bathroom, and I took more critical chawing about that. I don't know what's wrong with people these days! It seems like nobody wants to laugh at anything unless it's Woody Allen! What happened to the old "stick your hand in your armpit and make fart noises" routine? That was funny to me. But not anymore.

Q: I think that some of the cuts that were made in order to avoid an "X" rating from the MPAA really hurt the film. There's one sequence where you spend ten minutes getting this kid to where a guy is lying in a ditch. In the original cut, the guy's face just sloughed off when he grabbed the kid's wrist and sat up. After a ten-minute buildup, the audience is led to expect something big there, but when the guy just grabs the kid's wrist and you cut away to something else, it's rather anti-climactic.

KING: Tell me about it. You'd have to talk to Dino De Laurentiis about it. That's the only place where I felt I didn't get support from Dino and his organization. I went with Dino because Dino promised that he would support me, and he's a man of his word. He supported me everywhere, except with the ratings board. And if you ever see the thing uncut, you tell me what there is anywhere in that goddamned picture that even approaches *The Fly* for gore effects, or any of that stuff. There's a scene in *The Fly* where Jeff Goldblum breaks this guy's wrist arm wrestling, but he doesn't just break the guy's wrist—he practically tears off his hand, and we see that. We see him puking over his food, for Christ's sake. We see him puke onto another guy and melt his foot off. Next to that, what we had was tame.

All I know is that from the time we were doing the picture all the way up until we went before the ratings board—I'm like a car on an assembly line, you know? I've got to go in front of the Environmental Protection Agency just like every other car coming off this assembly line. Dino can't stop the line and argue for me without jeopardizing everything else that he's got coming along. So he didn't. Frankly, at that time I was exhausted, and maybe I didn't fight as hard as I could.

CHAPTER SEVEN

†

PERSONAL DEMONS

†

With Michael Hanlon *(1983)*

The house sits a little back from the road, old and dark red, the color of drying blood. In one corner is a tower with long windows from which a pale, anxious face might peer.

In the lawn behind the house sits a chair carved out of rock; it looks like a tombstone. The house seems to creak under the lowering September clouds.

It is the perfect setting for a horror story.

Two of them are taking place in the house right now, to the accompaniment of raucous rock music and the murmur of an electric typewriter.

They are being created by Stephen King, a thick-spectacled, thick-stubbled, thickly built man who has scared more people than the Mafia in the past 10 years. King has written *Carrie, The Stand, 'Salem's Lot, Night Shift, The Shining, The Dead Zone* and *Firestarter,* currently the number-one best-selling hardcover book in North America.

His readers shiver deliciously as the ordinary becomes evil, gentle children inexplicably assume strange powers and small New England towns—towns like Bangor, Maine—confront his monstrosities.

He's sitting on his porch this particular afternoon, chatting amiably, drinking Budweiser from a can, smoking a chain of cigarettes and playing a game with Star Wars figures with his three year old son, Owen.

His two other children, Naomi, 10, and Joe, 8, are indoors wrapping gifts for their father, whose 33rd birthday is but three days away.

Owen wins the Star Wars game easily and goes off to play with a horde of neighborhood kids who are fighting World War III behind the house.

"I write about 'what if'. . . ?" King says. "Literary writers, the high-brows, say 'what next?' I'm not interested in that. I'm a 'what if' writer.

"What if there's something there? What if it can take control? What if it's mad?"

King allows that he still makes a point of sleeping with his feet under the covers because he's afraid something will reach up from under the bed and clutch his ankle.

"Not some*one*," he stresses, "some*thing*."

He puts his beer can in his lap and points with his index and little fingers at some birds on the lawn and makes whistling bullet noises.

"Blackbirds," he says. "Give 'em the evil eye."

There are a lot of blackbirds in Bangor, Maine, and King makes the same gesture whenever he sees one.

It's natural that he should try to appear a little weird, like his books, but in fact he's very plain and very jolly, an affectionate husband, doting father and friendly fellow who likes to crack a few beers, as he puts it, and sit around and chat.

But he has the stern self-discipline that's almost as important to a writer as talent.

"I'm up at 6:30 every morning and get breakfast for the kids and get them off to school," he says. "Then I just walk around for about four miles, sort of sniffing at this book in my mind.

"I get back at 9:30 and write to 11:30. Everyday I write 1,500 words. In the afternoon I read and sort of gibber around."

He churns out words like a machine, rock music blaring from his stereo. By the time he's finished his daily stint, he knows what he'll be writing about the next day. When he sits down at his typewriter at 9:30 every morning (weekends included), the words flow as smoothly as the Bud he's drinking on his porch.

The "gibbering" in the afternoon often includes rewriting another novel that's in the works.

Right now in the mornings, he's writing the first draft of a novel to be titled *IT* (one character, a librarian, is improbably named Michael Hanlon).

In the afternoon he's rewriting another novel, next to be published, named *Cujo*, a twisted tale about a boy and his dog.

"I'm not as facile as I used to be," King says. "I wrote *The Shining* in two months."

The Shining was set in a rambling hotel in the mountains of Colorado. But it was while he was living in Boulder that King got the idea for *IT*, which is set in Bangor, renamed Derry for the novel.

"I had to go and pick up the car from the garage, the transmission was shot or something," King says. "Tabby offered to drive me in the other car but I said no, I'd walk.

"It was dusk and I had to walk over this little bridge and I thought to myself. . . what if there was a troll living under this bridge?"

King says he likes to live in the place he's writing about, which is why the King family last month moved back to Bangor and the 15-room rambling house that King says is "kinda creepy."

"We stole this house," King says. "We got it for a ridiculous price."

It's 130 years old, the oldest house on a street of huge elegant houses that once belonged to the timber barons of Bangor.

"One hundred and thirty-five thousand dollars," Tabby King says.

She grew up in Old Town, about ten miles away and both have lived in Bangor before. She has French-Canadian forebears whose name was Pinette before they changed it to Spruce at the beginning of the century when the local Ku Klux Klan was hunting down Catholics, she says.

"The literal translation was Little Pine, but that would have been exchanging a French Catholic name for an Indian one, so they settled for Spruce," she says. "The name change was a social device."

When the Kings were in Bangor before, Steve worked for a local laundry for $60 a week. Now he sends the laundry his shirts to clean. "That's the sweetest thing of all," he says.

The new novel, *IT*, fits in Bangor because it's a hard town, King says. "They busted a lot of people here during the Viet Nam war. They won't stand for much. It's a hard-drinking, working man's town.

"They're just as likely to set fire to your hair in a bar if they don't like the way you're talking."

King realizes we've run out of Budweisers and he won't drink the no-name beer from the supermarket so we walk down to the corner store for fresh supplies. King takes three empty cans with him to get back his deposit.

On the way back to the house, through a park where young teenagers are playing football, he suggests we "crack open a couple" from the six-pack and we sip from the cans as we walk.

It's small-town peaceful, but, as King points his fingers at blackbirds overhead, you can almost sense a story brewing. Yet, plodding along in his scuffed running shoes, constantly hitching up the jeans that keep slipping off his bulky hips, he doesn't look the man with the most lucrative and successful of fantastic imaginations.

"It's not enough to have imagination," he says later, back on the porch. "You have to be able to tap into it."

"I taught school and you could see the kids losing their imagination right in front of your eyes. I don't know whether it's peer pressure or some sort of governor they have. But imagination shrinks and shrinks and shrinks."

"I've never met anyone without a sense of humor but I've sure met people without any imagination at all."

King believes much of his creativity is inherited. "I know little about my father—he left us when I was two—but I know he wrote science fiction. He had a lot of rejection slips."

King has an adopted brother older than himself and hasn't seen his father since he deserted the family. "My mother tried to track him down a couple of times, just for support, but she never found him."

"I came home one day and my mother was absolutely white. 'I think I've just seen your father on the news,' she said. It was when there was all the fighting in the Congo in the Sixties and she thought he was one of a bunch of mercenaries. Maybe that's how he ended up."

Tabby—a short, round-faced, smiling woman who seems as little affected by King's riches as King is himself—sits beside him on the cane loveseat on the porch. Amber "the Maine shed-cat" jumps up on his lap.

King says he's thinking of having some unpublished short stories privately printed to send to friends at Christmas.

"But what do I say, 'Merry Christmas from the Great Me'?"

"Why not, you don't knit," Tabby says.

They had celebrated *Firestarter*'s number one position on the best seller list at lunch time this day with two bottles of Perrier Jouet champagne.

This evening they're going out for dinner. And when they get back at about 11 pm., Steve goes into his office and writes some more.

And sure enough, he's up early next morning, breakfasting with the kids, sitting at the kitchen table in a Chewbacca mask while three-year old Owen wears a Yoda mask.

As Naomi and Steve leave for school, King sets out on his walk to sniff at the book. Tabby goes with him and they pass "The Bangor standpipe" —a hundred-year-old water tower that may one day appear in one of his stories.

They explore an 1870 bird bath in the middle of a common, pass a variety store that's the setting for one of his short stories. When he gets back to the house he checks test papers that son Joe has brought home from school. At almost 9:30 he picks up his iced water and his vitamin pills and goes into his office off the dining room.

While Tabby sits at the kitchen table sorting out cents-off coupons with King's secretary, the name-brand writer puts on an album, sits before the electric typewriter with *IT* in front of him and *Cujo* alongside, switches on and begins his daily 1,500 words, knowing where he's going.

With Michael J. Bandler

Some folks along Bangor's West Broadway say that the Kings' rambling red and white Victorian house is haunted.

Tabitha King doesn't believe it.

"That's what the previous owner claimed," says the wife of Stephen King, the enormously prolific and successful author of a string of best-selling novels most accurately identified as horror tales.

The alleged ghost is a General Webber, who, before dying in his room about a century ago, announced firmly, "I'm not leaving." But Tabby King says the manifestations of his presence—strange noises, sensations, and the odor of cigar smoke—are "quite insubstantial."

If there is no General Webber, there is, nonetheless, an apparently endless parade of eerie, alarming, possessed characters many with awesome supernatural powers—marching out of Steve King's typewriter to glory on Publishers Row and in Hollywood. For the 34-year-old writer, horror isn't merely something he fixed upon and capitalized upon as an adult. As a niche of culture, it has been a lifetime companion, ever since his first close encounters with the classic EC comics and the cinematic kitsch of the Fifties.

You don't have to chat for long with the rumpled, rangy, sometimes bearded writer ("We know it's spring when he shaves off his beard and gets out his Caddy convertible," says Tabby) to realize how closely his life and career are linked with kids—his own and those he has created in his imagination. A child is a central character in such books as *Carrie*, *The Shining*, *Firestarter*, and *The Dead Zone*. And three children—Naomi, eleven, Joseph, nine, and Owen, four—are central characters in his and Tabby's home.

"To me the real purpose of having kids has nothing to do with perpetuating the race or the survival imperative. Rather, it's the way of finishing off your own childhood. . . . By having children you're able to reexperience everything you experienced as a child, only from a more mature perspective. It's like completing the wheel. At that point, you can give your childhood up."

Does he think about his own kids or use them in his books in any way?

"Sure, although probably I think more about what I remember from my own childhood than I do about them. But, for instance, Charlie McGee, in *Firestarter*, was very consciously patterned on my daughter, because I know how she looks, I know how she walks, I know what makes her mad. I was able to use that, but only to a certain degree. Beyond that, if you tie yourself to your own children, you limit your range. So I took Naomi, used her as the frame, and then went where I wanted."

The kids, and some of their friends, were flowing in and around the house on a typical Sunday in early spring as Steve patiently explained himself to the latest in a series of interviewers who have been travelling to Maine—either Bangor or Center Lovell, a town of only 640 that is 95 miles away, where the Kings have a summer home—to confront this one-man cottage industry. Actually, now that Tabby has published her first novel, *Small World*, also a horror tale, it's a two-person concern.

An open, forthright woman who exudes a sort of pioneer spirit, Tabby readily acknowledges that her budding career has been helped by the fact that she is Stephen King's wife.

"But I think we're both willing to say pretty bluntly that I put ten years into helping him advance in every way that I could, from socializing to reading the manuscripts and making suggestions, as he did with mine. We don't write each other's books. But there is a constant exchange going on, and it's all to the good, so far as I can see, I'm not ashamed and he's not ashamed to say, 'Ta-dum, here's my wife, she's pretty good, too.'"

When Tabby isn't pecking out the plot of her second novel on her typewriter, she sits on several committees at the University of Maine, notably on issues involving women. Recently she was involved in preparing a directory of women in various professions in the locale. "I think someday she'd like to get a place on the board of trustees," her husband suggests. "She doesn't talk about it, but I think she's laying the ground for a career in public service of some sort—not politics, but something close to it, something between being a Tupperware lady and being a senator."

Unlike her mother, eleven-year-old Naomi hopes to be a ranger when she grows up. She's a voracious reader but steers clear of horror books and movies, preferring science fiction, legends, heroic tales about animals, and stories like *Gone With the Wind*, which she recently completed. Nine-year-old Joe, Steve's faithful moviegoing companion, likes horror and hopes to be a writer like his dad. He's begun, in fact, and, says his mother, "The kid can write a story—he's really got the bones of the business." But he has encoding problems, a particular learning disability that results in poor spelling and punctuation. The Kings installed a computer to assist him in learning how to keep his thinking and writing in pace with each other. As for Owen, four, whose room is decorated with superhero and space adventurer posters and dominated by a formidable stuffed version of the Loch Ness Monster, he promises to be his dad's kind of guy. "You know what part I liked best?" he asked rhetorically about a movie he's just seen on television. "The bl-o-o-dy part!"

Naomi and Joe each have read some of the stories in their father's collection *Night Shift*, but none of the novels yet. Naomi watched *'Salem's Lot* on television but left the room of her own volition during the "scary" parts. She and Joe weren't allowed to see the movie *Carrie* when it was released, because, says King, "the movie and the book both have uncomfortable things to say about parents who hate their children and use them, and about children who are put upon by their peer groups. We thought it would be upsetting." As for *The Shining*, the senior Kings saw it and found it ineffective, so they permitted Naomi and Joe to see it. Only Joe went.

The Kings, naturally, have to maintain a careful balance between what their children routinely absorb as the offspring of a pair of horror novelists and what they feel the kids can tolerate. Tabby thought Joe saw *Jaws* too early. "I wasn't concerned about the blood," she explains. "I was opposed because of the overstimulation and the emotional intensity, which I felt was too much for him to take. But I'm usually overruled anyway."

Steve, an inveterate moviegoer from kindergarten days (Tabby saw her first movie, *The King and I*, when she was about ten and no others for years afterward), feels that horror is relative. "The movies that I remember affecting me, overstimulating me, and keeping me awake at night were not the *Black Scorpion* or *Screaming Mimi* types, but *Bambi* and *Fantasia*, particularly "The Sorcerer's Apprentice" sequence. The implied father-son relationship, and the idea that the son had disobeyed his master, made me cringe. Often I think that Joe in particular is made uncomfortable by things he sees in television sit-coms. I remember a *Laverne and Shirley* episode when one of them who was Queen of the Hop made her entrance and stumbled down a flight of stairs. He was very upset by it.

"Kids don't typify or categorize. They don't see things as either just funny or just horrible," King observes. "It's somewhere in between. A child who has just discovered the idea of peer groups and relationships can be very scared by the notion of someone doing things wrong. And right now Joe is sensitive to this."

These days King is feverishly trying to complete a multilevel novel he's been working on for what seems like ages. The title is simply *IT*—named for a monster inhabiting the sewers of a large city. It's the story of a group of youngsters who, in 1958, through some act of faith, go into the sewers and wound the creature. "It" decides to let them go and to deal with them after they've grown up. "Twenty years later," says King, "they come back and have to try to replicate what they did.

"I've written the book in two parallel lines: the story of what they did as kids and the story of what they're doing as grown-ups. That's what I mean when I say I'm interested in the notion of finishing off one's childhood as one completes making a wheel. The idea is to come back and confront your childhood, in a sense relive it if you can, so that you can be whole."

These native Down Easterners have come a long way from their wedding day in 1971, which was set to conform with the schedule at the laundry where Steve worked. ("We got married on a Saturday because the place was closed on Saturday afternoons. . . . Everyone wished me well, but I still was docked for not being in that Saturday morning.")

They have a staff of three people now, but the services performed are merely what is necessary to allow the Kings to pursue their craft.

A housekeeper is on the premises five days a week, and on those days prepares lunch. Tabby's sister, Stephanie, is Steve's secretary, and Stephanie's husband, Jim, is what Steve calls the majordomo. ("He does the lawn, repairs things, washes the cars, and plays tennis with me to keep my heart going.")

On the weekends, everybody pitches in. Steve happens to live to bake. "I don't particularly care for sweets myself," he says, "but if I make bread or coffee cake someone around here'll eat it." Actually he has an ulterior motive for getting involved in baking. "There's something sexy about kneading dough."

In truth, a brief visit to the Kings' $135,000 Bangor home reveals few examples of conspicuous consumption that set them apart from the average suburbanite. They're not clotheshorses ("I doubt my entire wardrobe retails for more than a thousand dollars," he says matter-of-factly). His kids have an Atari game, and he has a video cassette recorder, but they're becoming standard these days. He does have a giant-screen television console; but only this and his fleet of cars (the Caddy convertible, a beat up 1975 station wagon that "smells like someone died in it," a van, a motorcycle, and Tabby's Mercedes) hint at their real affluence. They have definite plans for remodeling the house—installing a solar-heated indoor pool at the rear, adjacent to a new office for Steve that will replace his cramped current quarters in the front parlor. And they have made certain that their children's education will be provided for.

"I'd also like to have a TV satellite dish put in at ground level," King comments, "but Tabby's disgusted by the whole idea of bringing more garbage into the house on the tube. I'd like to have a jukebox. I'd like to have one of those fancy Asteroids games, but haven't gotten around to doing much about it. You see, I am my work to a large extent. Work takes most of the energy. It's what gives me pleasure. It *is* the toy. I don't feel the need to fill up my life with tape decks and amplifiers. It's nice, but I can take it or leave it."

They think a lot about how his fame is affecting their children. "They're going to realize someday that there are people who will want their acquaintance only because their daddy's famous," she predicts.

"They haven't gotten to the hard part," Tabby observes, "the moment when they have to decide whether they're gong to rebel or imitate. We all come up against this, but it's a little more difficult when our parents are well known. It'll be interesting to see what happens."

With Bob Haskell

Like all reputations, Steve King's does not tell us everything. The readers of his books consider him the undisputed master of horror fiction—the writer who loves to scare your pants off.

But that is only one side, the famous side, of the man from Lisbon Falls whose name keeps popping up on all those bestseller lists and who has recently moved his family to Bangor.

For example, how many out there know that Stephen King is a bona-fide baseball junkie? All right, you five people can put your hands down.

The rest of you seem a little surprised. It's true. And nothing in sports captures his fancy more than the World Series, which is going on this week.

Far be it for me to embarrass the man by pointing out he could have been a sports writer. So can just about anyone who can count. It is safe to say that had Steve King hit the locker room circuit he would have added a new dimension to sports journalism comparable to what the Rev. Sun Myung Moon has brought to religion in this country.

He had his chance. He earned his first paychecks in his chosen field as the sports writer for the weekly *Lisbon Enterprise* during his junior and senior years in high school, recalled King following lunch Wednesday at his home on West Broadway. He's also had a taste of coaching with a Brunswick Little League team in the summer of '67 after his freshman year at Maine.

His observations as a mere fan however, are as extreme as the supernatural ideas he has developed into novels.

He despises the New York Yankees. "If someone were to ask me who I hate more, Bucky Dent or the Ayatollah Khomeini, I'd have to think about it.

"They ruined the Red Sox. Remember that single playoff game? It ruined me for four months. I was like the walking wounded."

He cheers for the Red Sox. He's been a fan for more than 15 years.

"I'm a white guy. I don't want to sound like a racist but Boston has always had a white team. The Red Sox give klutzy white guys something to root for. It shows that maybe white guys can do something in sports.

"They're an incredibly flaky club. Remember Bill Lee? I loved Bill Lee. And who can forget Pumpsie Green? He didn't even know what city he was playing in most of the time."

He likes the game itself because "the clock never wins. You have to win on your own. The saddest spectacle in sports is in college football when the quarterback falls on the ball or in high school basketball when a team freezes the ball to let the clock win for them."

Also: "You can watch an entire game, drink a case of beer, read a novel and never miss a thing. I love it because it's slow."

But we digress. It is the World Series which brings the baseball fan out of Steve King like sap seeping from a maple in March. By his reckoning he has not missed a Series game in 14 years, regardless of who has played. His earliest memory of any game was of Don Larson jumping into Yogi Berra's arms after pitching a perfect game for, that's right, the Yankees in the fifth game of the 1956 series with Brooklyn.

"Anyone who loves baseball comes to that love through the World Series," said King, who insisted he will see every game even though he will be away all weekend.

It is during the Fall Classic that King also starts thinking about growing his winter beard. He generally stops shaving after the fifth or sixth game, when he figures one of the teams is on the ropes. It is a sign of mourning. "A part of me dies when the World Series is over," he said.

CHAPTER EIGHT

†

BEYOND THE BRAND NAME

†

With Ted Koppel (1984)

His name is Stephen King. His novel *Pet Sematary* is number one on *The New York Times* hardcover best-seller list; another novel by Mr. King, *Christine*, is at the top of *The New York Times* paperback list. He is also, in case you didn't know, the author of *Carrie, The Shining, Cujo* and other novels that have all done extremely well. Mr. King is with us now live from Bangor, Maine. Did you ever suffer, did anyone not publish you ever?

KING: Oh, yes. A lot of people did not publish me ever.

Q: How could they have lacked the insight?

KING: You'd have to ask them, but the first four novels that I wrote, beginning at age 16, went unpublished. I became a published writer in the pulp jungle. The phrase belongs to Frank Gruber, who is a guy who published a lot of short stories and a lot of paperback originals. I began at age 18 publishing a story in a magazine called *The Magazine of Strange Tales*, which was one of the last of the pulp magazines, for $35. I worked my way up to those magazines, which, if you hold them up horizontally, the gatefold would fall out.

Q: I've heard of them.

KING: Yeah.

Q: Yeah. Tell me—

KING: The ones you see in barber shops.

Q: Did you—you mean *Police Gazette*. Did you ever have a formula in mind when you started writing, or did you just set out to write the best thing you could?

KING: No, I wrote out, I started out to write the things that I loved, which were mostly stories of fantasy, stories of horror, stories of make-believe. And as I grew and as the market shrank for short fiction, I found out that the only magazines left that were still publishing those things were basically the skin magazines. I published in *Cavalier*, I published in *Dude*, I published in *Gent*. The story that became *Carrie*, my first novel, started as a short story which I thought maybe I could sell for $200, $400. At that time I was working in an industrial laundry, and if a sale came in, what that meant was that if the baby, my daughter Naomi, got an ear infection, then we could afford the penicillin.

Q: Let me ask you a—it's a personal question, and if you choose to, answer it just in the most general of terms, but these figures are thrown around. What kind of money do you—or what—do you have an agent?

KING: I have an agent.

Q: What kind of money does he talk—I mean if he walks into a publisher now and says, "It's old Stephen King, you know him," can they even talk to you for less than a million dollars?

KING: Well, in the case of *Christine* they talked to me for a buck, because I got totally disgusted with the huge advances. I began to feel that I was participating in some sort of a pork-barrel operation that almost made the Pentagon look a charitable organization in comparison. So, you know, in terms of advances, I read in *The New York Times* that for the Judy Krantz book, *Princess Daisy*, that could have brought 60 first novelists advances of enough to take them off the streets. Now, nobody ever gave me a foundation grant or anything like that. But the basis of the industry is still royalty, what you get from the consumer, your percentage from the guy who goes in a B. Dalton or a Walden Books or the corner bookstore and says, "Okay, I'll pick up the book." And because I feel confident enough that they will go in and pick up the book, and because I don't want to give publishers the rolling interest or anything like that, I said let's publish the book for a buck, and that's what we did.

Q: And who gets the profit?

KING: Well, I get some of it, the publisher gets some of it, and hopefully the reader gets some of it from the book that they read.

Q: But you think these big advances, generally speaking, are harmful or helpful to the industry as a whole?

KING: I think they're very harmful to the industry as a whole when it comes to established writers, but I also think that if you gave a guy like the fellow who wrote *Endless Love*, I can't think of his last name now, Scott someone [Spencer]—but if you have a guy like that, if you have a first novelist who's waiting tables, whose wife is waiting tables in order to support his aspirations, that fellow has got to have enough to allow him to live his dream.

With William Robertson

Since almost no cultural phenomenon, popular or otherwise, escapes academic scrutiny, it was perhaps only natural that King's time would come. It did, in 1984, at Florida Atlantic University's fifth annual Conference on the Fantastic in the Arts. King's work was the subject of a number of papers and the author himself was a keynote speaker.

Q: Why do you think there's such large-scale interest these days in horror and fantasy?

KING: Well, I think people are scared. They're scared of a lot of things: war, poverty, inflation, deflation, deficit, arms race, whatever. And what you do when you've got a lot of things that you're really afraid of is you sublimate them into something that's not real or you find a place to escape—escape pure and simple. So you're talking about translating the real fears into symbolic fears so that you can deal with them in another way. That's one reason. The other reason is because we've become an increasingly secular society and that means that we don't have the traditional outlets for contemplating our own mortality, and saying. "Well, we're surrounded by forces, by an invisible world," or else "we're surrounded by nothing." And either one of those ideas is kind of. . . well, it's bigger than all of us, I guess.

Q: So in a sense fantasy and horror are taking the place of religion in an earlier time?

KING: Yeah, I would say that for a lot of people they have. Because these people will say, "No, I don't believe in God; no, I don't go to church. Church is bullshit. You go to church and the next thing you know somebody's telling you to march off to a crusade somewhere; people die and I don't believe in all that stuff. I don't believe that Jesus was the son of God, I don't believe in Buddha, I don't believe in any of those things. But at the same time I'm going to go see *The Amityville Horror* and I'm going to go see *The Shining* and I'm going to read *The Dead Zone* and all these other things."

I go see a movie like *Amityville* in New York, and there's this kind of respectful silence and you look and you say to yourself, "The Church of Times Square is now in session." Because these people are trying to touch something that's supernatural or beyond the bounds of ordinary rational, empirical life as they know it, but they're trying to touch it in a very secular way, in a way that sort of short-circuits ideas of God, the devil, satanism, all that stuff.

Q: What do you think about the essays and the papers being given at this conference on your work?

KING: I haven't seen any of them in advance so I can't say.

Q: Do you have any feeling about that generally?

KING: Sure, unreality.

Q: Unreality?

KING: Yeah, that anyone should care to write a paper about my work.

Q: Why do you say that?

KING: Because I'm just a storyteller, basically. I mean the work ought to have some resonance. I guess in a way resonance is the only thing you need to produce any kind of academic paper in the field of American literature today. It better be all you need because if you need much more there's going to be too many academics trying to write papers on too few subjects. I suppose in a way that's why they've gotten around to me. It's like if you have enough mouths to feed sooner or later you'll even eat the stunted corn [laughter]. You hear what I'm saying?

Q: Yeah, right.

KING: Anyway, my interest has always been in telling stories. The stories themselves may be unbelievable. But within the framework of the stories I'm concerned that what people do in those stories should be as real as possible and that the characters of the people should be as real as possible. So in that context you probably could generate some insight about literature or symbolism or allegory or whatever you want it to do.

Q: The Latin American novelists work with fantasy and Gabriel Garcia Marquez, for instance, has said, "Well, you think it's fantasy, it's supernatural, but it's everyday reality down here." Is there any of that going on in your work?

KING: Sure. There is. There's a lot of it. I'll tell you something I just put into a story that I read in the newspaper probably eight months ago now, maybe a little bit longer. There's this guy who came into a doctor's office in San Francisco, and he says, "I'm having these terrible headaches." Well, he was a Type A. He was in college, he was approaching final exams in his senior year. You know, just the type you'd expect to have migraine headaches, but still you check it out. So they gave him the X-ray series to make sure he wasn't growing a tumor in there.

The guy effectively had no brain. I mean he had a skull case that was filled with cerebro spinal fluid, and he had a cortical twist like a macrame drape roll that was running his—what do they call them?— the functions that you don't have to consciously control, like your breathing and your heart rate. But that's all he had. And somehow the spinal fluid was conducting impulses or storing memories or something. I mean the guy was an A student and apparently the headaches had nothing to do with his brain condition. They were migraines and they went away after his senior exams.

He had no brain is what I'm saying. This guy had no brain. So compared to some of the stuff that I've written in the past, if I tried to write something like that...you know people say, now, "King could publish his laundry list," but I couldn't publish that. That's like a physical impossibility in a world where, when we look around us, craziness is all we see everywhere. Somebody asked Isaac Singer, "Why do you write about demons and dybbuks and all these things?" and he said, "Because it puts me in touch with reality." It's not a bad answer, really.

Q: But this guy without the brain? Was that written up in any of the medical literature?

KING: I read it in the newspaper. But it was apparently something that the newspaper, the AP or whatever, got from the New England Journal of Medicine or something similar. Like Casey Stengel said, "You can look it up."

Q: A question on genre fiction: It isn't regarded as "serious" fiction by the critical establishment. How do you, as someone who writes in the genre, feel about that?

KING: I feel that's generally proper. There are some guys always who bust those genre lines open, like Edgar Allan Poe, who wrote both detective fiction and horror fiction—Ross Macdonald in our time. But mostly we're starting to see a blurring of the lines of what comprises a genre that is below our notice. Like in the old mystery novels, the domestic servants were supposed to be below suspicion, not above suspicion but below suspicion. They weren't worthy of suspicion. And genre novels generally in the past weren't regarded as worthy of critical notice. And now one of the things that is happening is that there have been a number of fine writers who have come out of several different genres, science fiction, mystery, the horror genre. It's interesting to me that there are some genres that haven't produced anything, so far, of note—something that is above that line, so that the critics take notice of it even to lambast it. Like several times my own work has been taken up either in the *New Yorker* or the *Village Voice* or *Harper's* or something like that, sometimes favorably, sometimes in the sense of "this suggests the continuing degeneration of American literature." But if you're taken up at all that means that you're above that line, somebody has noticed you, even if it's only "Look we've got to pinch this thing off because we don't want to let this get out of hand; it's like a weed." But I can't think of anybody, including Louis L'Amour, in the western field who has consistently written westerns that have been critically talked about in the last 20 or 30 years. And I can't think of anybody in the romance field, so far, who has produced anything. And it seems to me that any genre can produce fine literature. It depends if somebody wants to take it seriously on its own terms.

Q: How do you balance commercial and artistic impulses? Or do you?

KING: Boy, that's a really interesting question. Yeah, you do. You do. It's really a good question. I've never been asked that before and I don't know how to answer it. But there's a little voice inside that's like conscience—only I think it's almost more real than conscience—that always knows. Commercialism per se doesn't even enter into it so much, but that voice always knows when you took the easy way out—when you said something here because you could say it in one paragraph and you didn't do this because it would take three of four paragraphs and be much harder to write. The hardest thing I ever had to write in my life was a novel called *Cujo*. Part of the story revolves around this woman who's having an affair and her husband finds out. There's a scene where he goes home and confronts her with what he knows and they talk about it.

And that was the hardest scene I ever had to write in my life because I've never faced that situation, not even with a girlfriend—finding out that a girlfriend had been stepping around on the side let alone my wife seeing somebody. I wanted to work it out in a way that would be fair to both of them. That is, I didn't want to turn one of them into a villain. So it was very, very tough. It was easy enough to react to the man because I know how I'd feel if I found that out. It was tougher to react sympathetically to the woman. And that little voice said, "Well, have her say this and have her say that and have her say the other thing." And then you say, "I can't do that because that just slides by the central question." Because if there's anything artistic in what I do or what anybody does it's because you get to the point and you explore it whether you want to or not because that's really why you came there.

Q: How long did it take you to write that scene?

KING: Two days. As opposed to what would have ordinarily taken me an hour and a half. It was a lot of sitting and looking at the typewriter and looking at the page. But it wasn't the kind of thing where you're sitting there and trying to think how to frame a sentence. It was more like you're sitting there thinking, "Why did she do that?" And the answers are not perfect in the book as to why she did that. But what's there is honest enough, anyway. So that's in response to what you said about how you balance off art and commercialism. I guess I don't really know except you do it all the time, I do it all the time. And anybody who tries to write a commercial novel anyway usually doesn't succeed.

Q: Do you write fast? Do you work every day?

KING: Yeah, I work after breakfast until about a half hour before lunch. And then most nights I go back and work for another hour and a half. I'd rather work on something goofy at night. I smoke at night. I don't smoke in the daytime. I put the kids to bed at 8:30 and go and sit in front of the word processor for an hour and a half and write and smoke, drink beer. It's great.

Q: Your work seems to cut across all age barriers. What do you think accounts for that?

KING: I think a lot of people see the America they know in the stories. I've never written a novel that was set in England or Italy. I don't have any plans to do that. The people who I write about are generally speaking not very rich or very cultured, maybe because I'm not very cultured, because I don't have any idea what it is to be rich. In a manner of speaking I guess I'm rich myself, but I don't know what that means beyond, let's say, a bank statement, in real terms—like estates at Newport or being able to look back on your father and grandfather and having portraits in the hall. My father left my mother when I was two and I don't even know where the hell he is. He might be alive or dead. He was a merchant mariner. So I think they see the America they know and they may respond just because they like that feeling of touching the unknown that we've talked about.

Q: Do you take advances on your work now?

KING: Um-hum. But the big advances, there's no need of them. If you're successful and if the audience seems steady, the big advance is nothing but an ego trip and it's bad for other writers because it ties up a lot of available cash that could go into other advances. And I don't want to be that one who's guilty of swallowing that up.

I always used to see red. . . . I put myself through college. When I was a senior in high school I went to school days and worked in a mill nights to make money to go to college. When I got out of college I couldn't get a teaching job. I pumped gas, I worked in another mill, I worked in an industrial laundry, and I'd go to the library and I'd get a book and I'd open it up and in the front I would see something like, "The author would like to thank the Nathaniel Guggenhiem Foundation for the money to write . . ." and I'd think, "you fucking shithead, where do you get off taking that money so you can sit on your ass in some cabin in New Hampshire while I'm trying to write a book at night and I've got bleach burns all over my hands. Who the fuck are you?" Steam would come out of my ears I was so mad and jealous of these guys. And I would think it was all because they would all sit around and sniff each other's underwear in the literary sense. Some English professor says to his grad student, "You ought to go out and read some Nathaniel Hawthorne," and the kid comes back and says, "Gee, chief, Nathaniel Hawthorne's great. Will you sign my application for the Nathaniel Guggenheim scholarship?" I used to go crazy—like some people about Roosevelt in the '30s. But it's different if I don't take the money. In a way it is like the Stephen King fellowship. It's money that I'm not taking. My name doesn't have to get onto it. And I don't have to get involved. There's no political thing.

Q: So you will take less so that more money can be spread around?

KING: I'll take less but it doesn't make a goddamn bit of difference.

They just give it to each other in salaries and hire two or three more supernumeraries to fill worthless positions. They are the most uninformed, asinine bunch in American business.

Q: Publishers?

KING: Yeah. I mean here we have a business that is basically the business of American thought and it's very influential. And yet in a financial sense we rank just below the brassiere makers in terms of the input into the gross national product. We're not in the Fortune 500. Publishing is not one of the big American industries. And yet it certainly has a much more potent input into American life and the American course of the future than, say, the bra makers. Although the bra makers do have some, of course.

Q: Why do you think publishing houses are badly run?

KING: Because they're a bunch of guys who sit around—and their concern is books. We have editors who were president of the literary society at Brown University or Duke University, or someplace similar. Then they become editors and they wear tweed jackets with elbow patches. And they smoke pipes and they drink Perrier in restaurants. And maybe once in a while they go where the books are actually printed. At sales meetings they talk in the most vague terms about what people want. There are no marketing surveys done—there has not been an industry-wide marketing survey since 1968. So they run on inertia. It's a gentleman's business, and they have to run it like gentlemen and gentlemen don't get their hands dirty with things like market analysis.

Q: Well that's certainly the stereotype and it has been the stereotype for years. Do you really think it's applicable?

KING: It's more applicable than not. You ask people "Why does King sell so much, and who is he selling to?" They don't know. I have a much better idea than they do because I read the fan mail and they just pass it on.

Q: Where do you see your work standing, say, 50 years from now.

KING: Oh, it'll still be in the libraries—we're assuming there will be a world in 50 years. I'm not sure it'll still be in bookstores, in the paperback racks. The real test of how good a writer is, particularly a popular writer, is whether or not their work can outlast their deaths by five, ten, fifteen years. That remains to be seen, but I think a lot of this stuff will be in the libraries and 50 years from now or 100 years from now. After I'm dead some eleven year old kid will be going along through the stacks the way I went through the library stacks and discovered Richard Matheson and Algernon Blackwood, and he'll find this dusty book and he'll take it home and he'll lose an afternoon.

With T.N. Murari

Q: How did you happen to choose horror as your specialty?

KING: I didn't exactly choose horror. If anything, horror chose me. I'm not really interested in horror at all; I am sort of interested in fantasy. The stories I create are about people with magical powers to which they themselves are vulnerable.

Q: But your novels *are* scary. Do you enjoy frightening people?

KING: Yes, I do. When I've written a particularly spooky scene, I feel a great pleasure and have been known to chuckle with glee. A novelist must arouse the emotion of a reader—whether it's laughter or tears or tension. The imagination is an eye, a marvelous third eye that floats free. The job of a fantasy writer, or the horror writer, is to provide a single, powerful spectacle for that third eye. If I can scare my reader and keep him turning the pages, I have succeeded in my craft.

Q: Is there one idea that so frightens you, you'll never write about it?

KING: No—but some are precluded for reasons of taste. In 'Salem's Lot, for instance, I originally had a really gruesome scene with rats. My editor thought it was best excised, as it was quite tasteless. He was right.

Q: Have you tried to write other kinds of fiction—action, Westerns?

KING: Yes, and I still do. I also write some poetry.

Q: You've also written original screenplays. Do you enjoy that medium as much as novel writing?

KING: No. Once you've seen the film industry's workings from the inside, you realize it's a creative nightmare. It becomes difficult to understand how anything of quality—something like *Alien* or *A Place in the Sun* or *Breaking Away*—can be made.

Q: Have your children seen any of your movies?

KING: Yes, and they've liked all of them except the television version of 'Salem's Lot, which scared them badly.

Q: But isn't that what you really wanted to do?

KING: Yes, and the film succeeded a bit too well there. But the irony, I think, is that children are better able to deal with fantasy and terror on their own terms than adults are. A certain amount of fantasy and horror in a child's life seems to me to be perfectly okay, even useful. Because of their imaginations, children are able to handle it.

Q: In what ways has the fame affected your personal life and your relationships with people?

KING: I'm more wary of new acquaintances than I would be if I was not "famous." When people call me up, the first thought that flashes through my mind now isn't, "How nice it is to hear from this person," but "What does he want?"

Q: Do you still keep in touch with your old friends?

KING: No.

Q: You are one of the most prolific writers around. Do you ever get writer's block.

KING: No.

Q: Why do you write under a pseudonym?

KING: I wrote under a pseudonym for two reasons: First, because I had a number of books in manuscript that I thought were fairly good and I was afraid of flooding the market with "Stephen King" books. I didn't want to see them just moldering in a drawer, so the pen name seemed like a good compromise. Second, I wanted to see if I could achieve the same sort of sales success under another name that I had achieved as Stephen King.

Q: Why have your publishers now admitted that you wrote *Thinner*?

KING: My publishers did not admit I wrote the book, I did. There was growing speculation over the last three years that I was Bachman. Finally, a young bookstore employee in Washington, D.C., named Steve Brown, checked in the Library of Congress; the earliest Bachman book had copyright notice filed under my name—enough evidence to shoot a very large hole in the alias. I decided that further denials would be useless. The photograph on the jacket is of a man named Richard Manuel, a Minnesotan and an old friend of my agent's.

Q: Your wife is also a writer. Do you have any conflicts with her?

KING: No, we have no career conflicts. I think we have all the conflicts that happily married people have, but most of them fall into other areas—questions of child rearing, where to go on vacations, sometimes even politics.

Q: How would you advise a young writer trying to emulate your success?

KING: I would advise any writer trying to achieve success to ignore popular fashion as much as possible and write what he or she really wants to write. Of course, it helps to remember that writing is an act of communication. The more accessible your work is, the more people will want to read it.

Q: How important is critical success to you now?

KING: That's very difficult for me to say. I read my reviews fairly closely and get depressed by the bad ones, but on only two or three occasions have really awful write-ups interfered with my lunch.

Q: How would you like to be remembered?

KING: As a good storyteller.

With Mick Farren

In his suite at the United Nations Plaza Hotel, where he's taken up residence until the completion of Maximum Overdrive, *about the only thing that Stephen King has unpacked is his word processor.*

KING: Okay, I'm going to give you the Reader's Digest condensed version. What happened was I had written this story called "Trucks" back in 1974 and it got published in a men's magazine. I got 500 bucks for it, the most money I had ever gotten for a short story. It was always my favorite of those early short stories, which Dino De Laurentiis eventually bought up. He wanted to do *Trucks* and he wanted me to do the screenplay and I said I couldn't. He accepted that and started to develop another one of the stories that he'd picked up. *Silver Bullet* was in production when he came down—this was during Hurricane Diana last year—and he asked me again. He said, "I can't get anywhere with *Trucks*—do you have any idea?" Well, I had had an idea and that was to expand the story beyond trucks running by themselves, to *everything* running by itself, which is something that is inherent in the story anyway. I don't care why these things happen, it doesn't make any difference to me. But you have to give people a reason, whatever it is—if it's Sleeping Beauty falling asleep for 100 years, it's a poisoned apple....

So, I said it's a comet. Halley's Comet is coming around in 1985 and '86, so it's a comet. The comet comes and makes all these machines run by themselves. Dino said, "Why?" and on the spur of the moment I said,

"Because there are these invaders that send it and they want to use the techno-industrial society to sweep off all the bright people in the world and then they come and land and, you know, take everything over." And he said, "Stephen! Eez fantastic! You must a-write dees picture." I said, "Jesus, Dino, I can't." But he's really seductive, and the more I thought about it the more I really wanted to write it.

Q: Doing it right.

KING: Not doing it right, doing it wrong—you don't even think about that, you just think about *doin' it*, man. My wife and I'd had a thing for a long time about directing, she knew that I wanted to. Just once—because of all these people who write letters or say, "Jesus Christ, the book was good but the movie ain't shit." So I really felt like *Trucks* might be a good one to direct. I didn't take any money up front from him except the Director's Guild minimum. I didn't want to be looking like I was shaking the cherry tree when I didn't even know if I could do it.

Q: How long does it take you to write a book?

KING: Depends. Four months maybe, if it goes good, for a first draft. The work, all told, might take a year.

Q: There seems to be a tendency in horror and science fiction, where one equates a 90-minute movie with a short story—like *Alien*, like *Terminator*—real simple. But when you've got a complicated novel, it gets cut to shreds.

KING: Well, that's the big novel right there, if you look behind you [*SK points to a hefty pile of manuscript pages*]. That's a novel in progress; it's called *IT*. The only solution for something like that is to sell it to TV for a mini-series. We've had a lot of problems because it deals with children and children in jeopardy, which is one of the no-nos, but I think we've got that solved. The problem with *Trucks* was fleshing it out—that's a problem that I love to have. I've done screenplays for a bunch of my novels. The only one that *may* be produced is *Pet Sematary*, next spring or summer in Maine. The rest of them—I've done screenplays for *The Dead Zone, Cujo, The Shining*—none of them were used. I wouldn't touch '*Salem's Lot* with a ten-foot pole. To do a script of a novel that you wrote is like sitting on a suitcase that's full of shit and trying to get it on an airplane. It's a stupid business and I won't do it any more.

Q: The thing that worries me slightly is that over the years it seems like there has to be a constant escalation in horror. I mean, 40 years ago people were getting scared by Bela Lugosi as Dracula or Lon Chaney, Jr., as the Wolf Man, but today it's got to be Driller Killer.

KING: Now that's *dysfunction*. That doesn't work. Driller Killer doesn't work. There's a lot of stuff that can be real graphic but doesn't work a goddamn and doesn't sell a goddamn. You pick something that does work, a movie like *Friday the 13th*—I dicked on that picture at first. I said, "This is nothing more than a slasher picture—it's a snuff movie." But that isn't really what it is and I've changed my mind a lot about the picture. It's a classic camp story. On those grounds, it stands perfectly well and I don't have any problem with it whatsoever. And it made a lot of money. So, why not? By Christ, the first movie *ever* to be produced in the *world* was a horror picture. It was Thomas Edison's *Frankenstein* in 1912. So we go back to the start. The genre reflects so many concerns of the spike of moviegoers, say, seventeen-year-olds, that sort of thing. You know, these guys in Hollywood piss and moan about how their gate is off because of VCRs and things like that—it's not the truth at all. The reason why is because the audience that they had when *Easy Rider* was a hit, the audience that they had when *The Exorcist* was a mega-hit, isn't there anymore. The mega-hits now, the really huge whopper hits, are neo-Disney pictures. Spielberg. So you can get an audience for a horror picture, but more and more it's shrunk to this reliable, core audience, so that the people who finance films say, "Go ahead and spend the five million bucks on a film." You know, we're retracting gradually to a 1957 mentality.

Q: So this is getting back to *Invasion of the Crab Monsters*. . . .

KING: Yeah, that's what I'm saying. That sort of thing, with more graphic crabs. . . . George Romero is right, you know, the way to go with this is to produce directly for video cassette, then you'd get the same audience. But it can't be done with the system that exists now because we've developed a rental economy of VCRs.

Q: When I started going to the movies, there was a cartoon, there was a second feature, it was an all-night experience. This sounds very old-fashioned, but movies like *The Beast with Five Fingers* were terrifying, but now you're getting coeds and chainsaws.

KING: Yeah, but that's because when you saw those things you were four, five, six, seven, eight years old. Times change. You get older but the possibility to scare people with innuendo is still there. *The Change-*

ling was a great picture. So it can be done. It demands a commitment from studio and producer and that sort of thing because, you know, they're copycats—they say, "This is what sells, let's go for it." But Hollywood is caught in this double bind. They want gore, but you can't give 'em too much gore. They need an "R," because if they go unrated, they won't get any distribution. There's a scene in *Maximum Overdrive* that Dino says is probably gonna be an "X" and we're probably gonna have to take it out of the picture. We'll take it to the ratings board and all that and I'll argue with it, but it's like in *Scarface*—the thing with the kid and the chainsaw. The problem, I think, is that it's a kid who's holding the saw. The guy who actually takes the fall is this 25-year-old stunt man who happens to be small, and what gets run over is a dummy. But it's the effect that counts.

Q: An awful lot of these horror films just seem to be showing you something you ain't never gonna see. Do they want to turn the cinema into a Disneyland ride?

KING: What is that supposed to be?

Q: Well, that's what I wonder about. The Lucas *Star Wars* movies— those were great! All these spaceships coming—and that you can't duplicate on the TV screen.

KING: No. Not even if you get the tapes can you duplicate the experience. You can't duplicate the sound. The only thing that you can do with your VCR and your tape is if you miss dialogue or if you want to look at a scene again, you can rewind it and you can look at it, and even that spoils some of the magic. And I'm not saying that there isn't a place in the cinema for legitimate, intellectual work, for work that deals with human emotions in an artistic way, in an insightful way, and I think Spielberg tried very hard to do that in *The Color Purple*. I hope it works out for him and I hope he doesn't get shit on too bad for trying to do something serious. There's nothing wrong with that. *Jagged Edge*. It doesn't have to be a horror picture, but there's no reason why it can't be that.

Q: That's also a cheap solution though, isn't it?

KING: Not always. In a way it's like saying, "This crazy motherfucker director will do anything." And it takes off that curse of expectation— that place where you say, "This is what he will do and this is what he won't do." What I'm talking about is the difference between movies that are entirely entertainment, that exist just for that purpose, and pictures that also want to make us larger as human beings. But one of the things that I think makes us larger as human beings, or that improves our lives, is the ability to dream. To just dream. Why not? I mean, why does the dream have to be a socially conscious thing or anything like that? It can just be, you know, *The Road Warrior.*

Q: It's the difference between *The Road Warrior* and, say, *Rambo*—it's the difference between dreaming and pandering to the worst in people.

KING: Yeah, I think that's true. The pandering aspect of it disturbs me a lot.

Q: What really disturbs me about it is that you're taking a premise that people are stupid, let's go to the lowest common denominator. . . and it's a planned exercise. I mean, it's like pornography.

KING: It is. *It is pornography.* There are fuck movies, there are suck movies and there are snuff movies. And there are also movies that are like invitations to a kind of knee-jerk hate reaction. To me, that was what *Rambo* was. And it's also a ridiculous picture. "All I want is for my country to luv me as much as I luv my country." Give me a break.

Q: I've been really interested in the concept of a 20th-century return to magic. The old movies were very Victorian—Dracula, Frankenstein, the Wolf Man, with all the crosses and posts. We had a resurgence of this in the Seventies starting with *The Exorcist.* But now you've got haunted Plymouth Furies and all kinds of good stuff that is uniquely 20th century. Has that been conscious? Even *'Salem's Lot* is putting vampires up against. . . .

KING: But the crosses still work in *'Salem's Lot.*

Q: Well, that's in the rule book.

KING: It isn't in the rule book. I've always tried to work out this concept. One of the things that's always interested me is magic. But what magic is is power. Magic and power are equal. Always the same thing. So whatever the talismans are of magic, these are the talismans of power. I like to work with that at the same time as concepts of good and evil. Now in *Christine* it's a Plymouth Fury and all this other stuff, but at the end of the book, it's not in the movie but it's in the book, the girl says to the hero, "Be my knight," and she takes the scarf from her hair and ties it around his shoulder. It's a power symbol. . . . You can talk all you want to about self-image and say that you put on your leather and say that it changes you into a different person because of some kind of "cultural image"—I don't give a fuck about that. What I care about is that it changes you—it's magic. And Jesus Christ, if we ever needed any magic, we need it now, in the life that we live today. 'Cause man, it's scary. Everything. From the technology to the possibility of total annihilation.

Q: And if somebody wants you to build in a rationale for what happens in your stories, you do it, but you basically don't care, right?

KING: I don't give a shit. You give 'em a little rationale and maybe at MGM they're happy. I don't care.

Q: I don't think the kids care either.

KING: Nah. No, they don't care. If it happens, it happens—Santa Claus comes down the chimney.

Q: Prior to your work it was always, "Oh, we just dug up something in Assyria. . . . " It was as though we had buried witchcraft, good and evil in the modern age, but a Plymouth Fury's a whole different ball game.

KING: It's not. It's the same thing. And I don't care why—I care about the nature of the evil and where it comes from. When you deal with people against supernatural forces, you reflect people's dealings with real forces of good and evil. You know there's such a thing as "outside evil." I know there is. Say you have a 22-year-old sister who starts forgetting things, goes to the doctor, has a CAT scan and is told she has a brain tumor and six months to live. Well, what happened? God hit her with a cancer stick? That didn't have anything to do with whether she was good or bad or anything else. Whereas you might make a conscious decision to become, let's say, a dope dealer or something like that. And you get into trouble because of that. That's inside evil. The talismans remain the same—good and evil—the issues are the same. The magic is a constant, but the use of it can change. Whether it's a Plymouth or a vampire or whether it's an out-of-control robot or car or something, it's all the same stuff. . . . A lot of it has to do with people groping, groping around for something outside of themselves. I went to see *The Amityville Horror* on 42nd Street. Man, it was the quietest 42nd Street theater I'd ever seen a horror movie in. I thought to myself, "Shit, these people are not seeing a horror movie, they're experiencing the unknown the way maybe your father or your grandfather experienced the unknown when he took communion."

Q: I was reading an interview you gave where you talked about having an obsession with Charles Starkweather at some point, which I kind of shared, and it seems that Bruce Springsteen also shares it. But he was essentially the baddest James Dean there ever was. . . .

KING: That's right. Well, there's an attraction to emptiness, and Charles

Starkweather, to me, was totally empty. My mother was sort of horrified with my fascination with him, but I was examining the human equivalent of a black hole and that's what really attracted me to Starkweather. Not that I wanted to be like him, but I wanted to recognize him if I met him on the street.

Q: When you've finished writing something particularly nasty, how does it feel? Is there a kind of catharsis, or do you stand back and say, "Jesus, did I just do that?" I mean, say the sex killer in *The Dead Zone*.

KING: Don't feel either way. There's no real thrill in it. There's part of you that's just standing off and just watching it happen. You hypothesize the situation and then you watch it develop. I've learned a lot of my craft from the naturalistic writers, Theodore Dreiser and Frank Norris and people like that, and the idea that I picked up was "Never back up, never flinch, never look away, see everything until you become this sort of disinterested observer."

Q: Do you ever think about the mechanics of terrifying people?

KING: I know what they are, but I don't think about it.

Q: What are they?

KING: Let's see. You put characters in a situation where the audience can't help them and where the audience will say, "I wouldn't do that." When the lady starts to go upstairs and you say to yourself, "Shit, man, I would never do that." Or in *Halloween* where she bludgeons the guy and then drops whatever she hit him with and the audience goes, "No, don't do that! I'd never do that!"

So you put on that situation, but you can't horrify people unless you can make them *love*. Basically that's the end of it. Otherwise, you've got a snuff movie—watch 'em fall down, watch 'em die, how inventively can we kill these people? But if you make them love the characters. . . that's what's so awful about *Pet Sematary*, why it's such a dreadful book, because you're welcomed into this family. It's a domestic drama. It's Mommy and Daddy and the little daughter and the baby son. The reason that you grow to love them is that I loved them. And then it all falls down. And people say, "Well, how could you do that?" Or they'll say, "How could you let that little boy die in *Cujo*?" The reason is that sometimes they do. That's the truth. It's like me saying, "I want to show you something." I put my arm around your shoulder and take you around the corner and show you something that's the most gross awful thing you ever saw. It's a very twisted sort of thing to want to do.

Q: How do you feel about being a figure in 1980s pop culture?

KING: It's true! Me and Bruce. . . . People'll read that. It'll be in the interview and people'll say, "That conceited son of a bitch," but it's actually the truth. I have been subsumed by the popular culture. There's a thing in *Fletch*, the Chevy Chase movie, where he goes into this old house and he hears a dog and he says, "Cujo?" and the audience laughs.

Q: Was there a point when you were a kid when all this gore was triggered? Or was it always there?

KING: I like that question because it presupposes certain assumptions about the entire genre that says, "There's a warp in your record somewhere and all of this comes out of it." Peter Straub, with whom I collaborated on *The Talisman*, has said that he thinks that a lot of horror stories and horror novelists are created by unrealized expectations, and by conflicts that are not settled, which is a pretty Freudian idea. I don't really subscribe to it. It may be there, but it may not. I had a mundane, rural childhood. One of the reasons that I've been left alone is that my books are fairly asexual.

Q: Do you do that deliberately?

KING: I tried once to write a porn novel when I was in college eating fried Cheerios—I just couldn't do it. I mean, I did about 50 pages and I just said, "Fuck, I can't do this." The words were there, but I couldn't handle it. I just collapsed. It was so weird. I got to the point where the twin sisters are making love in the bird bath and I just said, ". . . I'm sorry."

CHAPTER NINE

†

RECENT YEARS

†

With Elaine Landa

At a previous *Inside* meeting early last fall, the idea arose to do a story on the Modern Master of Horror, Stephen King. The interview was arranged for April 2, 1986.

When I arrived, I was ushered up to Mr. King's comfortable study and greeted with a warm welcome. The atmosphere was quite inviting. Everything was bright and cheery. Mr. King is an extremely nice man. Pleasant to be around, with an incredible sense of humor.

I took with me twenty questions which were prepared by the faculty and students. The first question was: How do you want to be remembered as a writer?

KING: I'd just like to be remembered. 'Cause I got a piece about some writer whose name I think was Joseph Hergeshimer or something like that, who was a big bestseller around the beginning of the 20th century. And I'd never heard of him. Nobody's ever heard of him. And that does happen.

Q: How do you avoid being bored by money?

KING: There is no way to be bored by money in that sense. I don't really even think of it very often. Like last summer when I was making this movie, it suddenly occurred to me that I was getting what they call a per diem, which from the Latin means per day, as a salary. And they just gave me an envelope at the end of the week that's full of cash. And in my case, I was making like $1,500 a week. And all at once after about three weeks I said, "This is ridiculous. Something has to be done." I was carrying around like $4,500 in my pockets because I was spending

$2.77 a day. I would stop every morning on my way out to location and get a McDonald's big breakfast. That was it. Because otherwise I did nothing but work and eat at the commissary and fall into bed. So it's not a question of being bored or anything else.

Q: Describe your typical day.

KING: This is it. I work in the morning. I eat lunch with my wife. I do whatever I have to do for my correspondence or if there's an interview or something like that, I do it in the afternoon. And then I groove with the kids at night.

Q: What kind of student were you in school?

KING: I graduated I think something like 17th in a class of about 190 or something like that. I was not number one in my class or number two or anything like that. I was not a total dip either. I got in trouble off and on because I wrote things about teachers or something like that and so I did standard number of detention halls and stuff like that. I tended to be a little bit of a class clown, a cut-up, goof off sometimes. And I worked really hard on all my hard courses like math and physics and that stuff. But in the other stuff, like the reading courses, English, writing, or whatever it was, I had this tendency to just sort of slide by. So that when I got to college I got this rude awakening and I got an 'F' on the first piece of composition that I had written.

Q: Describe your teaching career at Hampden Academy.

KING: It was brief. I taught two years at Hampden. And they were good years. I liked it. When we start teaching—that isn't what you're going to do—?

Q: Teach?

KING: —when you get out of college or whenever you finish? You going to teach or anything like that?

Q: No.

KING: Well, they start you off, it's a seniority system. You start off as a freshman teacher with a class you're least capable of handling. Which is to say you get the courses that nobody else who's got more seniority than you wants. So that you end up with large blocks of kids who are majoring in smoking area and stuff like that. But I liked it. I thought it was really nice. It didn't pay well enough, but everybody knows that.

Q: What authors do you read?

KING: They're there. I don't know, I read John D. Macdonald a lot. It's hard to say. I don't read just specifically horror.

Q: You don't have a favorite author?

KING: A favorite author. Do you?

Q: Hm-hmmm. Edgar Allan Poe.

KING: Edgar Allan Poe. He isn't my favorite. I guess—jeez, it's tough to think of all the good guys—probably William Faulkner. I go back to him a lot. I like Thomas Hardy a lot. Of modern guys I like a lot of detective novelists—Raymond Chandler—I think he's fantastic. I never understand after I finish the book what happened, but I love his voice. I dry up on that question because there are so many people that are good.

Q: Do you include yourself?

KING: I like my stuff—you know, it's funny, I'm reading one of my own books right now, *The Dead Zone.* I've only gone back and read them about three times. I read *The Stand* over again and *'Salem's Lot,* but it's weird.

Q: What do you think of academics dissecting your work? Is this amusing, gratifying, or both?

KING: It's amusing, gratifying, disturbing. It's a little bit like in *Tom Sawyer* where everybody thinks that Tom Sawyer and Huckleberry Finn are dead, they come back and they go to their own funeral. So you read these things, it's a little bit like that. The only thing is, see, I haven't done the critics yet the convenience of lying down and being dead and then I can't dispute anymore what it is they say about me. I wrote this story called "Children of the Corn" and I went to a symposium down in Florida and all these guys stood up and read papers about my work and this one guy stood up and read this paper. It was not a doctoral thesis, thank God, but it was something on the weight of that, about Stephen King's symbolic view of the Vietnam apocalypse in "Children of the Corn". And the idea of Vietnam had never crossed my mind when I wrote the story. And afterwards, after they read all these papers, you're invited to comment and I would not have commented unless I was forced to, and I said the thought of Vietnam never crossed my mind. And you could see this guy's face fall to the floor. And that wouldn't have happened if I'd been dead, but I was able to add that what goes on all around you while you're writing something must have some sort of an influence, which is sort of a saving thing, so the guy said, "Oh, yes, he said it never crossed his mind, but really it did. He just didn't know it."

Well, I'll see. But it's really weird to have your work criticized on any kind of a deep level. And one of the things that comes to mind, too, when it happens is how hard it is to make yourself understood—even when you supposedly, according to enough people who read the books, I must be being understood by somebody—and yet a lot of times the criticism that comes back, it doesn't seem like you really are.

Q: It's true, you were mentioned on *Entertainment Tonight* and they said something about you love yourself.

KING: That I love my self?

Q: Yeah, and it shows in your work or something like that.

KING: Oh, yeah.

Q: Yeah.

KING: Gee. Well, there are two ways to look at it. You can say you love yourself and you're totally conceited or you can say that you love yourself, that you're at home with yourself.

Q: Yeah, that's true.

KING: Like you're your own friend.

Q: If you don't love yourself, I don't think you can be confident.

KING: I think you at least have to be on good terms with yourself. And I must be because I think that the people who aren't are the people who get into all sorts of odd psychological states, who end up committing suicide and stuff like that. Like, I don't think I would have had a character in one of my books commit suicide because I can't really understand the mindset that leads up to it. That might be an interesting thing to explore.

Q: Do you explore the psychic or anything along that line?

KING: Do I explore it?

Q: Yeah, meditation—interested in anything like that?

KING: Ummm, not really. I get interested in things for a little while or I will think what if this happened or this, that or the other thing. But if people ask me if I even believe in psychic phenomenon, my answer is I think that I do. There seems to be enough evidence to suggest that something like that's going on, but I don't think about it that much. And ah, meditation, no, I've never really done that. The closest I get is writing, which is like a semi-hypnotic state anyway depending on how deeply you are into it.

Q: What would you have most like to have written?

KING: Oh, man. Of all the books in the world?

Q: Yeah.

KING: *Lord of the Flies* maybe. I wish I'd written that. A *Separate*

Peace, I wish I'd written that. *Catch-22.* That's a good question, too, because sometimes you feel such a feeling of jealousy when you read a book and you say, "God damn, why him? What about me?" Or sometimes you read a book where the guy did something that was so much above you in terms of either the idea or the execution of the characters. And you say, "Aw, no. I want to hide my head." The one by Steinbeck, *Grapes of Wrath,* I feel that way about that book. You just read it and push away. It's like a guy that's having a perfect day at the plate. You just say you can't beat him. It's almost like perfection. There are a lot of books I'd wish I had written, but I guess maybe *The Grapes of Wrath* more than any of the other ones. Except maybe *Light in August* by William Faulkner. And then I'll think of some more if I don't shut up.

Q: Do your books have a place in the high school curriculum?

KING: I don't know. I think that on one level they do. The problem with the books from the high school standpoint is you get into a volatile situation sometimes with parents because the books, while they're not terribly sexy, they're full of all sorts of vulgarity because they deal with people in situations that are very stressful a lot of times. And people have a tendency when they get into a situation like that to say all sorts of things. But a lot of times parents say, "What is this vulgarity? What's this awful trash that you're shoving down my kid's throat? It doesn't have any business in the schools," that sort of thing. On the other hand, the books are accessible or at least the mail says they're accessible to a lot of kids who don't read very well. That they will grab on and continue in spite of their reading problems because they want to know what happens. So for that reason, the question is answerable both ways. I think that teachers have enough problems without having to battle constantly to get a book into the curriculum. Some of them have crept into the curriculum just the same—*'Salem's Lot* is taught in schools. And *Christine* shows up in schools.

Cujo has been banned in a number of schools and I'm not even talking about teaching, just in the school libraries and the same thing is true of *The Shining.* Those are the two that have a tendency to get banned the most. So then I get letters or I get phone calls from school librarians saying, "They've taken your book out of the school library. Do you want to say anything about this?" And I say it's fine. It's a school library, the parents pay the taxes. The school legally is *in loco parentis,* which means that they are the parent because the kids are minors. And if they feel that the book has no place in the library and if they can fill out a form that explains why, then go ahead, by all means take the book out of the library. But I think that every kid in that school should know that it's been taken out and should immediately break their legs getting either to the nearest bookstore or to the public library to find out what it was that their parents didn't want them to know. What it was that was so bad or so awful for them that it had to be taken out of their hands. Because those are the things that you really ought to know, what people don't want you to know. If they want to take it out, that's fine, because they generally do that. They run to find out.

Q: Would you like to write more original screenplays, direct more films?

KING: If an original screenplay came up that had an idea I really liked, I would. As far as direct more films, I don't think so.

Q: Why do you stay in Maine?

KING: Because I'm a hick.

Q: There's nothing here.

KING: That there's nothing here, well. There really isn't and that's one of the reasons that I stay.

Q: It's a beautiful state. It really is.

KING: It is and it isn't. You see these sweatshirts that say the Maine National Bird. It's got a black fly on it. Stuff like that. You oughta get one. One of the reasons that I live in Bangor is because if somebody wants to get to me, they have to be really dedicated. They have to really want to come here. It isn't like if I lived in New York or L.A., somebody could just pull my chain whenever they wanted to. You don't take people to the best restaurant in Bangor because there isn't one. You don't take people to see the sights because there are no sights. You don't put 'em up in the best hotel because there's no best hotel. The only thing that comes close is the Phoenix Inn and they don't even have any TVs. So I stay here because there's no distractions whatsoever. I have my family. I'm a guy who sells a lot of books and is fairly well known and yet my kids can go to public school and they're not—after the original shock wears off, there's no problem, there's nothing odd about it. They're just kids. We lead ordinary lives and there's no hassle about that. But I grew up here and I went to school, a one-room schoolhouse. You know there were outhouses to go to the bathroom. There was no running water or anything. I graduated at the top of my class because there were only three of us up until high school and one of them was retarded, Arthur Oscar. Poor

Arthur. "All right Arthur, I'll help you with your math." I don't know. I am a hick and this is where I feel at home.

Q: Let's see. What do you do with all your money? You can tell some of these questions aren't mine.

KING: That's okay because like money to Americans today—in a way a question like that is sort of sweet. Because—

Q: You don't have to answer if you don't want to.

KING: No, no, no, hey, what I'm trying to say is that it used to be nobody would ever talk about sex and today the big no-no is money. Nobody's even supposed to admit that somebody earns money or that there is such a thing as money. The answer is that I don't really do anything with it except to buy books and awful socks like the ones that I'm wearing and stuff like that. This used to be the top of the barn and we had it renovated and I think it cost like $18,000 or something to do it, but like, I have a business manager in New York and he invests in things.

So what I do with my money basically is I get papers at the end of the month that say "This is where your money is and this is what your money's doing" and all this other stuff. And so finally like about five years ago, Arthur, who's the business manager, said "I think we oughta invest in gold," and I said "Okay." And a little while later he said, "Well, we did it. We invested in gold and there was so many dollars or whatever in gold." And I said, "Well, where is it?" And he said, "What do you mean where is it? Well, it's somewhere. You get a paper that says and then they adjust the books." And I said, "No, that's no good. I want to have some of my gold." And he said, "Well, what good is that?" I said, "What good is it if I can't have that or feel that or anything?" So finally, under great protest, huge amounts of protest, he sent me some of my gold. And then I discovered I didn't have anything to do with it. So depending on the market data, it's like 600 bucks. But it depends on the day, you know. Or was 600 bucks. Now I think it's about 320 bucks. So he gave it to me. And I said, "Oh, that's it."

The only thing that I do with money and the only thing I think money is any good for is to give you a little security. You have a roof over your head. You know your children are going to be fed. You know that they can go to school to someplace that will fulfill their potential. We were talking about why I stay in Maine. Like I went to college in Maine and the reason why I did was not that I couldn't have been or wasn't accepted at anyplace else, but because this is where I could afford to go and my kids are going to have other choices, which I guess is good.

Q: Are you happy as a writer?

KING: Yes.

Q: Do your kids read your books?

KING: Yes. Not all of them, though Joe is reading *Christine* now and I don't think any one of the three of them have been through all of them. But all of them have been through two or three of them. And they like 'em.

Q: What advice do you have for a high school student who wants to be a professional writer?

KING: Read a lot. Write alot. But it's like if you want to be a pro writer, you have to write a lot. It's like if you wanna play the piano. You play an instrument?

Q: A little piano.

KING: You practice?

Q: I used to.

KING: You don't like it?

Q: Oh, yeah, I liked it. I used to play for a long time. I just couldn't, you know, I wanted to play saxophone.

KING: Yeah, there's a girl who plays saxophone with Quarterflash. But she quit playing the saxophone because she said she was going to have to have plastic surgery for her cheeks or something like that. But she was a great horn. I wouldn't mind playing the sax myself. Hey Big Man, I could be just like Clarence Clemons. That's what I want to do if I couldn't be a writer, I'd want to be a rock and roll guy, but I'd want to be black. Like one of these guys in the Temptations and have all these moves and everything.

Yeah, you gotta read a lot and you gotta write a lot. But writing a lot is like practicing on the piano or something like that. It isn't practice if you like then it's something to get doing because you just enjoy doing it, 'cause it's self-fulfilling in itself.

Q: Who cuts your hair?

KING: I get it cut at Great Expectations. Is that a plug?

Q: It's just a question.

KING: I was just wondering if that was a plug.

Q: Well, no, people have said that time to time you have a different look. That's what I think the question was.

KING: Well, I shave off my beard when the weather gets warm and I have a tendency to keep it off longer now because everything's turning gray. And a lot of times months will go by and I don't get a hair cut and my hair gets really long. And the last time that that happened, I went in and I said to the lady "Punk it." She said, "What? Are you sure?" And I said, "Yeah, but do it real quick because I'm gonna change my mind if you don't." And she said, "Do you want it to be radical?" And I said, "Yeah. Do it." And so she did it and I look at myself and I couldn't believe what I was seeing and I came home and I didn't know what my wife was going to say and she says, "Isn't it cute? My husband looks like a baby duck."

Q: When you write do you have a particular audience in mind?

KING: Yes, myself.

Q: Is there an imaginary particular person you write for?

KING: No, just me. Which in a way says something about my success. It suggests I must have the perfect mid-cultural mind, just this total drone, right through the middle of everything.

Q: You seemed to be attracted to humor and to family relationships. Would you like to write a book on either topic without any touch of the occult or horror?

KING: Well, my idea about the difference between humor and horror is that it stops being funny when it starts being you. If you see the Three Stooges and they're going *boink, quack, quack, quack*, it's funny. Except if somebody walked up to you and started going like that, it would be awful, particularly in public.

Yeah, I'm attracted to family relationships because I live in a family and I'm still trying to figure out what I'm doing or what's happening. But, yeah, I couldn't sit down and deliberately write a funny story, but I've written some funny things by accident because I do have a tendency to see the funny side of things. And a lot of times the stuff that people think is really horrible are things that I think are sort of funny. I wrote this story called "The Revelations of Becca Paulson" and it was about this country woman, this sort of fat, back-country lady whose cleaning the top of her closet and she comes up with this gun that her husband won at an Elks drawing or something about three years ago. And she's standing on a step-ladder and looking at it and she's got it turned around and she's sort of pointing it at her head and she's looking into the barrel to see if it's loaded because she's convinced that if it's loaded she'll be able to see the bullet. And she doesn't see anything so she thinks that it isn't and she backs down the stepladder and steps on the cat who is at the bottom and falls down and the gun comes up and she shoots herself with a .22 right in the head. And wakes up about five hours later and she seems to be perfectly fine, but she goes into the bathroom and she looks and sure enough there's this little hole where the bullet went in. I got kind of interested because I'd read somewhere that sometimes people actually get shot in the head and live. In fact, even the bullet can go right through and come out and nothing happens to them. Nothing. So I had her go in there and you're just writing along and in your—in that state where you're partially imagining and partially sort of watching like watching a real event. It's like crazy people in a rubber room except I get paid for it. So I can see this woman looking at this hole at her head in the mirror the way you would look at a mole or a pimple or something like that.

Q: What do you think about American high school students thinking you are a great writer?

KING: I do see myself as a Dickens.

With Jo Fletcher

Q: You write about fear, about putting ordinary people into extraordinary situations and watching the way they react. It permeates your work, but does it also play a major part in your real life?

KING: Fear. Well, I will take you way past the stop sign, I will take you beyond the things you think you want to know about, right down into the very depths. I will touch your darkest phobias. You may *think* you want to know, but by the time you realize you don't—well, sorry buddy, but it's just too damn late. . . Deep down inside, most of us are afraid. I can still find fear—in fact, I can find more fear now than I used to. I'm afraid the world will blow itself up. I'm afraid of flying. I'm nervous when I don't know where my kids are and I'm still afraid of what's lurking under the bed. I write about fear. Other guys go to psychiatrists and pay a lot of dough to lie on an imitation leatherette couch and spout on about all their crazy terrors and weird ideas. Well, I get to do all that in my books and I get paid for it. It's sort of like expiation, if you will. It's a marketable obsession.

Q: Both your movie *Maximum Overdrive* and your latest novel *IT* have received pretty unenthusiastic reviews, even though the former is doing well in the provinces and IT hit the bestseller lists almost before it was published. Do you care about what the reviewers say? Does criticism bother you?

KING: Of course I care about reviews, and any writer or creative person who says he doesn't is a goddamned liar. And secondly, if they are really disregarding what the critics say, they are making a terrible mistake. Although the way the business is set up now—and it is a business; both criticism and creation have become *big* business—you have to take it with more of a grain of salt, because critics have a tendency to buy the celebrity syndrome, in the same way the public does. So you are evaluated on the basis of whatever your celebrity status seems to be. That's a bit like trying to get shortwave radio through an ionized atmosphere. It's ridiculous to have to deal with that, or to have a critic begin a review of a book or a film with "Stephen King, multi-zillionaire hack" or "horror writer," or whatever the label happens to be. It's stereotyping; it's a type of shorthand critics should be forbidden, and yet they are not. British literary critics are much less prone to it than Americans, but British film critics are much more prone to it.

The trade press reviews of IT over here in America were bad, but I think they were bad mostly because a lot of books review badly. I think at *Publishers Weekly* they jumped all the way up to $27 for a review. Now you can make $27 by reviewing *The Brave Little Toaster*, which is 73 pages long, or you can make your $27 by being assigned *IT*, which is 1248 pages long, and it tends to put reviewers in a bad humor. But the trade reviews of *IT* really didn't make any sense. In one they said "King has written about seven stereotyped characters, in fact, each one is a type. There are two handicapped persons." Well, that makes sense, there is a stutterer and there is Eddie, who has asthma. And then you have a token woman, that's Beverly, and you have a token Jew, Stanley Uris, and you have a token fat kid, Ben, and a token black kid, Mike, and then they said there was a token gay or effeminate, and the only one left is Richie Tozier and Tozier has been married and there is this whole thing about his vasectomy that didn't work and if that's effeminism, I missed something somewhere. So it makes you wonder, did the reviewer read this book? Did he read the book I wrote? Because the book I wrote was on what it's like to be a kid and what it's like to be a grownup and where the two meet. I thought that people would get off on that, and also on what it was like growing up in the Fifties. So maybe they are reading the book they expect, the celebrity version or something. Maybe they are looking for a celebrity book; maybe they are looking for a bad book—I don't know. On the other hand, maybe I'm too close to it and maybe they're right.

Q: You are labeled a horror writer, and you are firmly placed on the horror shelves, and yet your best books work on many more levels. In a recent television interview, you stated very firmly that your next novel, *Misery*, has no supernatural horror at all. Does this labeling bother you?

KING: You can call me anything you like, but I've always been a fairly subversive horror writer. I remember doing an interview about eight years ago, just after *'Salem's Lot*, when the lady interviewing me said, "As a horror writer, do you think..." and then she stopped and kind of recalled it and said "Oh, do you mind?" It was as though she had said, "As a nigger, oh sorry, as a black..." And I said no, you can call me anything you like.

When people ask me if I am ever going to write anything else, well, I wrote *The Dead Zone*, which is a love story, and I wrote *The Stand* and *Firestarter* and *The Dead Zone*, which are all political novels, and *The Gunslinger*, which is a high fantasy. To me a book is a book. Well, I get letters from 13 and 14 year olds. Does that make me a children's novelist? Maybe, but that's fine.

Q: Do you write now to make money, or do you write because you have to?

KING: I didn't write *Eyes of the Dragon* with a view to publication, I wrote it for my daughter Naomi. Well, I have never offered anything for publication that I didn't feel warranted, but that is not to say that I never sat down to write something just on the chance that I might enjoy it. I think of writing as an act of communication with other people, as an act of getting in touch with them. And people seem to like what I do and I have always wanted to please other people. I was raised to please people. That was one of the things my mother taught me to do; that I was not to live life for myself is another way of putting it. That is not to say that my writing is a selfless act, because obviously it has made me very wealthy, not wealthy by the standards of the Vanderbilts. Vanderbilt himself, at the turn of the century, was heard to say that so-and-so, just because he'd become a millionaire, acted as though he were rich. I don't really think that any writer is going to become a Rockefeller or a Hughes, worth umpty umpty millions of dollars, but we are comfortable and that's nice.

But it's actually worth more to me, as a writer, when people write you a letter and say, "I stayed awake all night—you scared the shit out of me," or you get a letter from a woman who says, "My kid never read anything and now he's insatiable and he reads all your books; now he's even started to read some other things. Thank you." And your critical reward for that sort of reaction, to turning kids on that don't read, is to have *Time* magazine calling me the Master of Post-Literate Culture, which seems to me to be a little bit hard. But I guess I'll keep writing anyway.

And I should say that having this money means that I can go off and do other things if I want and that's great.

Q: One of the "other things" you have been involved with was the movie *Maximum Overdrive*, which you directed. Did you enjoy the experience?

KING: You know, Graham Greene, my favorite writer when he talks about writing, says a writer lives for 21 years, then spends the rest of his life writing about it. He said writers write books they can't find on library shelves. And that's why I made this picture: it was the kind of picture I'd go see, the kind I'd pay money for. It isn't the kind of picture like *The Big Chill* or *2001*, where people sit up all night and talk about it; it's just the sort of picture where you go see it and you say, yeah, that was good, that was fun.

In the cities, in New York, L.A., Washington, the critics lacerated it. I think a measure of my success at doing what I wanted to do was that the *New York Daily News* said they would give it zero stars, and furthermore, there was a bathroom scene that is vulgar beyond description, and I thought damn, I've succeeded! Once you get outside the big cities the reviews improved drastically, because I think people seemed to understand that what I was doing was in a spirit of fun.

Q: Did you enjoy the chance to direct your own movie, and is that something you would want to do again?

KING: Well, yes, I think I would do it again, but not for a long, long time. I mean really, I hated it—it was too much like real work. You're looking at a man who's been retired for ten years. I can't see myself doing it again until my children are all grown up. It took too much time. I was away, I wasn't a husband, I wasn't a father for a year. It would have been a little different if it had worked out the way we had foreseen. We thought that we would film the beginning of September, and the shoot would last through October and November and maybe the first two weeks of

December, to make the movie on location in North Carolina, and to make it mostly outdoors. But we made it in the summer time and that was sheer insanity. Two of my three kids were at camp and for all of them to get down, my wife included, meant that they had to commute— which they did. I got a chance to come back once, for five days, which I did, but otherwise it was incumbent upon my wife to get in a private plane and shepherd the kids down so they could spend some time with their father. So it made things difficult for Tabby and it made it difficult for me, it made it difficult for the marriage and the kids and I just can't see going through that kind of thing again. Not under any circumstances while I have children that I can enjoy and a wife that I can enjoy. It would be one thing if she were a bitch and I wanted to get away, and it would be one thing if the kids were a bunch of spoiled rotten little monsters and I didn't like them, but the fact is I do and I like them better than the job. And I don't like having to work for a living. And that's what it is.

Y'know what? I discovered what a producer is. A producer is not only a man who funds pictures and puts packages together. He is the guy who directs from the comfort of his air-conditioned office, while you stand in the hot sun with sweat running down the crack of your ass and into your Keds.

I would spend the day out on set, then we would come back and Dino would say, "Stephen, you comma-into-my-office." And he'd tell you what you were doing wrong and how to fix it and maybe you'd argue a little, and sometimes you'd win, but mostly he'd win. And nine times out of ten you'd realize at the end of it all that he'd been right. He is an honest man. He says what he's going to do and he stands by it.

Q: So what were the things that you enjoyed about making your own film?

KING: Blowing things up! No, really, it did have its highs. It was a pleasure to work with Emilio Estevez and Pat Hingle. Pat Hingle taught me much about directing, in a very gentle way. He was not going around saying, "Hey, you're wet behind the ears, I'm going to dry you off," it wasn't that way at all.

The first sequence of the movie features a bridge going up and there were two drawbridge keepers. One was a guy who was a fairly nice guy and the other was this woman who was like a dragon at the gate. The other guy would go as far as he could for us. I wanted to go up one day and do points-of-view shots for this dump truck driver at the top of this drawbridge. The bridge is counter-weighed and in reality you couldn't go up that far with a truck on it, but we asked the operator how high we could go up. And he asked how much the cameraman weighed, and how much I weighed, and how much the camera weighed, and then he said no problem, he'd take us up as high as we wanted. So the bridge goes up, very very slowly, and it's near the beginning of the shoot and I didn't understand that camera operators are suicidal—that's why they go to places like Vietnam, and that's why sometimes they get killed. So we're going up and you can feel the machinery and some movement, but that sensation goes away very quickly because you get used to it. So I'm saying to the cameraman, like "How is it for you, darling?", you know, it's a bit like making love, and he says can we go a bit higher and I say sure. The only sensation I'm feeling, and like I'm getting off on this too, is feeling the weight shift from flat feet onto the balls of the feet and then onto the toes.

I don't know how much further he would have taken us, but finally I hear the continuity lady screaming "Stephen, for Godsakes, make him stop it, make it stop," and I hear a lot of other people yelling and screaming. And I looked around and we were up to about 57! and I felt this urge to just lie down and clutch at this grating. It was scary, but it was very exciting too. Oh, and I got to blow up a milk truck on my birthday—that was cool!

At the end of making the movie, Dino says to me, "Hey, Stephen, whenna-you-gonna make-a you next-a picture?" And I told him, "Dino, I think about the year 2000." But he said no, I'd want to do it again. He told me it's addictive, like cocaine. And he's right in lots of ways: there is an addictive quality to filmmaking and his simile is correct, it is not a benign addiction. But I can't see myself doing anything like this again, at least not until my family has all grown up. I want to be around to enjoy them while I can.

Q: You have fame, you have fortune, you have an ever-increasing row of books on the shelf: what ambitions do you have left?

KING: I don't have any long-term ambitions—stay alive, stay married, stay writing. . . I live day by day. I think perhaps I'm done writing about kids the way I have been doing, particularly in "The Body" and IT—in many ways the latter was an extension of what I'd been doing in the novella. One of the reasons I have written about kids so much is because

I have my own, but they are growing up now, so my interest in childhood is fading.

You live your childhood twice if you have kids, once as you live it yourself and the second time as you raise your children and watch them. You get a kind of perspective on what your own childhood meant, what you went through. There is a need to finish being a child and I don't think that can be done until you have kids and they have finished with it completely.

At the same time, coincidentally, I think I am about done writing about monsters. It was like an orals exam: if I was going to say it, then I had to say everything I was going to say and screw the critics if they didn't like it. But I will listen to them, and if they don't like it, well, they won't have to face that sort of thing again.

Going back to Graham Greene again, the one time in my life I ever went against writers writing what they couldn't find on library shelves was when I wrote the fantasy for my daughter. She doesn't like horror stories and she had never read very much of my stuff and what she had read was because her mother sort of pushed her at it, like carrots, with the idea, well, this was a better way for her to know her father. And she did it, but not with much enthusiasm, so, I thought, Goddamnit, if the mountain won't come to Mohammed. . . I knew that she liked fantasy, she had read some of the Conan comic books and Piers Anthony and stuff like that and in the end I really got into it. And I did her the courtesy of writing *Eyes of the Dragon* for myself too, because if you are writing just for someone else, you always write down.

Q: You obviously don't have much privacy any more: you are one of the highest profile writers around and I know you get mobbed at football games, or even when you're in the public lavatory. Is this making you more of a hermit?

KING: I'm still a fan at heart and one of the things which is real rough is not being able to go to a convention and go into the hucksters' room and look around, maybe pick up some copies of *Weird Tales* or other pulps without having people come up for autographs, or to talk about something they've written, or you've written. They're hitting on you all the time and you try to be polite and you try to talk to them but often you are just thinking to yourself, "Why can't I be like these other people and just be allowed to browse?" You've become the browsee instead of the browser, kind of like a walking, talking book. But I haven't totally stopped going to conventions. I like to meet my peers, people like Peter Straub, Ramsey Campbell, Whitley Strieber. I like to sit around with these guys and shoot the shit and have a few beers.

So I haven't quit and I won't retreat from my own ideal, which is that I am no better and no worse than anyone else. I should be allowed to live a life which is not necessarily more private and not necessarily more public than anyone else's, but just simply a life.

I guess to me public life is when I leave this room and I walk down the street and someone I don't know just passes me and says, "Hi, Steve, loved your book," and walks on. That's just fine.

And I guess I am going to continue writing, but I think the public has got a bit of Stephen King overload at the moment, or will have by the time everything currently scheduled has come out, so I think it's about time to shut up for a while.

With D.C. Denison

Q: Your books are very funny, in addition to being horrifying. Do you think that humor and horror are related?
KING: They're very close. They are the two most childish things that people make art out of. They are the artistic equivalent of mud pies. Humor and horror are also the only two things that elicit instant audience gratification. If you're in one of these cinema complexes, and you hear the audience make a noise in the next theater, you usually don't know whether it's horror or comedy, but you know it's one or the other. Because those are the only kinds of movies that cause people to make noises out loud.
Q: Out of all the horror movies you've been associated with, what actress has impressed you as the best screamer?
KING: Dee Wallace, who was in *Cujo*, comes immediately to mind. You have to be unabashed, get into it, and let yourself totally go to get a good scream. It's tough to do. A lot of people are very inhibited about screaming. Would you like to know the greatest scream scene of all time?
Q: Sure.
KING: It's Bette Davis in *Hush...Hush, Sweet Charlotte*. She sees

Joseph Cotten at the top of the stairs, and she thinks he's dead. And so she crawls down the stairs screaming in that wonderful cigarette-hoarse voice, "Ahhhh!, Ahhhh!" It sounds like a dying crow. It's great.

Q: Is it getting more difficult to frighten people these days?

KING: No, I never think about it—honest to God, I never do because a scare just comes up. And when it comes up, you milk it for everything that it's worth. You know what to do at that point. You tease, and tease, and tease, and then when it comes, it has to be as absolutely bad as you can make it. In *Misery*, it's pretty short just a few words long actually, but I think it works. I got a letter yesterday from a woman who passed out in the beauty parlor while reading *Misery*. They decided that she had had an epileptic seizure, and they ran all these tests. But two or three days later the doctor came in and said, "I read the book that you were reading at the time, and my diagnosis is that you fainted out of fright." I should frame that letter.

Q: Are there any traditional scary things that have lost their clout?

KING: Not in books. There's always a different way to do it. But in movies I would have to say that the werewolf has probably had it. It's been tried several different ways, cleverly in many cases, but without great success. *An American Werewolf in London* was a very clever picture, but it didn't make money. My own *Silver Bullet* was so-so, with ho-hum boxoffice. It made about $900,000, which I don't think the major studios care about. They want Spielberg pictures; they don't want to make $900,000.

Q: Have you ever discussed literary prolificacy with Joyce Carol Oates?

KING: No. She gets a lot of ink because she's a very good writer, a classy writer. And I get a lot of ink because I make a lot of money. I'm a salami writer. I try to write good salami, but salami is salami. You can't sell it as caviar. Updike I'm not, thank God.

But there are very good writers who are much more prolific than both Oates and me: Evan Hunter writes about four novels a year. The late John D. MacDonald used to do about two a year.

Q: What's the key to your productivity?

KING: Nothing in particular. I don't take notes; I don't outline; I don't do anything like that. I just flail away at the goddamned thing. I start with an idea, and sometimes I even have an idea of where I'm going, but it usually turns out to be someplace else that I end up. For example, I'm working on a story now about a kid who is home sick with the flu and sees his cat outside playing with a little tiny man, rather than a mouse. I know something about this teeny guy, but I still haven't figured a lot of things out. I don't know whether the book will be publishable, but it will probably get done, and that's all I care about. I've worked on a lot of busted novels over the last year.

Q: Horror movies are often defended as being psychologically cathartic. Do you buy that?

KING: I take it with a huge grain of salt—about the size of a salt lick. It's too often an excuse to get away with cutting people up and slicing and dicing and peeling and chopping and then saying, "That's Okay, everybody's got to get their ya-yas out somehow." That's crap. That's just feeding a sickness. Yes, there is catharsis involved, but only in work that is strictly moral, and strictly artistic. Otherwise, it's simple pandering. You really have to be careful about this catharsis stuff if you're in the business, because it's too easy to excuse everything.

Q: What is your motivation—to scare people plain and simple?

KING: No, that isn't my motivation at all. If my motivation was just to scare people, I wouldn't know how to begin. I get ideas for stories, that's all. And a lot of times they are fantasy stories, because I'm very childish. I like to go away. So I make stuff up, and I tell stories, and what comes out, a lot of times, is scary stuff.

Q: What have you discovered about human nature in the course of your writing career?

KING: Well, most people are good, there's no question about that. That's comforting. And I think that the success of my own fiction suggests that, because you can't scare people by setting up ducks in a shooting gallery and knocking them down, you need real people in real danger. There isn't any shadow unless you provide a bright white background. I've always tried to create people who were ordinary decent human beings.

Q: Do you every worry about inspiring psychopaths?

KING: No. You hear stories, like the guy who saw *Psycho* five times and then went home and stabbed his grandmother 60 times with a pair of scissors, but my argument is that this is a crazy person who would have done it anyway, but found a more creative way to do it by plagiarizing from a work of art.

Now maybe that's a self-serving justification that will allow me to go on doing what I'm doing, but I don't believe that's so. I don't believe that

John Wayne Gacy, in Chicago, did what he did because he read a novel—or Juan Corona, or Ted Bundy. It's built in. We're always looking for a quick exterior solution. What the American people want is fast, fast relief. When it comes to complicated questions like violence in society, there has to be an easy way, and an outside reason. But that's not the case, usually. It's bred in the bone.

Q: With all the work you do in New York and Hollywood, why do you and your family live in Maine?

KING: I have a very obscure answer to that: I think a place is yours, when you know where the roads go. They talk my language here; I talk theirs. I think like them; they know me. It feels right to be here. Also, it's not that easy to get up here. So when people want to see me, they have to shuck and jive. The great intestinal tract of air traffic in America narrows to a single urethra up here in Bangor.

Q: Are you afraid of the dark?

KING: What can I say? Yes. And you are too, if you're honest. Set me down out in the woods at night and, yes, I'm afraid of the dark, and so are you, and so is everybody.

With Ed Gorman

Q: Will you tell us why you wrote a psychological terror novel at this time? And will you tell us about *Misery*?

KING: I wrote it for the reason I write anything: it occurred to me as a story I wanted to hear myself. No sermon, moral, or Great Truth was intended. I do remember thinking that it would be a great pleasure to finally have another character like Randall Flagg in *The Stand*, who was utterly and completely gonzo. Willing to do *anything*, not only to her "pet writer" or any "dirty bird" who happens to get in her way, but to herself. Halfway through, as in *Pet Sematary*, I realized I was trying to express some of my own deepest fear-feelings: the sense of being trapped, the sense of having come from someplace like Africa and knowing I would never be able to get home, and trying to figure out what it was I was doing, how I was doing it, why I was doing it, and why people were responding to it. But mostly I was doing it for the same reason I do all my stories: I'm havin' a blast.

Q: In many of your autobiographical/literary pieces you refer to key suspense writers as having influenced you. Would you tell us about some of your favorites past and present?

KING: Ira Levin; Richard Matheson; Robert Bloch; these are the writers associated with my genre who seem to generate the most raw, sweaty-palmed suspense in me. But there are others, not always genre-related, who also do it: Daphne Du Maurier, Mary Higgins Clark (when she's telling a story that's on the mark and not ridiculous), Joseph Hayes, Thomas Chastain, Robert Parker, Jim Thompson, David Goodis, John Fowles, P.D. James, Ruth Rendell (the best suspense writer alive, I think), Robertson Davies...man, I could rock on all night. Oddly enough, the two best suspense novels I've ever read aren't "horror" or "mystery/suspense" novels at all. They are *The Lord of the Flies* by William Golding, and *The Sound of His Horn*, by a French fellow named only Sarban.

Q: There is an ongoing argument about the Hitchcockian style of suspense versus the gore of today. What is your feeling?

KING: On gore, I feel pretty much as Hitch did. If you need to let it flow, man let it *go*. This is particularly effective if you do it well near the beginning of a novel or film (see for instance John Farris's *All Heads Turn When the Hunt Goes By*, where the only scenes of really explicit violence occur at the beginning and the end). Violence for the sake of violence is of course immoral and thus pornographic; to shy from a violent scene necessary to the story is equally immoral and equally pornographic.

Q: *'Salem's Lot* is the seminal popular novel of this century. It gave writers the courage to push against the walls. As you were writing it were you aware that you were altering the shape of commercial fiction?

KING: No, I was not aware that I was altering the course of and/or shape of commercial fiction when I wrote *'Salem's Lot*. As it happens, I think you just might be right; at any rate, a lot of blueback contracts got written and signed and a lot of money changed hands as a consequence of those bluebacks. Without *'Salem's Lot*, that might not have happened. I also think it energized a certain number of writers, set them free to write what they had thought would be greeted with ridicule. But I disagree with your lead-in, which smacks of "Are you still beating your wife?" The idea that *'Salem's Lot* is "the seminal novel of this century" is clearly not true. It's just a good story. Even *I* still like it. But any relationship between it and art is purely coincidental.

Q: When you look at today's bestseller list and you see genre writers—yourself, Clive Barker, Dean Koontz, Arthur C. Clarke up at the top. Why do you think genre fiction has replaced the more sedate bestsellers of our youth?

KING: *Sedate bestsellers of our youth? Are you kidding?????* Man, the stuff on the lists has always been the cutting edge of every moral and social question our society needs to deal with. That's why people buy them. Think of some of them: *Peyton Place, Gentleman's Agreement, The Jungle, The Last Angry Man* ("'Old man,' the drunk kid across the street kept yelling, 'you ain't nothing but SHIIIIIIIT!'"), *The Naked and the Dead, The Valley of the Dolls, God's Little Acre.* If these books look sedate now, it's only because you've forgotten the social context of the times. Stick *Peyton Place* next to the Mouseketeers, put Selena Cross next to Annette Funicello, and you'll see what I mean.

Q: What are your plans for the next few years?

KING: To try to stay alive. Work for political candidates who don't want to blow up the world.

Q: Is it still more fun to be famous than not to be famous? What's the upside? What's the downside?

KING: Being famous sucks. There is no upside. The downside is when you realize that the only reason everything on the buffet is free is because they're planning on having you for dessert.

Q: You mention Max Brand many times in your essays. Your books are filled with the same kind of reverence for nature his books displayed. Do you think there's too much "lean" fiction today and not enough that honor the old verity place?

KING: I love Max Brand-Frederick-whatever-his-last-name was. Frank Gruber tells a fabulous anecdote about him in his book, *The Pulp Jungle.* He says Brand (which was a pseudonym) worked at one of the major studios as a "grind" rewriter. Every day, the coworker who told Gruber the story said, Brand would arrive with a very large steel thermos filled with pure vodka. He would open it, pour a cup into the red top, and begin to write. He wrote all day without stopping except to go to the bathroom (and to refill his Thermos, from some source in his car, apparently, at noon). He never ate lunch. He never exhibited symptoms of drunkenness. He wrote with hardly a single strike-over. He would finish a quart or two of straight vodka each day, the writer who shared Brand's office said, and he would finish his "grind-work" by 1pm or so. For the next four hours he wrote either Dr. Kildare novels or Westerns. And some of those Westerns are damned good stories. You can't put 'em down, because the characters actually seem real.

Q: What do you think makes *Misery* different from your other novels?

KING: Nothing, really, except there's a novel inside it and the cast of characters and locations are both really small. Actually, when I got to the epilogue, I got agoraphobia. I'd spent the whole novel dealing with only two people, and all those people in New York City scared me!

Q: Many of your novels seem to have great chunks of autobiography in them. Does *Misery*?

KING: I decline to answer the question on the grounds that the answer might tend to incriminate me. Which is to say, no. Which is also to say you're damned tooting.

Q: Would you give us the names of some writers you think we ought to be reading but aren't?

KING: Don Robertson. Thomas Williams. I would have said Charles Willeford, but now he's getting the star treatment. Jim Thompson. Shane Stevens, David Goodis. Dan J. Marlowe. Donald Hamilton. Peter Rabe. Horace McCoy. In the horror genre, if you've missed Gary Bradner, you've missed a treat. The same with Richard Laymon (although he's *really* uneven) and John Coyne (who gives steady value). In SF, Joe Haldeman, Wade Hawkins (best pulp since Doc Smith), Greg Bear, David Brin, Susy McKee Charnas, Marta Randall, George Alec Effinger. When it comes to pushing it way over the line, Shane Steven's *Rat Pack* and *Dead City* are particularly good. Oh, and don't miss Jonathan Carroll. He defies genre, but he reads *good*.

Q: If CBS gave you 60 seconds to give the world a message, what would it be?

KING: If it shoots or if it can blow up, put it down right now. Pull the plug. Bulldoze it under. Quit shitting where you eat. Stop killing the animals that breathe the same air you want to keep breathing. Buy a great big Oldsmobile and drive it to Mexico. Ask yourself once every five years or so if you're happy. If the answer is *no*, you're in trouble, son. If the answer is *not much of the time, but sometimes, yeah*, relax. Winston Churchill said "The world's work is done mostly by tired and unhappy men and women." It's true. Stop picking your own mental scabs. If you got your head up your ass, get it out before you asphyxiate.

With Martin Booe (1989)

It is cold this time of year in Bangor, Maine, and best-selling horror novelist Stephen King has just returned from the doctor.

"The kids all had strep," King reports by phone, "but I was lucky—I tested negative."

What is *not* negative these days is the prolific writer's bank account. The sum is officially a secret, but the *New York Times* reported that American Library paid the author of such blockbusters as *The Shining*, *The Stand* and *IT* a whopping $40 million for his next four books.

"The Bible says the laborer is worthy of his hire, so we took what we were offered," King remarks dryly, adding that the terms of his contract forbade him to disclose the sum.

But $40 million?

"Only the Pentagon gets those numbers," King laughs, shirking the question. "I don't think anybody would pay that for the Bible II."

Whatever the amount, one can safely assume it's enough to keep the ghouls, goblins and other deranged denizens up to their ears in designer gore.

While the 41-year old King isn't about to wax sentimental for the days when a job in a Laundromat was all that stood between his family and starvation, he admits that Big Money can mean Big Pressure.

"There is a real rush to get a book out so the publishing company can recoup what it put out. So the editor can suffer and the work can suffer because you're under pressure.

"It's a little like being a free agent in baseball where you know everybody's saying, 'They paid X million dollars for this guy. We wanna see a home run every time he gets up.' Well, at least with a baseball bat he gets 450 at-bats a year, where I only get one. And it had better be a home run."

King's output—23 novels since 1974—must place him among the *least* blocked writers in history.

However, he's no stranger to the dark side of the creative process. It's an area he tapped for his novel *Misery*, in which a writer of horror novels is held captive and tortured by an ardent fan who demands that he write a novel the way she wants him to.

A similar preoccupation fuels *The Dark Half*, his novel-in-progress, to be published in November. In it, King lashes his imagination to a chunk of autobiography and lowers it unflinchingly into his nightmarish pit.

The impetus for the story was the real-life "demise" of one Richard Bachman—the pen name King used for several novels after his publisher cautioned him about glutting his own market. An enterprising (and curious) law student was the culprit who blew King's cover by doing research at the Library of Congress.

"I sort of wondered what would happen if the pen name was the writer's meal ticket. . . . And then I started wondering what would happen if the pen name didn't wanna stay dead and took on its own identity—and not a nice identity. And that led me to the real question of who writers are when they write.

"So I started this novel called *The Dark Half*, which is basically about a writer's nasty nature on a rampage."

In the meantime, King is anticipating the April 1989 movie release of *Pet Sematary*, for which he wrote the screenplay.

"I think it's a much more serious scary picture than *Friday the 13th* or *Halloween*," he says.

That's saying something, coming from King, who's typically modest to the point of self deprecation. Nor has he been one to pull punches when it comes to assessing the movies made from his books.

"I've always thought of screenplays as work for idiots," King muses. "It took me about five days to do *Creepshow*. Screen-writing is like skating on top of a frozen pond in the winter, whereas writing a novel is like swimming—you have to dive in and get wet."

But King has done more than scratch the surface of show biz. He dived in headfirst two years ago by directing *Maximum Overdrive*, in which a group of men are held hostage in a truck stop by rampaging semi-trucks. The movie bombed, leaving King with mixed feelings about trying directing again.

"It's an awful lot of work," he groans, "and I'm basically a lazy person."

Lazy and turning out 3,000 words a day?

"Well, writing is a different kind of work. No heavy lifting. When you're directing you have to cope with being someplace at a certain time, fragile egos, the whole works. And when I'm writing at my word processor, the special effects always work—they're right there in front of me."

One wonders if, after producing such a plethora of novels in the horror genre, King might be at the end of his rope. Is he ready to tackle something else? A political thriller, perhaps, or a contemporary *Babbitt*?

"Novels in the horror genre have been accepted as serious novels the way romance novels never are," he says.

"I've been able to talk about the American way of death in *Pet Sematary*. I've been able to talk, in another book I'm working on, about American business and American consumerism. The interesting thing is you can take these things to their furthest limit just by introducing a little bit of nightmare."

Still, King admits, the idea of making a foray into another genre has occurred to him.

"I tell myself if I wanted to write a novel without any supernatural elements that it would meet with pretty good acceptance," King says, then hastens to sprinkle on the usual self-deprecation. "But maybe I'm just kidding myself."

There's no apparent danger of King's creative well running dry. He says he's usually at least "one idea ahead, which is the most any writer can ask for."

"Working on a new idea is kind of like getting married," he muses. "Then a new idea comes along and you think, 'Man, I'd really like to go out with her.' But you can't. At least not until the old idea is finished."

Speaking of marriage, King may count himself among the lucky ones whose marriage has survived the precipitous rise in fortune. He married his wife, Tabitha, after graduation from college. They now have three children.

In weaving his nightmarish tales, King has variously employed the likes of vampires, blood-lusting dogs, killer cars, telekinetic teenagers. A couple of years ago, he astutely observed that the one truly universal horror of the Eighties was cancer—as evidenced by such visceral portrayals of *Aliens* as parasitic creatures taking root in human stomachs.

Universal horror for the Nineties?

"Addiction," King says, who himself gave up drinking a couple of years ago. "Everybody lives in total horror of it. I think you'll see that subtext used more and more. So far the only thing I've seen is Larry Cohen's *The Stuff*. But it seems to be that's what people are worried about."

EPILOGUE

†

HAS SUCCESS SPOILED STEPHEN KING?

†

With Edgar Allen Beem

Horror superstar Stephen King and rock superstar Bruce Springsteen were out on the town one night following one of The Boss's concerts. They stopped in at a little Irish bar, an out-of-the-way steam table affair, and were enjoying their anonymity. Some joker even approached the pair and tried to sell them some coke. Nice to be treated like an ordinary human being, hunh Bruce?

Well, it wasn't long before a 14 year old at a nearby table was hit by the shock of recognition. ("It was like stars exploded in her eyes.") Attracted by the irresistible magnetism of celebrity, the little girl got up and made her way toward the table where The Boss and The King were seated. As the dazzled fan approached, Springsteen reached for a pen, but. . . the little girl looked right passed Springsteen to King. "Aren't you Stephen King?" the teeny-bopper blurted out in the time-honored manner of star-struck ordinary people everywhere. "My God! I've read all your books!"

The point? Stephen King is FAMOUS. Forget his "Do you know me?" commercials for American Express, Stephen King has entered the twilight zone of pop culture celebrity. He is to popular literature what Bruce Springsteen is to popular music, what Steven Spielberg is to motion pictures, what McDonald's is to dining out. His string of horror bestsellers now stretches back over a decade from *Skeleton Crew* (1985) through *Pet Sematary, Christine, Cujo, Firestarter, The Dead Zone, The Stand, The Shining,* and *'Salem's Lot* to *Carrie* (1974). There are an estimated 60 million copies of Stephen King books floating around in the world at this very moment. Eleven motion pictures—most notably, *Carrie* with Sissy Spacek and *The Shining* with Jack Nicholson—bear King's paw print as writer and actor, and he is about to make his debut as the director of *Maximum Overdrive.* And, as if that's not enough. . . .

"You want a laugh?" asks Maine's master of the macabre. "*Carrie* is being made into a Broadway musical."

Stephen King has ceased to be the local-boy-makes-good story of the Seventies. In the Eighties, his success has taken on a life of its own. There are now almost as many words written *about* Stephen King as *by* Stephen King. If he isn't the most famous man in Maine, who is? And what impresses many people about King's phenomenal success is how well he seems to have handled it. Why hasn't success spoiled Stephen King? That's what we wanted to know, so we visited King in Bangor recently to ask him.

Stephen King has lived in a 24-room Bangor mansion with his wife Tabitha and their children since 1980. The mansion is lavish by Maine standards, but modest on the scale of world-wide wealth. The two Mercedes and the new Harley-Davidson parked outside can hardly be considered luxuries when one considers that Stephen King is worth "at least $20 million" (according to a year-old *Newsweek* article). The master of this Bangor estate is a slouching 38-year old man with the physique of a sleep sofa, his six-foot-four-inch frame hunched into a space a six-footer could occupy. At the moment he is in his stocking feet amusing himself with a yoyo. His dress is All-American working man— blue jeans and a Harley-Davidson t-shirt. Not your average unapproachable millionaire.

Ask the big guy with the yoyo what celebrity means to him and don't be surprised by a thoughtful response.

"The bottom line," says King, "is that a lot of the time now I'm too busy *being* Stephen King to write."

Being Stephen King, for example, means that he is going to have to miss a local graduation he wanted to attend because he is needed in New York to guest host an MTV program featuring AC/DC, the rock group that recorded the soundtrack for his new movie, *Maximum Overdrive*. Being Stephen King also means he had the chance to direct that film.

As he candidly told reporters from *American Film* magazine, "I didn't get this job because I could direct or because I had any background in film; I got it because I was Stephen King."

Directing *Maximum Overdrive* kept King in North Carolina most of last fall and winter. He did not enjoy the separation from his family and, from the sound of it, he isn't likely to try directing again too soon.

"It's a very primitive way to create," says King of his directing experience. "Eighty people standing around with their thumbs up their ass drinking GatorAde because the sun's behind a cloud is a primitive way to create."

Plastered on a bathroom door is a motion picture poster featuring King's menacing buck-toothed squint.

"I feel like something raised by Frank Perdue these days," he says as he disappears behind the door. When he reappears he is still thinking about the meaning of celebrity.

"The apotheosis of real pop culture celebrity was finally reached last week when someone called from Merv Griffin with an offer to do either *Hollywood Squares* or *The $10,000 Pyramid*," he reports. "The medium is the message all right, but with a writer that's just not the way God intended it."

Clearly, King has been forced to think a great deal about the meaning of fame. He hasn't shied away from it, but then he hasn't abandoned himself to it either. If he had, this would be a story about a Maine boy in Hollywood snorting cocaine through hundred-dollar bills and being serviced by a bevy of starlets.

"The problem," says King of fame, "is only the extent to which . . . the disturbing extent to which . . . we've started to attach this hollow idea of celebrity to people, mistaking what people *do* for what they *are*.

"Up until *The Dead Zone* and *Firestarter* (1979–80)," says King, "I had the situation Robert Frost talked about—where what makes a man happy is when his work and his want are the same things."

As a writer, he says he is haunted by the knowledge that bestselling schlockmeister (not his choice of words) Harold Robbins was once "a pretty good little proletarian novelist." That was before the monkey demons of fame, fortune, and ego jumped on Robbins's back. King sounds sincere when he says he doesn't want to become another Harold

Robbins or Jacqueline Susann. Being a huge popular success does not often endear a writer to literary critics, however, and King has already taken his lumps for appealing to lumpenproletariat. He has been called "the master of post-literate prose" and one critic even updated an old Truman Capote chestnut about Norman Mailer ("That isn't writing; it's typing") saying of King's prose, "That isn't typing; it's word-processing."

"I don't think that's true yet," says King of the charge.

One of the reasons that very few people begrudge Stephen King his outrageous good fortune is that he has a very clear perspective on his own work. He knows the difference between a best-selling American novelist and being the best American novelist, which is like saying he knows the difference between sex and love.

Back in 1976, when King was experiencing his first heady rushes of major success, he wrote an essay in *The New York Times Book Review* that earned him a lot of respect in many circles. In "The Guest Word" column, he confessed to feeling a bit guilty that some better novels did not sell as well as his own books, but he also pleaded "not guilty," explaining his commercial success as a function of the accessibility of his storytelling. Specifically, King compared sales of *'Salem's Lot* to those of David Madden's *Bijou* ("a better book").

"If *Lot* was that water off a bit of Maine beach," King wrote, "it would be extremely warm water, easy to slip into, pleasant to stroke around in for the next 400-odd pages. *Bijou* is a cooler ocean, and the footing underneath shelves off much more suddenly. To get through *Bijou* you have to make a commitment; to get through *'Salem's Lot* all you need is a sunpad and a pair of eyes and you're in business."

It took a big man to make such a public admission. *'Salem's Lot* remains King's favorite by his own hand. He cites New Hampshire novelist Thomas Williams (*The Hair of Harold Roux*) as his favorite writer, but having said that he launches into a string of favorites Ed McBain, John D. Macdonald, Paul Scott, Sax Rohmer, Edgar Rice Burroughs, William Burroughs, Don Robertson... trailing off only as the pen cannot keep up—that makes it clear the prolific writer is also an omnivorous reader. Former University of Maine at Orono classmates remember the student King as a hulking presence shuffling around the campus with his nose in one paperback and two others, ready and waiting, stuffed into the back pockets of his jeans.

These days the paperback stuffed in blue jean pockets, purses and beach bags are very apt to be by Stephen King. Even publishing at almost a two-book-a-year clip hasn't kept up with King's voluminous production. You figure it out. If King writes six pages a day (1,500 words), he produces over 2,000 manuscript pages a year. If he only published one book a year, he'd already be booked into the 21st century.

When you achieve the kind of success that Stephen King has, you get to write your own rules. King is the first major best-selling American author to demand and receive a licensing contract for his novels. From now on, instead of signing away the rights to his books for the life of the copyright (life plus 50 years) in exchange for royalties, King will license his books to his publisher for 15 years. If he is happy with the way the book has been treated after 15 years, he will renew the license to publish for an additional fee.

"We're not selling the books anymore, we're renting them," says King.

First came wealth, then came fame, now comes power . . . all of which are said to corrupt. But Stephen King has kept his head. Indeed the only real whiff of spoilage that comes from his success is traceable to *Castle Rock*, the monthly Stephen King newsletter. Faced with a mounting volume of fan mail and requests for information, King was more or less forced (in wife Tabitha's words) to "institutionalize his relationship to his fans." *Castle Rock* (named for the fictional Maine town of *Cujo* and *The Dead Zone*) is an eight -to 12-page newsprint tabloid that began publication in January 1985. The 3,000-subscriber newsletter is a family affair. The editor and publisher is King's sister-in-law, the managing editor is his brother-in-law, and the circulation manager is his mother-in-law. But the source of the spoilage is not the nepotism or the fact that an entire monthly newspaper is devoted to Stephen King. It is the content of *Castle Rock* that exudes a funny smell.

Okay, so *Castle Rock* is a fan magazine—Stephen King news, Stephen King interviews, Stephen King trivia contest, Stephen King parodies, Stephen King reviews, Stephen King favorite lists, even Stephen King classifieds. But it is the adulation and uncritical embrace of all that is Stephen King that is so nauseating. Stephen King has an intelligent perspective on his own writings, but some of his fans do not. When sycophantic *Castle Rock* contributing editor Tyson Blue gets to the point of arguing at length that Stephen King is a more important writer than John Updike, F. Scott Fitzgerald, or Norman Mailer, you'd hope King himself would start to get queasy.

The fact that a man who could afford to live anywhere in the world elects to live in Bangor, Maine, intrigues some people.

"This is home," says King of Bangor. "The kids like it here. I like it here. We've lived here long enough that everybody's seen us. It's like shoes. It takes awhile to break them in, but once you've broken them in, they're comfortable."

Stephen and Tabitha King say they sometimes feel as though they're living in a goldfish bowl when the tour buses pull up out front and some local motels supply guests with maps to their West Broadway home, but local residents are used to having celebrity in their midst. To move elsewhere would mean having to break in a new town all over again.

The King's house, a "must" stop on many a Bangor Halloween route, is no secret. Someday it will be marked by a plaque and known as the Stephen King House. Right now it is Stephen King's house, and it's conspicuously marked by a distinctive wrought-iron fence featuring spider webs and bats.

"The famous fence," insists King, "was Tabby's idea."

"The fence," says Tabitha King, "is a psychological statement. It says, 'That sidewalk is as far as you come, but I'll give you something pretty to look at.' It's no accident that it's five feet high."

Aside from the big house on West Broadway, Stephen King's other major presence in Bangor is radio station WZON, better known as "The Z" or "The Zone." King purchased the station in 1984 as something of a preservation effort. A great rock fan, King valued the fact that the station was one of the few AM (62 on your AM dial) stations with a rock 'n' roll format and he wanted to keep it that way. The Kings are justly proud that "The Zone" was the first station in the country to play Bruce Springsteen's hit, "Dancin' in the Dark."

His home, "The Zone," and a summer place on Kezar Lake have been King's major investments since striking it rich. He did make inquiries about purchasing *Maine Times* at one point, but decided against going into the newspaper business because he felt he didn't have enough time to devote to it.

A lot of money and not much time—that would seem to sum up in a crass way what success has meant to Stephen King. But he does find time and money to support a number of worthwhile (often liberal) causes.

"We're on every left-wing sucker list there is," says Tabitha King.

King himself is uncharacteristically guarded when talking about his charitable activities, not because he views money as sacred (and not because he doesn't want to be inundated with begging letters), but because he doesn't want to blow his own horn.

"Let's put it this way," says King of his philanthropic life, "if someone were to dig out my income tax returns and look at my charitable contributions, I wouldn't be embarrassed."

Mainers know, for instance, that King was active personally and financially in helping to defeat the recent obscenity referendum. Not only is King philosophically opposed to government censorship, but he had the experience of having his own works censored. *The Shining* was removed from a junior high school library in Washington state because some felt it contained excessive vulgarity.

On his own, King has already sought to assure that one major motion picture will be filmed in Maine. Since his financial success allows him to call the shots now, King reportedly passed up a $1 million offer for the screen rights to *Pet Sematary*, preferring to take $1,000 up front and a partnership interest in the project with the producer. The *Pet Sematary* film contract specifies that the movie be made in Maine and Laurel Productions has already done location work in Orono.

King has also used his influence on behalf of other writers in Maine. Last year, *Maine Times* reported that King had been instrumental in getting Michael Kimball's *Firewater Pond* published despite the fact that he had never met Kimball. In 1979, King also introduced Rick Hautala, a friend from his college days, to agent Kirby McCauley. McCauley managed to get Hautala's first book, *Moon Death*, published and now Hautala is perched on the edge of major paperback success. His forthcoming ghost story *Nightstone* will reportedly have a first printing of 600,000 and will be the first mass market paperback with a hologram cover.

"I think I'd still be unpublished if it weren't for his help," says Hautala of King's role in his career.

King is also giving a lot of young people a leg up in the world through his interest in education. Because he and his wife had to struggle to get through college, King now provides four $2,000 scholarships a year to graduates of Hampden Academy where he taught school before *Carrie* freed him to write full-time. But his support for education is not entirely parochial. When a young black girl from California wrote to him explaining that cutbacks in federal education funds mean that she would not be able to go to college, King wrote to her school, secured her records, and decided to help. He is now sending the young woman through the University of Southern California. In return for his support, King expects the girl to "do some good work" when she graduates.

As for his own aspirations at this point in his life, Stephen King's wants are modest.

"I'd like to write a really good book. I'd like to live to see my kids grow up. I'd like to stay as happily married as I am now, which is very happily. I'd like to slow down, maybe finish [Paul Scott's] *The Raj Quartet*, which I've been reading since March. But you know I never really wanted anything except to write."